What Readers Are Saying

"Without a doubt, *Adventism's Greatest Need* is the outpouring of the Holy Spirit into our hearts, first to make us the kind of people we ought to be—and then to provide power to finish the work Christ has given us to do. Only when the Holy Spirit knows that He can trust us with power will He give it to us. This book addresses this important sequence, which makes it needful for all of us to read and seriously consider its message, with fasting and prayer."

Jack J. Blanco, Professor Emeritus
Southern Adventist University

"Dr. Clouzet weaves biblical history with the Adventist story to demonstrate that 'the Spirit, surprisingly, is not sent to the world, but instead, He is sent to the church. It is as He works through the church that the world is brought to Jesus.' This book reinvigorates my desire to experience the latter rain power of the Spirit of God and see Jesus come again in this generation."

Debra Brill, Vice-President for Ministries
North American Division

"I started reading this book to give my opinion, but suddenly, I became absorbed in it. Before I knew it, I had finished reading it. Reading this book was really good for me: as a Christian, as a child of God eager for the finishing of the work, and as a minister. Ron was inspired to write about the marvelous Person of the Holy Spirit in a simple yet profound way. He doesn't get lost in theology or in history but engages the reader experientially. After reading the book, I sense an urgent need to be filled with the Spirit so the work of God can be finished in my life, in the life of the church, and in the world."

Alejandro Bullón, Evangelist
South American Division

"*Adventism's Greatest Need* by Ron Clouzet is a captivating, challenging, inspiring portrayal of the greatest need in the Adventist Church—the outpouring of the Holy Spirit. From the opening paragraph, your heart will be captivated with a desire to experience this greatest of all blessings. Backed by sound Adventist theology, the book exposes many of the false theories on Holy Spirit manifestations, while challenging us to seek this power that will not only transform our lives but send us forth to reap earth's final harvest. This book is a must read for every Seventh-day Adventist searching for that deeper walk with Jesus and for the empowerment of the Holy Spirit for the reaching of the lost."

Russell Burrill, Author and Former Director
North American Division Evangelism Institute

"If you want to encounter the power of the Holy Spirit in the life of your church, this book is a must read! Its practical and relevant nature, coupled with its evangelistic application, is extraordinarily useful for the church, both individually and collectively. I highly recommend it to church administrators, pastors, and members alike."

Carlton P. Byrd, Speaker/Director
Breath of Life Television Ministries

"Dr. Clouzet appeals both to his fellow ministers and to the young and old in the church: Knowing about Jesus and getting all the doctrines just right is not enough. Far from it! Fulfilling the gospel commission in Matthew 24:14 is more than 'proclaiming' a message—the message is understood only when its messengers are personal witnesses to its validity and trustworthiness. That means that those who profess these truths are transformed by them and are not mere spokesmen! We are God's messengers if we listen to the simple instructions of the Holy Spirit. . . .

"This book will help us understand that God cannot send the latter rain on unprepared people any more than He could or would in previous times. The latter rain does not fall on ground that has not experienced the early rain."

Herbert Edgar Douglass, Author, Editor, and Administrator
Seventh-day Adventist Church

"Dr. Ron Clouzet is an effective pastor, a competent scholar, a successful evangelist, and a gifted writer. His broad ministerial background and depth of experience provide a backdrop for his new book, *Adventism's Greatest Need.* The title itself speaks volumes. With the skill of a scholar and the heart of an evangelist, Ron shares his passion for the need of the infilling of the Holy Spirit in each of our personal lives and in the corporate life of the church. His insights into the ministry of the Holy Spirit are solidly biblical, presented with a freshness that will touch your heart as well as stimulate your mind. My prayer is that the Holy Spirit will draw you closer to Jesus as you read these pages."

Mark Finley, Assistant to the President
General Conference

"Do you often feel a profound spiritual thirst for God? Maybe a longing to walk more intimately with your Savior, Jesus Christ? If so, I invite you to read this book and be led to what the Word of God has to say about the meaningful and satisfying work of the Holy Spirit in your life today."

Bob Folkenberg, Jr., President
Upper Columbia Conference

"In reading *Adventism's Greatest Need: The Outpouring of The Holy Spirit,* I was drawn to the conviction of my own personal spiritual need. Dr. Ron Clouzet's excellent and thorough study of the work of the Spirit is a 'must read' for every serious Seventh-day Adventist.The book draws powerful lessons from the history of the church that are compelling, when evaluated in terms of the present needs and state of the Seventh-day Adventist Church today. A foundational appeal in this writing comes in the form of a direct question that we must answer both personally and corporately: 'How much longer will we be asleep in the light, while the world is asleep in the dark?' I highly recommend this book to all who would dare to be confronted by the Holy Spirit and who, in turn, will commit themselves to heralding the message of the Spirit to a world in need."

Daniel R. Jackson, President
North American Division

"You'll love this brand-new book! It's timely, needed, well written, and very practical. The labor of love that went into its preparation is welcome, because the message is filled with hope and encouragement. Ron Clouzet's messages are personal—deep enough for discoveries and wide enough to answer many of the common questions. You'll find a personal message that is life-changing. We believe this book will be a great source of light. And hope."

Ruthie Jacobsen, Director
North American Division Prayer Ministries

"*Adventism's Greatest Need: The Outpouring of the Holy Spirit* is one of the most significant and life-changing books I have read for some time. It has answered questions that I have had concerning the Holy Spirit, and it has helped me understand our church history that I never knew, as it has related to the Holy Spirit. Knowledge was just a small part of the message of this book. While reading it, I found myself several times stopping to apply what I was learning to my own life and getting on my knees to pray for forgiveness and for the Holy Spirit to come more fully into my life. My time with God has become much more purposeful and meaningful as a result of Clouzet's book. It is a must-read for every Seventh-day Adventist who is looking forward to the soon coming of our Lord and Savior Jesus."

Don James, Associate Director
North American Division Evangelism Institute

"The author has not only researched the topic of the Holy Spirit, he has let the Spirit search his own heart and life. This transparency has produced an inspired piece of work that creates in the reader a hunger for more of God, a reminder of the fruit of a partnership with the Holy Spirit, and the heartfelt cry to say, 'Let It Rain!'

"Every pastor and church leader should make provision for their members to read this book. The research is solid, the stories will inspire, and the Holy Spirit will convict and empower.

"WARNING: Reading this book is likely to lead to drastic changes in your habits and priorities. It is recommended that you make this journey with a small group—include your family, and your friends at school."

Esther R. Knott, Ministerial Association Associate Secretary
North American Division

"If ever the world needed a wake-up call, if ever those who believe they have been entrusted with God's last message of joy and warning sense the need for a similar wake-up call, this book by Ron Clouzet is the answer!"

Justin McNeilus, President
Generation of Youth for Christ (GYC)

"Every end-time follower of Jesus needs to read *Adventism's Greatest Need*. The last great revival will not happen as a result of human wisdom or man-made strategies. We all need to experience the life-transforming presence and the world-changing power of the Holy Spirit. Read, pray, and then give God permission to use you to impact the world."

Derek J. Morris, Editor
Ministry Magazine

"A powerful book! The Lord has used Ron's teaching and preaching on spiritual revival and reformation over the years to deeply inspire and change me and thousands around the world. This book is an excellent summary of those practical insights and biblical principles so needed by all of God's last-day people to really break through with Him! Invest the time to read this book and apply its principles, and it can make an eternal difference for you, your loved ones, and your church!"

Jerry N. Page, Ministerial Secretary
General Conference

"Clouzet tackles the important topic of revival and reformation in a most instructive and engaging way. His pastoral heart flows throughout the book with kindness and a sincere concern for the spiritual well-being of the church. He examines the work of the Spirit free from any sensationalism, while at the same time recognizing that the Spirit works and will continue to work in and through the church in increasingly powerful ways. Those who are also interested in the question of the nature of the Spirit will find here useful and reliable information. This volume could be very helpful for personal as well as for group study."

Angel Manuel Rodríguez, Director
Biblical Research Institute

"I was thinking, as I read Dr. Clouzet's book, that here's another 'safe' treatise on the Holy Spirit, written for nice church people who need a spiritual nudge every now and again. But hold on! Because a few chapters in, the reader is confronted not with a simple need of the Holy Spirit but with their sheer desperation for Him. This book is readable and ready to guide every believer into a journey of deep intimacy with the Spirit."

Fredrick Russell, President
Allegheny West Conference

Adventism's Greatest Need

The Outpouring of the Holy Spirit

Ron E. M. Clouzet

Pacific Press® Publishing Association
Nampa, Idaho
Oshawa, Ontario, Canada
www.pacificpress.com

Cover design by Gerald Lee Monks
Inside design by Page One Communications

Copyright © 2011 by Pacific Press® Publishing Association
Printed in the United States of America
All Rights Reserved

You can obtain additional copies of this book by calling toll-free
1-800-765-6955, or by visiting http://www.adventistbookcenter.com.

ISBN 13: 978-0-8163-2489-7
ISBN 10: 0-8163-2489-1

11 12 13 14 15 • 5 4 3 2 1

Dedication

I don't know if I'll write another book and have the opportunity then to dedicate it to my wonderful family. But I'd like to dedicate this book to God the Holy Spirit, without whom I would never have known Jesus or had any desire to be remade in the image of God.

Acknowledgments

No book is written by just one person—it takes an entire network of friends.

The first thanks go to Russell Burrill, former director of the North American Division Evangelism Institute (NADEI), author of a dozen books, and as of this writing, my right-hand help as manager for NET 2011. He warned me about how hard it would be to write something decent in only a few weeks, but after he did, he faithfully gave me feedback on each chapter, becoming First Cheerleader.

I'm greatly indebted to my mentor and friend, Jack Blanco, former Dean of the School of Religion at Southern Adventist University and author of *The Clear Word*, for paying attention to details, for timely counsel, and for expert feedback. Jack counsels with head and heart combined. This also goes for Herb Douglass—servant of God extraordinaire as professor, editor, and author of a myriad books, including the now-classic *Messenger of the Lord* and his latest titles, *The Heartbeat of Adventism* and *Red Alert: Hurtling Into Eternity*—who had the courage to point out weaknesses and the kindness to express faith in this project. These three men have taken hours of their valuable time to help this book be better. No weakness in this book, whether theological or stylistic, can be attributed to anyone but myself.

Thanks also go to a soul mate in matters of the Spirit, Pastor Kevin Wilfley. His comments made me think and clarify things, I hope, for the better. To my colleague at the Seminary, John Baldwin, who also provided me with valuable feedback, and to Angel Rodríguez, from the Biblical Research Institute, for insightful theological pointers. And to my faithful colleague at NADEI, Don James, who spent time he didn't have to help me craft questions for personal reflection and for use by small groups.

To everyone who had the courage and kindness to endorse the book, I am in your debt. These men and women of God who do marvelous work for the church are in my prayers, and they should be in yours. And I want to thank my long-time friend and pastor, Dwight Nelson, for writing such a gracious Foreword.

Scott Cady, from Pacific Press, a friend from my California days, has been patient and very helpful in guiding me along the journey from ideas to publication, and Ken McFarland provided expert editing.

Last, I thank my wife, Lisa, who not only was the first to read each chapter and catch my most obvious gaffes but was the one who endured in the flesh a husband out of commission for a number of critical weeks.

But the real thanks go to the Holy Spirit, who so gently and lovingly led me over so many years to know God better and love Him more. I only regret the many times I chose to listen to my wants instead of His voice, and I pray that this proclivity fades more and more with the passing years of His loving presence.

To God be the glory!

Contents

Foreword

Question: How long does it take to write an epic book on the Holy Spirit, such as this one?

Answer: It takes a lifetime.

I have had the privilege of knowing the author of this book for half a lifetime. Ron and Lisa Clouzet were young seminarians when I moved to Andrews University to become the pastor of the Pioneer Memorial Church. And from those halcyon days of his first pastorate, Ron has distinguished himself as a spiritual leader ignited by a deepening passion to know Christ—and a thirst to be filled with His Spirit.

That is why what you are about to read is not only faithfully biblical and rigorously theological—it is also deeply personal. As Frederick Buechner once observed, "All theology is biography"; that is, what an author struggles to articulate, by necessity flows from the depths of his or her private walk with God. You will sense those personal depths, as Ron with transparent candor and refreshing vulnerability chronicles his own spiritual search to "be filled with all the fullness of God" (Ephesians 3:19).

But this is more, much more, than a private journal, as valuable as those can be. This is a spiritual manual for the people of God—for God's last apocalyptic community on earth. And as such, it will perhaps be the most practical "how to" book on the Holy Spirit you have ever read—ranging from how to be personally filled daily with the Spirit of Jesus, to how to become a small group or even an entire congregation anointed with the mighty Third Person of the Godhead, to how to earnestly plead for the fulfillment of God's "latter rain" promises. I was particularly stirred by the detailed chronicle of what happened to one congregation, when they, along with the author, embraced God's promise of the Holy Spirit and obeyed Christ's command to "ask" as never before. Fasting and prayer, miraculous conversions, and explosive growth—could it happen in my campus congregation, too? Ron's personal testimony is evidence that it can—that it must.

Given the third millennial world you and I now cohabit—with its precarious flux and imploding upheaval—isn't it high time that we as a people storm the gates of Heaven on behalf of this Gift "that brings all other blessings in its [wake]" (*The Desire of Ages*, 672)? What else did Jesus mean, when He declared: "The kingdom of heaven suffers violence, and the violent take it by force" (Matthew 11:12)? We have namby-pambyed our spiritual way for decades. Surely, this is the right time for the Seventh-day Adventist Church to take utterly seriously God's call to revival and reformation within our apocalyptic community. On our knees with Bibles in hand, shall we not band together (don't miss his chapter on united prayer—it's worth the price of the book) to militantly plead for the divine outpouring that alone can reach 7 billion human beings with the glad and urgent tidings that the Savior of the world is soon to return?

Ron Clouzet believes that we can—that we must. Will you join me then in joining him in this relentless pursuit of Christ's greatest promise? What else are we waiting for?

Dwight K. Nelson, Senior Pastor
Pioneer Memorial Church
Andrews University

Introduction

Most of us live our lives gasping for air, as if drowning three inches below the waterline. We have grown so accustomed to this condition that we are oblivious that a whole new world exists just above us. We long for more—we find distractions and entertainment suitable only for the moment and ultimately unsatisfying. In our quiet reveries with God, deep down, we know another dimension could be ours if we chose it, or if we knew how to get there.

After forty years of successfully restoring many truths ignored in the Bible, the Adventist Church became adept at theological sword fighting, but real life was missing from many members. They had the truth, but somehow, it did not make them free. Preachers proclaimed the law until the church was dry "as the hills of Gilboa." For years, Ellen White urged the church to look to Jesus. Finally, in 1887, she penned her famous statement:

> "A revival of true godliness among us is the greatest and most urgent of all our needs. To seek this should be our first work. There must be earnest effort to obtain the blessing of the Lord, not because God is not willing to bestow his blessing upon us, but because we are unprepared to receive it. Our Heavenly Father is more willing to give his Holy Spirit to them that ask him, than are earthly parents to give good gifts to their children. But it is our work, by confession, humiliation, repentance, and earnest prayer, to fulfill the conditions upon which God has promised to grant us his blessing. A revival need be expected only in answer to prayer."[1]

Several things immediately jump out when you read this appeal. Note that the first sentence contains three superlatives: "the greatest," the "most urgent," of "all" our needs. Is anything greater or more urgent than this need? Actually, Ellen White also mentions elsewhere that faith, divine grace, and converted families are the greatest of all our needs. But when the greatest need is also "the most urgent," she reserves the expression to speak *only* of the endowment of the Spirit in the church.

You notice, too, that if the outpouring of the Spirit on the church is not taking place, it is not because God is unwilling to bestow it. She says that "to seek this should be our first work." So it will take work. This work has nothing to do with obtaining salvation—that is *God's* work—but it has to do with letting go, with coming to the point where God can bless us as never before. And what does this work consist of? Four things: confession, humiliation (surrender), repentance, and earnest prayer. And this implies one more thing: This work is also something that happens together, with other people.

A lot of misunderstanding exists today about the person and work of the Holy Spirit, let alone what may constitute the outpouring of the Spirit, or the latter rain. Some of that is because the Christian world at large is still trying to figure it out, but even in our church, there is confusion. One thing is certain: Without the outpouring of the Holy Spirit in our lives and in our church, we're going nowhere. "What we need, what we cannot do without, is the power of the Holy Spirit to work with our efforts."[2]

Why Another Book on the Holy Spirit?

My interest in the subject of the Holy Spirit started when I was a young pastor in California. For the last twenty years, I studied it for devotional as well as academic reasons; especially, what Ellen White said about the *baptism* of the Spirit in our lives. My interest in writing this book now is threefold:

1. To rectify wrong notions some hold on the work and ministry of the Spirit in our lives and in the church.

2. To give a somewhat comprehensive picture of the many-faceted work of the Spirit in our lives; particularly as it relates to the body of Christ, or the local church.

3. To provide content and insights that may spark a revival and a reformation in the reader's heart, along with those of friends and fellow members of the church.

The book is divided into four sections: Promise, Person, Praxis, and Power. For some readers, it may start slowly, because at first what's needed are biblical and historical foundations. But if readers persist, they'll be amply rewarded, in my opinion, in the last two sections of the book.

At the end of each chapter are questions that may stimulate group discussion and personal surrender. To be honest, my hope is that this book will be read not only individually but also in groups. I'd envision groups of young adults, young couples, university students, or simply groups of friends getting together to read it and pray. It would also be good for regular church groups to get together: small groups, Sabbath School classes, ministry groups, the church board, or board of elders. In larger churches, or in conference offices, I could imagine leadership—pastoral, or administrative staff—reading the book together, or at least gathering periodically to share comments and pray together about its contents.

Whether you choose to read this together or on your own, plan to spend time looking up texts in the Word, and as you read each chapter, pause to thank Jesus and talk with Him as the Spirit moves. Read it with pen in hand. Make the most of it. Do not let this opportunity to go by without surrendering all to Jesus, the lover of your soul.

May God richly bless you, as you read and ponder what the Spirit may be saying to the church.

NOTES:

1. *Review and Herald*, March 22, 1887, par. 1, also in the better-known reference: *Selected Messages*, bk. 1, 121.

2. *The Home Missionary*, November 1, 1890, par. 26.

Promise

CHAPTER ONE

God's Great Longing

Gao Hung Tse, a laborer who lived in the country, had been baptized. He had no family and no education, and not only was he illiterate, he had such a poor memory that he couldn't remember what people had read to him. But Gao loved Jesus, and he longed to share God's love and His Word with other people—if only he could learn to read.

One Sabbath he decided that he'd plead with the Lord to do something—*anything*—so he could share his faith, so he spent hours praying for the Holy Spirit to empower him. Suddenly, Gao heard a voice say, "Read Psalm 62." He protested that he couldn't read, but the voice came again. It didn't discuss the problem or argue with him. It simply told him again to read Psalm 62. So Gao took the Bible that someone had given him at his baptism and opened it to Psalm 62. Then, to his amazement, he found that he was able to read, so he read the whole psalm.

Gao couldn't contain his excitement. He ran out of his shack and across the village, where he told the church elder, "God taught me to read!" Then he recited the whole psalm from memory. God had miraculously given him the ability both to read and to memorize.

What did Gao do with his new, God-given abilities? He proclaimed the love of Jesus to everyone who would listen. He opened the Bible and read it to others as if each word came from heaven. And because this common laborer boldly placed his trust in God's promises, God used him to bring healing and hope to multitudes of people. Hundreds came to the waters of baptism due to his testimony and ministry—180 in the first year after he was baptized!

The Promise of the Spirit

Ellen White plainly stated that "the dispensation in which we are now living is the dispensation of the Holy Spirit."[1] So apparently, the Holy Spirit is now working on earth in a special way. Are we taking advantage of it? Are we asking for Him to fill our hearts and homes? Are we, like brother Gao, insisting that the Lord fill us and fit us, and are we refusing to take No for an answer?

On the Passover night, just hours before His crucifixion, Christ promised His disciples that the Holy Spirit would come. "I will ask the Father," He said, "and He will give you another Helper, that He may be with you forever; . . . the Spirit of truth, whom the world cannot receive, . . . [for] He abides with you, and will be in you" (John 14:16, 17).

What an amazing passage! Jesus promised to ask the Father for the Holy Spirit on our behalf. When did He do that? It must have been on the morning of the day He was resurrected, when He met with His Father (see John 20:1, 15–17).[2] That night, when He appeared to the disciples huddled in the Upper Room, He told them He was now "sending forth the promise of the Father" (Luke 24:49), and He breathed on them the Spirit as a pledge of Pentecost (see John 20:19–22). He impressed upon the disciples the sacredness of the work of sharing His character with those to whom they would present the gospel.

What else did Jesus promise them? John 14 tells us that He said He'd send "another Helper." The Greek word translated "Helper" or "Comforter" is *paraklētos*, which literally means "one alongside." We use *para* today in words such as *para*llel—something that runs alongside something else—and *para*legal—someone who "parallels" a lawyer, who does some of the same things that a lawyer does. The implication is that the Holy Spirit is Someone like Jesus, but Someone who'll be with us forever. While Jesus serves as the Second Adam, representing humanity in heaven, the Holy Spirit, the *paraklētos*, serves on earth as God with us.

I'd like you to notice one more thing from our text. Jesus changed the preposition that tells how the Spirit relates to us. He didn't say that the Holy Spirit would merely be *with* us, as Jesus was with the disciples. Now the Spirit is to be *in* us. When I give seminars on the Holy Spirit, I usually pause at this point, allowing this thought to sink in. And then I share an analogy. Every mother knows the difference between her child being *with* her and her child being *in* her.

What's the point?

Jesus intends our reception of the Spirit to be so powerful, so concrete, so life-transforming, that it is like going from having life *with* you to having life *in* you. Just as the bearing of a child changes a woman forever, so the reception of the Spirit changes us forever. He lives *in* us.

Time and again that Passover night, Jesus brought up the subject of the Spirit.[3] He told His disciples that the Spirit would teach them all things and bring to their memory what He taught them (John 14:26). He said that the Spirit would bear witness of Him, and thus they would themselves bear witness (John 15:26, 27). He assured them that the Spirit of truth would guide them into all truth and that the divine Helper would disclose to them what was to come (John 16:13). He told them that His leaving was to their advantage, because it meant that the Spirit could come (John 16:7). In fact, looking to the day of the Comforter's arrival—the Day of Pentecost—Jesus tenderly said to them, "I will not leave you as orphans; I will come to you. . . . In that day you shall know that I am in My Father, and you in Me, and I in you" (John 14:18, 20). Jesus expected to be closer to His disciples *after* His departure than He was while He was physically present with them!

But wasn't the Spirit on earth already? Why then the promise that He would come?

The Spirit in the Old Testament

LeRoy Froom's book *The Coming of the Comforter* is a classic work on the Holy Spirit—perhaps the most influential Adventist book on the subject written to date. In this book Froom tells us that the Holy Spirit is mentioned 88 times in the Old Testament and 262 times in the New.[4] Based on the difference in size of the two testaments, then, the Spirit is mentioned ten times more often in the New Testament than in the Old.

But the Old Testament *does* mention the Spirit and what He does. We find Him acting at Creation (Genesis 1:2), involved in the work of regeneration (Genesis 6:3), giving talents and skills for ministry (Exodus 31:3–5), and working through signs and wonders (Judges 14:6, 19). He's most evident in the work of God's chosen leaders, such as Gideon (Judges 6:34), David (1 Samuel 16:13), and Elisha (2 Kings 2:9, 15; 8:14, 15), and particularly, the major prophets, such as Isaiah and Ezekiel (Isaiah 48:16; 59:21; Ezekiel 2:2; 3:12, 24). During this time, "the influence of the Holy Spirit had often been revealed in a marked manner, *but never in its fullness.*"[5] While we see God's Spirit at work in individuals at that time, we rarely see Him working in a corporate way—in other words, in a group of people.

We do find, however, expressions that reveal God's longing for the Spirit to work on earth among His people, along with Jesus, the Messiah. In the days of Solomon, Israel began a long relationship with idols. Through the voice of Wisdom, God told the king, "Behold I will pour out my spirit on you; I will make my words known to you." Then He warned about the results of rejecting Him: "Then they will call on me, but I will not answer; they will seek me diligently, but they shall not find me"—except that "he who listens to me shall dwell securely, and shall be at ease from the dread of evil" (Proverbs 1:23, 28, 33). This was more than 900 years before Christ came to earth. A century and a half later, God told Isaiah that the coming Messiah would have the fullness of the Spirit of God (Isaiah 11:1–13; 42:1; 61:1–3).

By the time of the Babylonian captivity five centuries before Christ, God's people had become thoroughly pagan. Through Ezekiel, God promised a change. He said He would "vindicate the holiness" of His "great name which had been profaned among the nations." He would "sprinkle clean water" on them, and cleanse them from their filthiness and their idols. In addition, God said that He would give His people a new heart, put a new Spirit within them, and "cause" them to walk in His statutes (Ezekiel 36:23, 25–27). Did you catch that? God would *cause* them to walk in His statutes. When Israel stood at the foot of Mt Sinai, hadn't they promised to walk in God's statutes? They'd said, "All that the Lord has spoken we will do"! (Exodus 19:8). But, of course, they failed miserably. Only with the power of God's Spirit could they succeed (Zechariah 4:6).

Finally, through Joel, one of the last Old Testament prophets, God called for revival and reformation. He said:

> *"Return to Me with all your heart,*
> *And with fasting, weeping, and mourning. . . .*
> *Now return to the Lord your God,*
> *For He is gracious and compassionate. . . .*
> *Blow a trumpet in Zion,*
> *Consecrate a fast, proclaim a solemn assembly,*
> *Gather the people, . . .*
> *Assemble the elders. . . .*
> *Let the priests, the Lord's ministers,*
> *Weep between the porch and the altar,*
> *And let them say, 'Spare Thy people, O Lord. . . .'"*
> *And the Lord will answer, . . .*
> *"Then I will make up to you for the years*
> *That the swarming locust has eaten. . . .*
> *"And it will come about after this*
> *That I will pour out My Spirit on all mankind;*
> *And your sons and daughters will prophesy, . . .*
> *"And even on the male and female servants*
> *I will pour out My Spirit in those days.*

"And I will display wonders in the sky and on the earth. . . .
Before the great and awesome day of the Lord comes.
"And it will come about that whoever calls on the name of the Lord
Will be delivered. . . ."

"So rejoice, O sons of Zion,
And be glad in the Lord your God;
For He has given you the early rain for your vindication.
And He has poured down for you the rain,
The early and latter rain. . . ."
(Joel 2:12, 13, 15–17, 19, 25, 28–30, 32, and verse 23).

On the Day of Pentecost, Peter recalled this marvelous promise that God gave through Joel (Acts 2:14–21). For the first time, we find God promising the Spirit to "all mankind"—men, women, young, and old. Through God's people, the power and presence of the Spirit would now be seen in the world.

Why could that not have happened in Old Testament times?

John tells us that "the Spirit was not yet given, because Jesus was not yet glorified" (John 7:39).

When was Jesus glorified?

After He suffered and died, as both He and His Father made clear only days before the cross (John 12:23, 24, 28; 13:31, 32). And just a few days *after* the Day of Pentecost, Peter, by inspiration of God, announced that Jesus was now glorified (Acts 3:13).

How was that accomplished?

On that day, Christ was enthroned as King of kings "amidst the adoration of the angels," completing His inauguration.[6] Paul adds to our understanding of this event by writing that at His ascension Christ took captives to heaven and gave gifts to men (Ephesians 4:8). This mirrors what kings of that time did when they returned home after defeating their enemies in battle. The subjects of the victorious king would line up to welcome him. Then the king and his army would parade into their home city, leading the enemy soldiers who were now their captives. And as they paraded, the king would have gifts—a share of the spoils—tossed to his jubilant people. The "captives" Christ took to heaven were the first-fruits of His resurrection (Matthew 27:52, 53), and the spoils were gifts of the Spirit showered upon the church for the advancement of Christ's kingdom.

Calvary Before Pentecost

What we've just seen, then, reveals that under no circumstances could Pentecost ever have preceded Calvary. Christ had to be glorified as

Conqueror over sin and death before His people could receive the fullness of His Spirit. The reason is quite simple: We desire the fullness of God *in* our lives only as we see the full sacrifice of Christ *for* our lives.

Christ had said that the objective of the Holy Spirit was "to convict the world concerning sin, righteousness, and judgment" (John 16:8). How does God accomplish that? Conviction of sin brings results in repentance. But do we repent simply because it becomes clear to us that we've sinned? If you're anything like me, the answer is a pathetic No. All too often we stare sin in the face, fully knowing it is sin, yet we continue in it!

Repentance is prompted by something other than our recognition that we're sinful. It comes by a demonstration of God's love for us. "The kindness of God leads you to repentance," proclaimed Paul (Romans 2:4). Think about it: Christ could well have died in the Garden of Gethsemane. He would just as soon have died there, where He was overwhelmed with the presence and power of our sin (Matthew 26:36–38). Had that happened, however, only heavenly beings would have had an appreciation of the kindness, the goodness, of God toward the fallen race. We humans would have missed it. It took the suffering of the Son of God—the shocking, lavish demonstration at the cross of God's love for us—to make us begin to pay attention. Then, and only then, could we really be convicted of our sin.

Let me illustrate. A number of years ago, when I was a young professor at one of our Adventist universities, I went to my office to do some research early one morning, hours before others arrived in the building. While I was there, I caught a glimpse of a well-known word picture that Ellen White "painted" of Jesus' sacrifice *for me*. It spoke of Christ being brutally abused *for me;* His head, His hands, His feet being bruised *for me.* Ellen White pointed to the "unutterable anguish that filled His soul at the hiding of His Father's face," and I realized it was because of *my sin*. And then, in a crescendo of painful reality, the author addressed the reader: "It is for thee that the Son of God consents to bear this burden of guilt; for thee He spoils the domain of death, and opens the gates of Paradise."[7]

I started sobbing right then and there. I tried to finish reading the paragraph, but I could no longer see; my eyes had become rivers of pain and sorrow mingled with relief. I dropped to my knees, reduced to a violent heaving that wouldn't stop, and I cried aloud, "Why, Lord? Why would You love *me* so much? Who am I that You'd give Yourself up for *me?*"

I cried and cried that morning until I ran out of tears. I'd grasped the love of my Savior, my Master and Lord, more fully than I ever had before. I'd been a pastor and Bible teacher for years. I had grown up in the church, constantly exposed to the work of Christ on behalf of sinners. I had led hundreds of people to the foot of the cross. And I had read that passage a number of times before. But that morning, the windows of heaven cast such a flood of light on God's grace that it overpowered me.

I stayed on the floor of my office for the better part of an hour, weeping out my sorrow that my sins had caused Jesus' death, that I had gone on wantonly sinning with no care for what that sin does to Him, and that I had lived for so long without fully appreciating what God had done for me. How could the God of heaven, the King of kings and Lord of lords—the One to whom we owe *everything*, from our every breath to eternal life—yield His life, His all, *for me?*

To tell you the truth, I was so overwhelmed by the love of God that day that I dared not move or speak for a while. It seemed to me blasphemous even to say Thank You. My holy God gave Himself *for me.* I silently prayed that He'd stay His hand, because I imagined that if I were to discover more of His grace on my behalf, I could only explode, being unable to contain it all.

What do you think I did when I began to recover? Do you think I returned to living my life as carelessly as before? That I sought out secular distractions? Oh, no. I surrendered myself fully—at least more fully than I ever had before. "Lord," I said, "if You are willing to love me this much—I don't deserve it; I never will. If there's something You can do with me for Your glory, do it. I surrender all. It's my privilege and honor to surrender all to You. I'm nothing, and You're everything, but You've chosen to treat me as if I were worthy."

Do you see why John said the Spirit had not yet been given, for Jesus had not yet been glorified? (John 7:39.) The supreme, humble, gracious work of the Spirit is to show us Jesus as He really is. The law of God on which the universe runs is the law of self-sacrificing love—but until Calvary, only God knew how much He loved us. After the cross, the Holy Spirit could finally show His love to us in ways unknown before. That's why it was that the Spirit was poured upon *all* humankind at that time.

We live in a different era today—the era of the Spirit. Should we then expect the church and each follower of the cross to reflect that difference?

We should.

God does. .

NOTES:

1. Ellen G. White, *Testimonies to Ministers and Gospel Workers* (Mountain View, CA: Pacific Press, 1944), 511.

2. See Ellen G. White, *The Desire of Ages* (Mountain View, CA: Pacific Press, 1940), 790.

3. Ellen White wrote: "Christ, the Great Teacher, had an infinite variety of subjects from which to choose, but the one upon which He dwelt most largely was the endowment of the Holy Spirit" (*Selected Messages*, bk. 1 [Washington, D.C.: Review and Herald, 1958], 156).

4. LeRoy E. Froom, *The Coming of the Comforter*, rev. ed. (Hagerstown, MD.: Review and Herald, 1956), 27.

5. Ellen G. White, *The Acts of the Apostles* (Mountain View, CA: Pacific Press, 1911), 37; emphasis added.

6. *Ibid.*, 38, 39.

7. The entire paragraph is found in *The Desire of Ages*, 755, 756. It reads: "The spotless Son of God hung upon the cross, His flesh lacerated with stripes; those hands so often reached out in blessing, nailed to the wooden bars; those feet so tireless on ministries of love, spiked to the tree; that royal head pierced by the crown of thorns; those quivering lips shaped to the cry of woe. And all that He endured—the blood drops that flowed from His head, His hands, His feet, the agony that wracked His frame, and the unutterable anguish that filled His soul at the hiding of His Father's face—speaks to each child of humanity, declaring, It is for thee that the Son of God consents to bear this burden of guilt; for thee He spoils the domain of death, and opens the gates of Paradise. He who stilled the angry waves and walked the foam-capped billows, who made devils tremble and disease flee, who opened blind eyes and called forth the dead to life,—offers Himself upon the cross as a sacrifice, and this from love to thee. He, the Sin Bearer, endures the wrath of divine justice, and for thy sake becomes sin itself."

Questions for Reflection or Group Study

1. What impressed you most about the story of Gao Hung Tse from China?

2. What does it mean to you that the name Jesus gave the Spirit was the Greek *parakletos*, meaning "one alongside"?

3. What are the implications of John 14:17, about the Spirit being *in* us, not *with* us?

4. What about the Holy Spirit in the Old Testament?

5. Reread Joel 2:12–32. What is the prophet saying about the Spirit?

6. Describe the glorification of Jesus after the resurrection.

7. Why couldn't Pentecost happen before Calvary?

8. Read *The Desire of Ages,* 755, 756, found in the footnotes. What is your response to such love?

9. What is, in essence, the work of the Spirit?

10. In summary, what is "God's Great Longing"?

CHAPTER TWO

What It Takes to Birth a Church

Everything changed after Jesus was resurrected. Atonement for fallen humanity was now accomplished. Heavenly angels were assured that sin would now be finished. And God's people—His church—would also never be the same again.

The night of His resurrection, Christ breathed on His disciples the Holy Spirit (John 20:21, 22) because they needed His aid to understand, in a short time, centuries of Messianic prophecies. "When you have received the baptism of the Holy Spirit," Ellen White wrote, "then you will understand more of the joys of salvation than you have known all your life hitherto."[1] That night, He began opening "their minds to understand the Scriptures" (Luke 24:45). For the next forty days, Jesus unveiled to the apostles the Great Commission.

In the Bible we find four versions of the Great Commission. Most people think of the one found in Matthew 28, with the command to "go and make disciples," but a more complete picture is seen, when you include the other three. On resurrection night, the Commission was to proclaim "forgiveness of sins," and the first thing to do was not to *go*, but to *stay* in the city, until they were "clothed with power from on high" (Luke 24:46–49). The second and third times were during their meeting in Galilee, some days later.[2] Christ here emphasized their need to "Go into all the world and preach the gospel to all creation" (Mark 16:25) and to "make disciples . . . baptizing them in the name of the Father, the Son, and the

31

Holy Spirit, teaching them to observe all that I commanded you" (Matthew 28:19, 20).

The last time the Great Commission is recorded is just before the time of Christ's ascension, on the Mount of Olives. And the emphasis now is to *wait*, not to go. The text is worth quoting in full:

> "Gathering them together, He commanded them not to leave Jerusalem, but to wait for what the Father had promised, 'Which,' He said, 'you heard of from Me; for John baptized with water, but you will be baptized with the Holy Spirit not many days from now.' So when they had come together, they were asking Him, saying, 'Lord, is it at this time You are restoring the kingdom to Israel?' He said to them, 'It is not for you to know times or epochs which the Father has fixed by His own authority; but you will receive power when the Holy Spirit has come upon you; and you shall be My witnesses both in Jerusalem, and in all Judea and Samaria, and even to the remotest part of the earth'" (Acts 1:8).

A full picture of the Great Commission, then, includes the commands to *stay*, to *go*, and to *wait*—as well as a broader-than-expected spectrum of objectives, such as to "proclaim forgiveness of sins," to "preach the gospel," to "make disciples," and to "witness." But even though Jesus spent forty days explaining these things to the disciples, there were some things they kept missing.

Second Coming, or the Coming of the Spirit?

Let's look at that Acts 1 text again. For weeks, Christ talked much about their need to share the gospel with the world and emphasized how, in order to do it effectively, they would need the Holy Spirit. The last words they heard Him say before they went to the Mount of Olives pointed to their need to wait in Jerusalem until they received the fullness of the Holy Spirit. He even told them they would be baptized with the Spirit "not many days from now." But the disciples' response misses Christ's point entirely. Instead of asking about the Holy Spirit or about witnessing, they asked if at that time His kingdom would be restored! He had already plainly declared to them that it was "not His purpose to establish in this world a temporal kingdom,"[3] but they had a hard time switching their thinking to new ideas.

Jesus' reply is interesting. He told them not to worry about "times and epochs which the Father has fixed by His own authority" (Acts 1:7). This is reminiscent of the time He told them about the signs of His return, and the fact that "that day and hour no one knows, . . . but the Father alone," and to "therefore, be on the alert" because they would not know, exactly, when the Lord would come (Matthew 24:36, 42).

This interchange resonates with many in the Seventh-day Adventist

Church today. Since 1844, multitudes have been fascinated with the possible time of Christ's return. Books and lectures revealing the latest insights on the understanding of the times have always been popular and well attended. If this book were entitled *Twelve Reasons Why Jesus Will Come Before 2020*, it would likely become an instant best seller. I remember from a few years ago a sincere man who loved the study of the Spirit of Prophecy and the Bible, who became convinced Christ would come by or before May 15, 2003. He based this on questionable exegesis of the Old Testament, but it didn't matter. He was persuaded, and I would be responsible for the loss of souls if I did not embrace his view and began warning others within my sphere of influence. He was so convicted about his prediction that, if it were not to take place as he outlined it, he pledged to eat his socks. Well, you know the outcome: That date came and went. And a couple of weeks later, he saw me in the church foyer and sought to hide behind a column. I was really tempted to go up to him and ask, "How did those socks taste?"

We place a great deal of emphasis on the coming of Christ and for good reason—we are *Adventists*, after all, waiting for the return of our Lord. But notice that this was *not* Christ's emphasis during the last weeks with His disciples. His emphasis was to wait for the endowment of the Spirit, in order to have power to witness. Christ is far more interested in our *fitness* for His return, than we should be in the *timing* of His return.

The coming of the Spirit into our lives precedes the coming of the Lord to our world. And the baptism of the Spirit is necessary for His coming. Why? you ask. Because the Spirit is the only One who can convict the world of sin, righteousness, and judgment (John 16:8). But the Spirit, surprisingly, is not sent to the world but instead, He is sent to the church (v. 7). As He works through the church, the world is brought to Jesus.

John the Baptist, a man full of the Spirit from his mother's womb (Luke 1:15), gave a wonderful promise:

> "As for me, I baptize you with water for repentance, but He who is coming after me is mightier than I. . . . He will baptize you with the Holy Spirit and fire" (Matthew 3:11).

God is so serious about our need of the Spirit's baptism that it is the only promise mentioned in all four of the gospels (Matthew 3:11; Mark 1:8; Luke 3:16; John 1:32–34), as well as twice in Acts (Acts 1:5; 11:16). No other promise is given such preeminence in the New Testament. Even God's last-day messenger gives it the utmost importance.[4]

Fortunately, the disciples decided to obey. They waited in Jerusalem until the coming of the promise. They did not tarry for ten days; that is, they tarried for as long as it took until the Spirit came, which, unknown to them at first, was a mere ten days later.

Would we do the same today?

What Brought About Pentecost?

I wish you could take the time and read carefully the chapter entitled "Pentecost" from Ellen White's *The Acts of the Apostles*. A careful reading reveals marvelous insights about how the disciples spent that time together. Here is an excerpt from that chapter:

"As the disciples waited for the fulfillment of the promise, they humbled their hearts in true repentance and confessed their unbelief. . . . They called to remembrance the words [of] Christ. . . . Truths which had passed from their memory were again brought to their minds, and these they repeated to one another. . . . Scene after scene of His wonderful life passed before them. . . . They meditated upon His pure, holy life. . . . They sorrowed for having ever grieved Him. . . . But they were comforted by the thought that they were forgiven. And they determined [to] bravely confess Him before the world.

"The disciples prayed with intense earnestness for a fitness to meet men and in their daily intercourse to speak words that would lead sinners to Christ. Putting away all differences, all desire for the supremacy, they came close together in Christian fellowship. . . . They were weighted with the burden of the salvation of souls. They realized that the gospel was to be carried to the world, and they claimed the power that Christ had promised.

"The Spirit came upon the waiting, praying disciples with a fullness that reached every heart. . . . And under the influence of the Spirit, words of penitence and confession mingled with songs of praise for sins forgiven. . . . Lost in wonder, the apostles exclaimed, 'Herein is love.' They grasped the imparted gift. And what followed? . . . Thousands were converted in a day."[5]

Have you ever experienced anything like that? This is what brought Pentecost. This is what it took. The first thing that comes to mind is the fact that they did not focus on the Holy Spirit as much as they did on Jesus. Jesus' words, Jesus' character, and Jesus' works, they remembered and repeated to each other. They meditated on who He really was and the legacy He left with them. The second thing is that this filled them with love for Him, which made them determined to share Him with others. And there is one more thing. But first, allow me to list a summary of these pages—something you might find helpful if and when you choose to get together with others seeking the infilling of the Holy Spirit. Take note of the clear and simple nature of their actions:

▸ They gathered together to wait for the promise.

▸ They humbled their hearts in true repentance.

▸ They confessed their unbelief.

▸ They recalled the words of Jesus regarding His sacrifice.

▸ They repeated to one another the truths they remembered.

▸ They meditated upon Christ's holy life.

▸ They determined to share Jesus with the world.

▸ They prayed with intense earnestness to lead sinners to Christ.

▸ They put away differences and came close together in fellowship.

▸ They praised Jesus in song for sins forgiven.

▸ They contemplated with wonder the love of God.

▸ They took hold of the imparted gift.

The last thing that is striking about these pages is their *togetherness*. Few doubt today the value of prayer and of meditation on Jesus. We are clearly told it would be well for us to do so every day for an hour.[6] But what we miss, especially in the West, is the *togetherness* factor. Corporate prayer and searching after God will never replace the need for our personal, daily time with Jesus. But only when we choose to do this together are we finally getting serious about a radical change in our lives, families, and churches.

Above the Arctic Circle in Russia is an oil town called Murmansk. A miserable place, its winters last most of the year. In the mid-90s, there was a dying Seventh-day Adventist Church there. They once had twenty-two members, but because people don't move there unless they must, the attrition rate was severe, and they ended up with only eight members—the pastor and his wife and six men who worked in the rigs.

They did a reality check and concluded they were destined to die unless something radical were to take place. But what to do? How can you share the gospel in a place like that? They decided not to look to their circumstances but instead, to the Lord. They began to pray for the Holy Spirit and to yield their lives in full consecration to Jesus. But in this frozen tundra, they needed encouragement and accountability. So they came up with an idea.

Every icy morning at six, the seven men met at the Walrus Club, stripped to their shorts, walked onto the frozen lake to a designated fishing hole, and submerged themselves in the hole, one after the other. Then they knelt around the hole, arms on each others' shoulders, and earnestly prayed for the fire of the Spirit to melt their hearts with love for souls. Why such eccentric behavior? you may wonder. Couldn't they have met in someone's living room, by the fire, to have prayer? Perhaps that is what most of us would have done. But the men of Murmansk wanted to hold themselves accountable to God. The daily dip in the freezing waters was their pledge that they'd be ready to lead people to the waters of baptism every single day—rain or snow or ice. They would not wait until summer to receive God's Spirit. Their daily routine was to hold each other accountable in the service of God.

Did anything happen?

Everything happened. Within a year of this practice, they brought eighty people to the waters of baptism, a 1,000 percent rate of growth. Through the next few years, the church planted at least six more churches in the area. And this in a place where there are more vodka bottles than people!

> "It is the absence of the Spirit that makes the gospel ministry so powerless. Learning, talents, eloquence, every natural or acquired endowment, may be possessed; but without the presence of the Spirit of God, no heart will be touched, no sinner be won to Christ. On the other hand, if they are connected with Christ, if the gifts of the Spirit are theirs, the poorest and most ignorant of His disciples will have a power that will tell upon hearts. God makes them the channel for the outworking of the highest influence in the universe."[7]

Two Premises for Church Life

The way the early church was born was the same as when a child is born. It takes two to become one, in order to produce another one. This constitutes the first premise for church life: unity. This is why so much emphasis is placed in Acts on being of *one accord* (Acts 1:14; 4:32; 5:12).

The concept is eternal. Have you even wondered why God is three Persons? This is not the place to discuss imponderable issues such as the nature of the Trinity, but we could learn about ourselves by looking at the Godhead. If God is love (1 John 4:8), and love cannot become a reality unless it is shared with others, then it makes sense for God to be one in three Persons—Persons who practice and express perfect love in perfect humility. You cannot love no one, or nothing, and still assume you love. Love exists because there is someone *to* love.

So God has always been in three Persons, in order to love another, before there was any creature to love. When you read in the Bible about the relationship between Father, Son, and Holy Spirit, you find that they are each always seeking to give honor and preeminence to the other. They think of each other—and others—first. The Holy Spirit exalts Jesus, Jesus exalts the Father, and the Father exalts both the Spirit and Jesus by being equal to them (John 16:13–15). They were the first Community.

So when God created mankind, He could not have it otherwise. Look at the story of Creation. In the first chapter, everything is pronounced "good" after each day (Genesis 1:4, 10, 12, 18, 21), and on the sixth day, after the creation of Adam and Eve, it was "very" good (Genesis 1:31). You can expect that; after all, it comes from the hand of a perfect, loving God. However, in the second chapter, something is "not good," even though it is part of the Creation. "Then the Lord God said, 'It is not good for the man to be alone; I will make him a helper suitable for him'" (Genesis 2:18).

Why would God allow something *not good* to be part of His *good* Creation? Because Adam was made in God's image (Genesis 1:26, 27), and as such, he reflected God's character of love. God wanted Adam himself to figure out that unless he had someone to love, he would be incomplete.

God knew by personal experience the need for another, but He allowed Adam time to sort it out on his own. Once God made Eve, Adam thought of her as part of himself—"This is bone of my bones, and flesh of my flesh"—and he called her *Isha*, the Hebrew word for "woman," because she was taken out of *Ish*, "man" (Genesis 2:23). And since, according to Genesis 5:2, *Adam* is the generic name for mankind and not just a male name, then in a very real sense, Adam was not an individual man until Eve was made a woman. And one of the clearest evidences mankind was made in God's image was the fact that they were able to *re*create in *their* image (Genesis 4:1). That's something even angels cannot do.

If you've ever wondered why your sibling is different than you, or why in marriage opposites tend to attract, the root cause goes back to this concept. God intends for all of us to live in community; that is, with people not just like us, so it will demand a choice to love and cherish those around us. This is what it means to be made in God's image.

The church is to function the same way. At a time of disharmony and petty jealousies between the disciples, Jesus gave them one more commandment: "Love one another, even as I have loved you." Why, Jesus? Because "By this all men will know that you are My disciples, if you have love for one another" (John 13:34, 35). Everyone in the world knows you love those who love you back—it is human nature to do so. But when you love the unlovable, when you care for the one who forgets you, when you forgive those who hurt you or dismiss you, that reflects what God's type of love is all about. That *is* what reveals we are sons and daughters of our heavenly Father (Matthew 5:43–48).

Spending that time in the Upper Room together all those days allowed the first disciples to discover what true love was all about. Those 120 people did not have a natural love toward each other. Men and women were there, with all that those gender differences imply. Peter was there, who thought himself spiritually superior (Mark 13:29), and James and John, who were like Thunder to others (Matthew 20:20, 21, 24). Thomas was there, who would not accept the testimony of his friends (John 20:24, 25), as were the brothers of Jesus, who had made a sport of mocking Christ and His followers (John 7:3–5). But there they were, together, and they became of "one accord" (Acts 1:14). The focus on Jesus united them.

Here is a statement a friend of mine pointed out to me many years ago:

"The sanctification of the soul by the working of the Holy Spirit is the implanting of Christ's nature in humanity. Gospel religion is Christ in the life—a living, active principle. It is the grace of Christ revealed in character and wrought out in good works. . . . Love is the basis of godliness. Whatever the profession, no man has pure love to God unless he has unselfish love for his brother. But we can never come into possession of this spirit by *trying* to love others. What is needed is the love of Christ in the heart. When self is merged in Christ, love springs forth spontaneously. The completeness of Christian character is attained when the impulse to help and bless others springs constantly from within—when the sunshine of heaven fills the heart and is revealed in the countenance."[8]

And that is what happened to the early church. Because community took place, the second premise of church life became possible: the baptism of the Holy Spirit. Think of it this way: In order to produce new life, two must come together in complete unity. When the church was united, new life was born. A church was born in the Spirit. Without these two premises—these two non-negotiables—it is impossible to be God's church.

The question is, would the relationship last?

NOTES:

1. Letter 33, 1890, in *Manuscript Releases*, vol. 5, 231.

2. For a brief commentary on chronology after the resurrection, see Francis D. Nichol, ed. *The Seventh-day Adventist Bible Commentary*, vol. 5 (Washington, D.C.: Review and Herald Publishing Association, 1956), 100.

3. See *The Acts of the Apostles*, 30.

4. Based on the Ellen G. White Writings Complete Published Edition (2007), 8,943 entries refer to the baptism of the Spirit or similar expressions. That would mean nearly one of every ten manuscript pages she ever wrote.

5. *The Acts of the Apostles*, 35–38.

6. See *The Desire of Ages*, 83.

7. *Christ's Object Lessons*, 328.

8. *Ibid.*, 384.

Questions for Reflection or Group Study

1. What are your thoughts about the four versions of the Great Commission? *You by reading & studying them all can then see the need to follow the Lords direction & wait upon the Holy Spirit, then go*

2. Why do you feel the disciples were more interested in the time of the end rather than the coming of the Spirit? How does their experience relate to us today? *They continued to resent the misconceptions drilled into them by the Saducies & Pharasics.*

3. What are the implications to the statement: "The coming of the Spirit in our lives precedes the coming of the Lord to our world?" *We must be fully prepaird by the Holy Spirit.*

4. What is the only NT promise mentioned in all four of the gospels and twice in the book of Acts? Why is this promise so stressed in the NT? *The promise of the outpouring of the Holy Spirit*

5. Review the twelve actions listed that the disciples focused on while waiting for the Holy Spirit. What common denominators do you see in their actions? *A focus on Jesus, and His Character, ect......*

6. Why is it so hard to seek God together? *Because we are different. Like team players we most meld by the Glue we call Jesus,*

7. What would it take for a similar experience to happen in our church? *A revival in attitude to dedicate ourselves to join and beseach the Holy spirit following the examples of the disciples.*

8. How does the Murmansk story relate to and affect you at this time in your life? *Listen to the Holy Spirit & Follow His leading.*

9. Reflect on the insights about the creation of Adam and Eve and on the implications of what it means to be human. *This is an absolute true story about God's perfectia which most Christians wont understand without Gods Holy Spirit.*

10. Reread John 13:34, 35. Why was it so important for Jesus to share that with His disciples? What is the primary reason we are to "Love one another . . ."? *So others will know we are christs disciples.*

11. Take a moment and contemplate on the 120 in that Upper Room—look at their differences in gender, age, occupations, attitudes, and personalities. How did they really become community, "one"? They were first To recieve Christs gift of The first rain ~to all the world preaching The gospel To all Creation,

CHAPTER THREE

The Little Revival That Couldn't

"**A**re the things you are living for worth Christ dying for?" *Yes*

Pause for a moment. Read that again. This poignant question is written on the tombstone of English evangelist and author Leonard Ravenhill. How would you answer it?

Perhaps the early church became what it was by keeping that thought in mind. The book of Acts is the record of the Holy Spirit's activity in the early church. The stories, the miracles, the mission adventures, the messages that swayed friend and enemy alike, are all a reflection of what God can do with a group of people who give themselves unreservedly to the leading of the Spirit.[1]

Is your church like that? *Not yet*

We hardly find a church today like the one described in Acts. The words of Carl Bates, one-time president of the Southern Baptist Convention, are applicable to the Adventist Church in America today:

"If God were to take the Holy Spirit out of our midst today, about ninety-five percent of what we are doing in our churches would go on, and we would not know the difference. Yet if God had taken the Holy Spirit out of the midst of the first Christian community, about ninety-five percent of what they were doing would have ceased immediately."[2]

43

The early church began to lose its first love before the close of the first century (Revelation 2:1, 4). Once the apostles were gone, much of the life and power of the church also disappeared. Spiritual leadership does matter. By the second century, the church began to compromise God's Word, which is a direct affront to the Spirit, since He is the Author (2 Peter 1:21). God's Sabbath was given equal footing with man's alternate day of rest. Bishops began their way up the clerical church ladder. The person of the Holy Spirit became a distant notion in the church, much like an influence or a breeze in an open field, but devoid of personality or relevancy to people's everyday lives.

By the sixth century, the church had thoroughly apostatized. Religious traditions trumped God's Word, the church became the ruling empire, and the mission frontier ceased to be just outside the Christian's front door. Then, the church went into "the desert" for over 1,200 years. Dark were those church ages, devoid of much of the Spirit. God did move, in spite of these conditions, wherever He was allowed into the hearts of men, especially during the Protestant Reformation. The Pietist Movement in Germany, the Methodist Movement in England, and the Great Awakening in America followed as examples of the Spirit's work with some in the world. But the full recovery the Spirit initiated with the apostles would wait until the nineteenth century.

The Millerite Movement and the Second Great Awakening[3]

By most accounts, the Second Great Awakening began in 1794 with Isaac Backus' initiative known as "the concert of prayer." Backus, a leading Baptist minister, deeply convicted by reading accounts of the Holy Spirit's activity during the First Great Awakening, sent out a plea for prayer to ministers of every denomination. Churches set every Monday aside for prayer, and revival soon followed in New England, then in the Western frontier. The denominated Kentucky Revival of 1800 put the nationwide revival on the map. It affected Congregationalist, Methodist, Baptist, and Presbyterian churches all over the country. God used preachers such as Lyman Beecher, Peter Cartwright, and Charles Finney in mighty ways to bring about a revival that went on for decades. The churches experienced phenomenal growth at this time. The awakening "continued for a full half century in an almost unbroken succession of revivals, thereby constituting an era of evangelism unparalleled in the history of the nation or the world."[4] God seemed to be preparing the new nation for the Advent Movement.

The Millerite Movement was the climax of the Second Great Awakening. But it went deeper and made an even greater impact on the people. This time, the Awakening became a *worldwide* phenomenon *and* became rooted in the study of Bible prophecy. Between 1840 and 1844, it seemed as if everyone had caught millennial fever, and the longing for God to come near became very tangible. So many expected Christ to come in 1844 that Ellen White remembered it to be "the happiest year of my life."[5] But there was another difference, in contrast with the excesses of previous revivals. She recalled that "of all the great religious movements since the days of the apostles, none have been more free from human imperfection and the wiles of Satan than was that of the autumn of 1844." That time was, indeed, "a glorious manifestation of the power of God."[6]

The Lord could have come shortly afterward. The world had received an unprecedented warning of His soon return through the first and second angels' message, taking it "to every missionary station in the world." The movement swept over the land like a tidal wave.[7] Nearly 100,000 souls in New England alone prepared to meet Jesus in the clouds![8] "The softening, subduing power of the Holy Spirit melted the heart as His blessing was bestowed in rich measure upon the faithful, believing ones."[9]

Yet few survived the Great Disappointment of October 22, 1844. Many Adventists lost hope in Christ altogether, some recanted their experience, and some took up fanatical practices that brought shame to Christ's other followers and lawsuits to themselves. Forty years after the fact, Ellen White believed Christ could have come after 1844, and she gave the reason why it had not happened:

> "If all who had labored unitedly in the work in 1844, had received *the third angel's message and proclaimed it in the power of the Holy Spirit*, the Lord would have wrought mightily with their efforts. A flood of light would have been shed upon the world. Years ago the inhabitants of the earth would have been warned, the closing work completed, and Christ would have come for the redemption of His people."[10]

The third angel's message had not been proclaimed by the time of the Great Disappointment, although evidence shows that several dozen Adventists were already keeping the seventh day holy, thanks to Rachel Oakes and her Methodist pastor, Frederick Wheeler. Even though the Adventists were receptive to the Spirit's leading regarding the Second Coming, most of them resisted the truth of the Sabbath, considering it unnecessary. Only six weeks before October 22, one of their major papers self-righteously proclaimed:

> "Many persons have their minds deeply exercised respecting a supposed obligation to observe the seventh day," but "we feel borne irresistibly to the conclusion that there is no particular portion of time which Christians are required by law to set apart as holy time."[11]

God's Spirit, however, would try again to wake up His church to finish the work, so Christ could return for His own.

The Message to Laodicea

The few dozen who survived the Great Disappointment chose to stay faithful to what biblical prophecy had so incontrovertibly affirmed, and they believed that their error was in the event and not in prophetic dating. This conviction opened the doors for more light from God's Word. Thus, the "little flock" studied and prayed, prayed and studied. By the end of the decade, the ministry of Christ in the sanctuary, the seventh-day Sabbath, and the non-immortality of the soul, along with the Spirit of Prophecy, became theological pillars of the remnant.

Consequently, the Sabbath became an important issue for this remnant. "But it seems that the attention on the Sabbath crowded out proper attention to nurturing the believers in spiritual growth."[12] In May of 1856, Ellen White received a vision about the condition of the remnant. When writing about it, she compared the present situation with that of the 1844 movement.

> "There was a spirit of consecration then that there is not now. What has come over the professed peculiar people of God? I saw the conformity to the world, the unwillingness to suffer for the truth's sake."[13]

What happened?

Seventh-day Adventists were becoming lackadaisical, worldly, Laodicean, just like the Christian world around them had become. The Industrial Revolution and the vast opportunities afforded in a virgin land, as people moved West, were so plentiful that many made riches with relative ease. The invention of the railroad and the telegraph, along with the discovery of gold in California, all contributed to an unprecedented age of prosperity. In his inaugural address, President James Buchanan stated that, because of the unparalleled success of the United States, "no nation ha[d] ever before been embarrassed from too large a surplus in its treasury."[14] Religious historian Warren Candler couldn't be more clear: "Men forgot God in pursuit of gold."[15] This affected the religious world in general and the Adventist faithful in particular.

As New England Sabbatarian Adventists moved West in search of better opportunities, they lost their vision for the soon return of Christ and became self-absorbed. Even effective ministers lost sight of the mark, as in the case of J. N. Loughborough, who—once found in Waukon, Iowa, working and building instead of preaching—elicited the stern and now-famous triple rebuke of the prophetess: "What doest thou here, Elijah?"[16]

In late 1855 Ellen White received a vision in which she "saw that the Spirit of the Lord has been dying away from the church" because God's people had trusted too much to the strength of argument.[17]

On October 9, 1856; the *Review and Herald* published an article wondering, for the first time, if the message to Laodicea was meant for "those who profess the Third Angel's Message" and not Christians in general. James White's article was followed by another one the next week, in which he concluded that "the Laodicean church represents the church of God at the present time." Two weeks later, David Hewitt responded with an appeal to families, children, and even preachers to "let Jesus in," ending with, "May the writer of this let him in."[18]

"The response from the field was electrifying," wrote Arthur White.[19] By the end of the month, the budding remnant had accepted this new light, even though it would be another six months before Ellen White published anything about it. Between November 1856 and December 1857, 348 articles appeared in the *Review and Herald* on the Laodicean message—most of them by lay members—a very high percentage, considering that only about 2,500 members made up the entire church those days.

However, the revival caused by the appeal of Jesus, the True Witness, (Rev. 3:14–22) did not last. By the summer of 1857, there were signs that many had not heeded the Laodicean message. The November 29, 1857, issue of *Review and Herald* carried an article from Ellen White in which she told of a vision of two groups. One prayed earnestly, sharing the truth "in great power" due to "the latter rain . . . the refreshing from the presence of the Lord, the loud cry of the third angel." But the other did not participate in the work of agonizing and pleading and eventually, they lost their way. Why? Because "the testimony of the True Witness has not been half heeded . . . if not entirely disregarded." In 1859, she gave a clear testimony as to why revival and reformation did not take place as the Spirit had planned:

> "I was shown that the testimony to the Laodiceans applies to God's people at the present time, and the reason it has not accomplished a greater work is *because of the hardness of their hearts*. But God has given the message time to do its work. . . . When it was first presented, it led to close examination of heart. Sins were confessed, and the people of God were stirred everywhere. Nearly all believed that this message would end in the loud cry of the third angel. But *as they failed to see the powerful work accomplished in a short time, many lost the effect of the message. I saw that this message would not accomplish its work in a few short months*."[20]

The problem with believers resided in their expectations. A few short months of the Spirit's work would not be enough for the thorough work He had in mind. She continued to say that the Spirit meant to fit them "for the loud cry of the third angel" and that God had sent "angels . . . in every direction to prepare unbelieving hearts for the truth."

Had angels been sent to prepare the world for the truth? Maybe.

The Laymen's Revival

On September 23, 1857, at the Fulton Street Church in downtown New York City, Jeremiah Lanphier had been hired as a missionary to reach the businessmen of the city. Not knowing exactly how to do that, he printed handbills, announcing noon prayer meetings, with the title, "How Often Should I Pray?" That first day, he was joined by six men. Within a month, over 100 people came. Six months later, 50,000 people were meeting every day at noon for prayer in churches all over New York and in other cities! Factories began to blow the lunch whistle at 11:55 A.M. to allow workers to dash to the nearest church for prayer, and then the whistle would blow again at 1:05 P.M. By February of 1858, conversions in New York alone were seen at a rate of 10,000 per week! Newspaper reports throughout New England revealed no unconverted adults in many towns. Estimates are that the 1857–1859 revival brought over one million people to conversion in America. A religious journal gave the following picture of the revival, in March 1858:

> "Such a time as the present was never known since the days of the Apostles, for revivals. The prostration of business, the downfall of Mammon, . . . [conviction] have come home to the hearts and consciences of the millions in our land with a power that seems irresistible . . . exciting the earnest and simultaneous cry from thousands, What shall we do to be saved? . . . The large cities and towns generally from Maine to California are sharing in this great and glorious work."[21]

Recent research has shown that the Prayer Meeting Revival, as it is sometimes known, made a universal impact. Although lacking a central organization, the awakening spread to dozens of cities in the Eastern seaboard, the South, and the frontier West, as well as to Canada, Ireland, the British Empire, Jamaica, South India, China, Japan, Indonesia, Uganda, South Africa, Scandinavia, Germany, and the Ukraine. It influenced scores of ministers and future missionaries and revolutionized the lives of college and university young adults all over the world.

God was awakening the world to receive the third angel's message, but the remnant church had not responded wholeheartedly to the Laodicean appeal made in 1856 and 1857. The church's failure was an unwillingness to persevere in faith for Christ to accomplish a deep work of repentance in their lives, in order to fit them for the loud cry of the third angel. Had the church surrendered thoroughly, Christ would have come.[22]

Ten years after the Laodicean message was meant to turn the little flock, Ellen White wrote: "God's unwillingness to have His people perish has been the reason for so long delay."[23]

How much longer will we be asleep in the light, while the world is asleep in the dark? The Lord, in His infinite love for the lost, would try once again to wake the church.

"Are the things you are living for worth Christ dying for?"

NOTES:

1. In my personal study of Acts, I have found fifty-five references to the Holy Spirit—forty-two of them in the first thirteen chapters alone—and twenty-nine clear and distinct references to church growth or specific conversions.

2. Cited by David Watson, *I Believe in the Church* (Grand Rapids, MI: Eerdmans, 1978), 166.

3. Much of this chapter and the next is taken from an unpublished paper I wrote and gave at the 2nd International Bible Conference in Izmir, Turkey, in July of 2006, entitled, "The Holy Spirit and the Finishing of the Work in Historical Perspective: Implications for Spiritual Leadership."

4. Frank G. Beardsley, *Religious Progress Through Religious Revivals* (New York: American Tract Society, 1943), 39, cited in Felix A. Lorenz, *Our Only Hope* (Nashville, TN: Southern Publishing, 1976), 52.

5. *Testimonies*, vol. 1, 54.

6. *The Great Controversy*, 401, 611.

7. *Ibid.*, 611, 400.

8. As estimated by Arthur L. White, in his *Ellen G. White: The Early Years, 1827–1862* (Hagerstown, MD: Review and Herald, 1985), 53.

9. *The Great Controversy*, 403.

10. *Ibid.*, 458, emphasis supplied.

11. *The Midnight Cry*, September 5, 12, 1844.

12. See Lorenz, 25.

13. *Testimonies*, vol. 1, 128.

14. Cited in J. Edwin Orr, *The Event of the Century* (Wheaton, IL: The

International Awakening Press, 1989), 1. Orr is considered by many as the greatest authority on the history of Christian revivals.

15.   Warren A. Candler, *Great Revivals and the Great Republic* (Nashville: Publishing House of the M. E. Church, South, 1904), 210, quoted in Malcolm McDow and Alvin L. Reid, *Firefall: How God Has Shaped History Through Revivals* (Enumclaw, WA: Winepress Publishing, 2002), 252.

16.   For the whole story, see White, *Progressive Years*, 348–349.

17.   *Testimonies*, vol. 1, 113.

18.   "Gold Tried in the Fire," *Review and Herald*, November 6, 1856. Hewitt had the reputation of being "the most honest man in town"—the kind Joseph Bates looked for when seeking to share the Sabbath truth at Battle Creek in 1852.

19.   White, *The Early Years*, 344.

20.   *Testimonies*, vol. 1, 186, emphasis supplied.

21.   Henry C. Fish, *Handbook of Revivals*, 77, 78, quoted in Lorenz, 55.

22.   In May 1856, Ellen White saw in vision acquaintances at a conference, and said about them: "Some food for worms, some subjects of the seven last plagues, some will be alive and remain upon the earth to be translated at the coming of Jesus," *Testimonies*, vol. 1, 131, 132. Clearly, in spite of the conditional nature of this prophecy, Ellen White expected the Lord to come in the very near future.

23.   *Testimonies*, vol. 2, 194.

Questions for Reflection or Group Study

1. Are the things you're living for worth Christ dying for? *Yes*

2. Reflect on the condition of your local church in view of the words by Carl Bates that nine-five percent of what we do in the churches may be regardless of the Holy Spirit.
   We need To join togather & Cry out for The Holy Spirit.

3. What was "the concert of prayer," and what did it bring about?
   1794 in New England led by Isaac Backus Set aside every monday for prayer

4. Why wasn't Jesus able to return in the wake of the Millerite Movement? *Gods people became discouraged instead of proclaiming The 3rd angles message.*

5. Describe the condition of the Adventist Church which led the Whites to identify it as the Laodicean church.
   The people became worldly Neither Hot or Cold

6. Read Revelation 3:14-22. What is the solution to our Laodicean condition? *Invite The spirit of The Lord into your soul*

7. Why did the Adventists of 1857 not see a thorough and lasting revival and reformation in their midst?
   The remnant Church did not respond wholeheartedly To The Laodicean appeal.

8. What was God's Spirit doing in the lives of other Christians while the church lost its revival momentum?
   Remained in darkness

9. Reflect on Ellen White's statement, "God's unwillingness to have His people perish has been the reason for so long delay." What does this tell you about God's love for His church? And what does it tell you about our love for God?
   That we must seek The Holy Spirit as a church, and not give up but hold fast To The Love of Jesus., as Jacob would not let loose of The angel, We must love & Cling To one Another.

Repentance = Gold refined by fire
(Faith & love Combined)

White Garments
(Christ's righteousness)

eyesalve
(anointing of The Holy Spirit)

Proclaim with
a loud voice The 3rd angel's message

We (I) must direct my eyes To The
divine Person of Jesus, His merits, and
His changeless love for The human family.

plead with God for His Spirit To decend
upon us as it came upon The disciples
upon the day of Pentecost.

CHAPTER FOUR

When the Church Shut Away the Spirit

In 1844, advent believers failed to accept and proclaim the biblical Sabbath—the reason for the third angel's message. Nevertheless, God led the disappointed remnant to more years of serious Bible study. This would help them realize their mistakes and more fully comprehend their commission. While glad to plumb the depths of doctrinal understanding, the early believers did not keep their eyes fastened on Jesus with the same intensity and single-mindedness that characterized their 1843–1844 experience. Their presumed Philadelphian experience—faithful, committed, mission-minded—had actually become Laodicean.

Once they discovered their condition, God sought to lead them to repentance and to buy "gold refined by fire," "white garments," and even "eyesalve," in order to see what God sees (Revelation 3:18, 19). The first item represents "faith and love combined," the second, "Christ's righteousness," and the last, the anointing of the Holy Spirit for spiritual discernment.[1] Again, they failed to obtain these to the fullest, because "many lost the effect of the message," having given up too soon the work God had begun in their hearts. So there was no third angel's message to the world, because there was no deep repentance in the church.

Paul clearly states that the only way to be led to repentance is by perceiving sufficiently "the kindness of God" (Romans 4:2). This would now be the Lord's next attempt—pointing the remnant to Jesus and His righteousness, to help them see their sin and need for repentance.

The Message of Righteousness By Faith

Shortly before James White died, God had forecast that things in the church were about to change. James, along with other early pioneers, had spent his entire life in the service of the church. The work done, the institutions built, were all very precious to them, to the point that James would "rather die" than see these mismanaged.[2] After White died, God gave Ellen White the strength to stay by her post, "with the understanding that God was to bring an element in this work that we have not had yet."[3] What could be new to God's young Adventist Church?

Although the message of righteousness by faith in relationship to the third angel's message was not exactly new to the Seventh-day Adventist Church, the angel told Ellen White that there were "but few, even of those who claim to believe it" who understood it.[4] And what was this message? Fondly, she remembered:

> "The Lord in His great mercy sent a most precious message to His people through Elders Waggoner and Jones. This message was *to bring more prominently before the world the uplifted Saviour, the sacrifice for the sins of the whole world.* It presented justification through faith in the Surety; it invited the people to receive the righteousness of Christ, which is made manifest in obedience to all the commandments of God. *Many had lost sight of Jesus.* They needed to have their eyes directed to His divine person, His merits, and His changeless love for the human family. . . . This is the message that God commanded to be given to the world. It is the third angel's message, which is to be proclaimed with a loud voice, and attended with the outpouring of His Spirit in a large measure."[5]

Too little of the Spirit and the power of God was evident in the church at the time; too much emphasis on the law of God, which brought no transformation of heart. The third angel's message is supposed to be given "not in whispered tones, but with a loud voice."[6]

In 1926, Arthur Daniells, past president of the General Conference, published the first comprehensive study of the subject, based on his knowledge and personal experience of the 1888 session. He admitted that the church had become blind and dull of heart.[7] The church, having lost sight of the nature of *sin*, was unable to perceive her true condition—thus her Laodicean state of affairs.

The emphasis on righteousness by faith at the 1888 General Conference session has been widely viewed by theologians and historians as a watershed event in the Adventist Church, "towering above all other sessions in uniqueness and importance." Christ was uplifted "as never before in our history."[8] At the time, the trappings of success were evident everywhere in the church. It had grown 646 percent since organizing twenty-five years earlier. From the late 1870s and through the 1880s, there was unprecedented progress in mission outreach and in the establishment of educational and health institutions. Ministers grew accustomed to defending distinctive Adventist doctrines with such skill "that it was difficult to defeat the Adventists in debate." Adventists had become "doctrinarians."[9] The result was self-satisfaction, leading to a spirit of lukewarmness.

This was the most important message ever given to the remnant church. Adventists believed in the twin truths of "the faith of Jesus" and "the commandments of God" (Revelation 14:12). The problem was that this was processed only at an *intellectual* level. The overwhelming love of Christ for the sinner and His work on his or her behalf was something far from being real at the personal level. Thus, the church taught accurate truth, while its members had little clue of its transforming power. What was needed were the commandments of God and the faith of Jesus in their proper framework. The angel guide said to Ellen White:

> "There is much light yet to shine forth from the law of God and the gospel of righteousness. This message, understood in its true character, and proclaimed in the Spirit, will lighten the earth with its glory . . . a power that will send the rays of the Sun of Righteousness unto all the highways and byways of life."[10]

Only two months before the Minneapolis Conference began, Ellen White sent off a letter to the church leaders, stating:

> "We are impressed that this gathering [about to take place] will be the most important meeting you have ever attended. . . . All selfish ambition should be laid aside, and you should plead with God for his Spirit to descend upon you as it came upon the disciples who were assembled together upon the day of Pentecost."[11]

She fully expected the latter rain power of the Spirit to start that year, in that place. On the second day at Minneapolis, early in the morning, she addressed the conference:

> "If we ever needed the Holy Ghost to be with us, if we ever needed to preach in the demonstration of the Spirit, it is at this very time. . . . The baptism of the Holy Ghost will come upon us at this very meeting if we will have it so. . . . Let us commence right here in this meeting and not wait till the meeting is half through. We want the Spirit of God here now; we need it, and we want it to be revealed

in our characters. We want the power of God here, and we want it to shine in our hearts."[12]

A Call to Magnify Christ

Before 1888, Ellen White had for years been calling the church to spiritual revival by focusing on the work and character of Jesus. In 1879 she said:

> "Golden opportunities are lost by delivering elaborate discourses, which display self but do not magnify Christ. A theory of the truth without vital godliness cannot remove the moral darkness which envelops the soul . . . the power of the Spirit of God is lacking."[13]

In 1880 she expressed her wish that ministers dwell more upon the cross of Christ, "their own hearts, meanwhile, softened and subdued by the Saviour's matchless love, which prompted that infinite sacrifice."[14]

Year after year and with increasing frequency, Ellen White begged the church to "look to Jesus" as the antidote to a pervasive and blinding Laodiceanism. Finally, in March 1887, she wrote the well-known, comprehensive appeal referred to earlier:

> "A revival of true godliness among us is the greatest and most urgent of all our needs. To seek this should be our first work. There must be earnest effort to obtain the blessing of the Lord, not because God is not willing to bestow his blessing upon us, but because we are unprepared to receive it. Our Heavenly Father is more willing to give his Holy Spirit to them that ask him, than are earthly parents to give good gifts to their children. But it is our work, by confession, humiliation, repentance, and earnest prayer, to fulfill the conditions upon which God has promised to grant us his blessing. A revival need be expected only in answer to prayer."[15]

Ellen White recognized that "the hindrances to strength and success are far greater from the church itself than from the world," and she appealed to members to "unite in earnest, prevailing prayer." She asserted that what Satan fears most is God's people clearing the way "by removing every hindrance, so that the Lord can pour out His Spirit upon a languishing church and an impenitent congregation," noting that "if Satan had his way, there would never be another awakening" to the end of time. Then she ended with great pathos:

> "There should be earnest searching of heart. There should be united, persevering prayer, and through faith a claiming of the promises of God. There should be, not a clothing of the body with sackcloth, as in ancient times, but a deep humiliation of soul. . . . O

my brethren, will you grieve the Holy Spirit, and cause it to depart? Will you shut out the blessed Saviour, because you are unprepared for his presence? Will you leave souls to perish without the knowledge of the truth, because you love your ease too well to bear the burden that Jesus bore for you? Let us awake out of sleep."[16]

The Start of the Latter Rain

This message was to be the start of the latter rain. "The loud cry of the third angel has already begun in the revelation of the righteousness of Christ, the sin-pardoning Redeemer," Ellen White wrote in 1892, adding that "this is the beginning of the light of the angel whose glory shall fill the whole earth."[17] Her guiding angel had revealed this fact to her in 1886, and she included it in one of her messages to those assembled at the 1888 General Conference:

"There is much light yet to shine forth from the law of God and the gospel of righteousness. This message, understood in its true character, and proclaimed in the Spirit, will lighten the earth with its glory."

But while 1888 was the *start* of the latter rain, the end of it was yet to come.

"The closing work of the third angel's message will be attended with a power that will send the rays of the Sun of Righteousness into all the highways and byways of life, and decisions will be made for God as supreme Governor; His law will be looked upon as the rule of His government."[18]

But more on this later.

The point is that God had set out to do something new in the church. For centuries, He'd been in the process of restoring neglected Bible truths lost sight of since the last of the apostles had died. He finally gave birth to the remnant of Bible prophecy (Revelation 10), a group of people raised up for the express purpose of preparing the world for the coming of Christ. The truths of the Sabbath, the non-immortality of the soul, the manner of Christ's coming, the sanctuary ministry and the investigative judgment, the validity of God's commandments, and care for the body temple were now restored, for a perishing world to understand the work and character of God. But not unlike the Jewish remnant after their return from exile, Seventh-day Adventists lost sight of the center. They lost sight of Jesus, just as the Jews lost sight of the Messiah. And just as the Jews felt proud of their understanding of God's law and their absolute resolve not to be deceived by following pagan deities ever again, Adventists were full of the law, without the heart of God. And this led to the shutting away of the Spirit.

Shutting Away the Spirit

The messengers God used in 1888 to bring revival by looking unto Jesus were rejected by a large portion of those present. Some feared that emphasis on the cross meant a de-emphasis on the distinctives that had identified them as a prophetic movement. Older leaders felt defensive with the assumption that this was "new light," remembering the joy in Christ they had experienced during the years leading to 1844. Years later, some still viewed the emphasis on righteousness by faith as nothing more than a mainstay of Protestant teaching.[19]

But this message was much more than mainstream Protestant dogma. In the words of one-time editor of the *Adventist Review*, Kenneth Wood:

"The 1888 message was distinctive and included far more than Luther's gospel of 'justification by faith.' It had a strong eschatological emphasis. It was designed to prepare a people for translation at the second coming of Christ. It called attention to the heavenly sanctuary. It emphasized the humanity of Christ, and declared Jesus to be not only our Saviour but our Example—One who lived the life of faith and showed us how to live that same kind of life."[20]

The message had greater implications than anyone then imagined: The message of Christ Our Righteousness was the third angel's message, which, if "given with a loud voice" would bring about the latter rain "power of the Holy Spirit."[21]

A generalized rejection of the message succeeded in shutting away the Spirit of God from our leadership at the time! Satan suspected as much, knowing that if people receive the message of the unmerited gift of God on our behalf, "his power will be broken."[22]

In 1896, Ellen White gave a chilling assessment of such a reaction:

"God would have every member of His creation understand the great work of the infinite Son of God in giving His life for the salvation of the world. . . . An unwillingness to yield up preconceived opinions, and to accept this truth, lay at the foundation of a large share of the opposition manifested at Minneapolis against the Lord's message through Brethren Waggoner and Jones. By exciting that opposition *Satan succeeded in shutting away from our people, in a great measure, the special power of the Holy Spirit* that God longed to impart to them. The enemy prevented them from obtaining *that efficiency which might have been theirs in carrying the truth to the world*, as the apostles proclaimed it after the day of Pentecost. The light that is to lighten the whole earth with its glory was resisted, and by the action of our own brethren has been in a great degree kept away from the world."[23]

This statement should stun every reader.

The resistance to the message resulted in the shutting away of the Spirit's power, meant to carry the gospel to the entire world! Ellen White was left pleading for prayer that "a few more years of grace" may be granted.[24] And God granted her request. Much work was to be done, mostly in the hearts of God's own people, to see the beauty of Jesus' love and surrender all to His keeping. In 1892, she addressed missionaries in foreign lands, saying, "Onward, ever onward! Angels of heaven will go before us to prepare the way."[25] Three years later, she lamented that the church looked for the outpouring of the Holy Spirit in the future, when it was her privilege to have it then.[26] In 1900, she wrote that "only a moment of time, as it were, yet remains."[27]

What happened next would show what God intended to do in the church and in the world.

NOTES:

1. *Testimonies*, vol. 2, 36; *Christ's Object Lessons*, 311; *Counsels to Writers and Editors*, 174, 175.

2. *Testimonies*, vol. 1, 107.

3. *1888 Materials*, 540. Years later, Ellen White would tie this revelation to the message Jones and Waggoner were presenting at the 1888 Minneapolis Conference. For an exhaustive study on this issue, see Ron Duffield, *The Return of the Latter Rain: A Historical Review of Seventh-day Adventist History from 1844 to 1891* (self-published, 2010).

4. *1888 Materials*, 165.

5. *Testimonies to Ministers*, 91, 92, emphasis supplied.

6. *Testimonies*, vol. 5, 252.

7. *Christ Our Righteousness* (Takoma Park, MD: Ministerial Association of Seventh-day Adventists, 1926, 1941), 6.

8. LeRoy Edwin Froom, *Movement of Destiny* (Washington, D.C.: Review and Herald, 1971), 187.

9. *Ibid.*, 182.

10. *1888 Materials*, 165.

11. *Ibid.*, 38, 40.

12. *Ibid.*, 72, 73.

13. *Testimonies*, vol. 4, 313, 314.

14. *Ibid.*, 374, 375.

15. *Review and Herald*, March 22, 1887. The entire appeal can also be found in *Selected Messages*, bk. 1, 121–127.

16. *Ibid.*

17. *Review and Herald*, November 22, 1892.

18. *1888 Materials*, 166.

19. For instance, L. H. Christian: "Some may ask, What was this teaching of righteousness by faith which became the mainspring of the great 1888 Adventist revival, as taught and emphasized by Mrs. White and others? It was the same doctrine that Luther, Wesley, and many other servants of God had been teaching," *The Fruitage of Spiritual Gifts*, 239. See also Froom, *Movement*, 605–612.

20. "Editor's Viewpoint," in *Review and Herald*, November 18, 1976, 2.

21. *Manuscript 16*, 1900, "To W. W. Prescott," February 17, 1900, also in *The Seventh-day Adventist Bible Commentary*, vol. 7, 980.

22. *Gospel Workers*, 161.

23. *Selected Messages*, bk. 1, 234, 235, emphasis supplied. The bulk of the statement was written in 1896; the first sentence in 1890.

24. *Testimonies*, vol. 5, 711–718. The context was the impending National Sunday Law debated in Congress in 1888.

25. *Gospel Workers*, 470.

26. *Review and Herald*, March 19, 1895, par. 14.

27. *Testimonies*, vol. 6, 14.

Questions for Reflection or Group Study

1. What did God forecast as "new" in the church, after the death of James White? Why would that message be "new"?

2. What was the reason that the church had lost sight of Jesus? Where are we today in our local church in relationship to this point?

3. What do you think it means "to magnify Christ"?

4. Reread the well-known statement from March 1887 about a revival of true godliness being the greatest and most important of all our needs. Reflect and discuss each component. What would it take for that to happen in your church?

5. What does it mean, in a practical way, to confess, to experience "humiliation," to repent, and to pray earnestly?

6. Why did the older leaders in the church feel that focusing on Jesus was not what the church needed?

7. Why was the Holy Spirit "shut out" at the Minneapolis session in 1888?

8. What could have happened, had the entire church accepted the righteousness by faith message in 1888?

CHAPTER FIVE

A Taste of Revival and Reformation

O n the last day of the Minneapolis meeting, Ellen White addressed the church leadership once more: "Now our meeting is drawing to a close, and not one confession has been made; there has not been a single break so as to let the Spirit of God in." This scathing rebuke was followed by resignation and a glimmer of hope. "If the ministers will not receive the light, I want to give the people a chance; perhaps they may receive it."[1]

If you've had a chance to read what took place in those turbulent years in the church, your heart may be gripped, as is mine, with sorrow and disgust. What in the world is wrong with us! Why can we not listen to the voice of the Spirit of God pleading, urging, begging us to reconcile with God! Who do we think we are to remain aloof to the words of life—the only means whereby any of us could possibly know what it is like to live "the abundant life" Jesus Himself has promised! Oh, when I discover in my own life the many times I have ignored the voice of God in order to give my will preeminence, I inwardly cry for not only ignoring, but also scorning, the counsel of my loving Savior. All He wants is my happiness, my best. All He desires is my joy, the full life in God we were all meant to enjoy as children made in the image of God. Yet we keep listening to the siren voices of foreign idols instead. But God is not done with us.

And He wasn't done with the church in 1888.

Revival Fires

Ellen White, along with A. T. Jones and E. J. Waggoner, set out to share the message of Jesus' love and righteousness with the rest of the church. They went to conference ministers' meetings, churches, and schools. The following summer saw them in a number of camp meetings. Individual victories were seen all around but not without great struggle by the opposition, coming from Uriah Smith and some other leaders who, by this time, thoroughly disliked Waggoner and Jones' quick rise in the church and even doubted Ellen White's wisdom for endorsing them. Yet in spite of this initial, open opposition, the brethren saw to it that this message would get a hearing.[2]

At the Battle Creek College's Week of Prayer, the message given was "not alone the commandments of God—a part of the third angel's message—but [also] the faith of Jesus, which comprehends more than is generally supposed."[3] The "week" was scheduled from December 15 to 22, but it lasted a month instead. Such was the gripping power of the message of God's love for those young adults. Yet the impact among Adventists was city-wide: the sanitarium, the publishing house, and the Dime Tabernacle Church.

One day, after speaking to the college students, W. W. Prescott, the college president, who once was in opposition to this message, "arose and attempted to speak, but his heart was too full. There he stood five minutes in complete silence, weeping. When he did speak, he said, 'I am glad I am a Christian.'... His heart seemed to be broken by the Spirit of the Lord." Later that day, Ellen White spoke at the Tabernacle, "and many bore precious testimonies that the Lord had forgiven their sins and given them a new heart."[4]

People began to change. Reformation followed revival. Some, under conviction, began to be faithful in tithes and offerings. Wrongs with others were made right. Tangible changes followed a revelation of God's love for sinners. Ellen White exclaimed, "Oh, what a changed atmosphere from four weeks ago. Jesus indeed was present."[5]

Revival followed next in South Lancaster, Massachusetts, the site of South Lancaster Academy, precursor to Atlantic Union College. As elsewhere, the factors involved were Christ-centered messages to our Laodicean condition, much prayer, and testimonies, including confession of sin and repentance. The Spirit of God was able to work freely, when these things were in place. Typical of what happened in those days is recounted in Ellen White's testimony:

"I have never seen a revival work go forward with such thoroughness, and yet remain so free from all undue excitement. There was no urging or inviting. The people were not called forward, but there was a solemn realization that Christ came not to call the righteous, but sinners, to repentance. The honest in heart were ready to confess their sins, and to bring forth fruit to God by repentance and restoration, as far as it lay in their power. We seemed to breathe in the very atmosphere of heaven. Angels were indeed hovering around. Friday evening the social service began at five, and it was not closed until nine. No time was lost; for every one had a living testimony to bear. The meeting would have continued hours longer, if it had been allowed to run this full course; but it was thought best to close it at that time. I was not able to sleep that night until nearly day. The Lord had visited his people."[6]

Such is the power of the Spirit in our hearts, when Jesus as a personal Savior is exalted. And all this, God had planned to do in His church, but soon after, major setbacks followed. Ellen White was asked to leave the United States in favor of new work in Australia. Some of God's key people, such as Jones and Waggoner, became discouraged, their weaknesses unsurrendered, eventually leaving the church. Others, such as A. F. Ballenger and the leaders of the Holy Flesh Movement took the message to some extremes, under the banner call of "Receive Ye the Holy Ghost." The Review and Herald publishing house, as well as the Battle Creek Sanitarium, burned to the ground, their success becoming their doom. Shortly after, Dr. Kellogg, after writing a book laced with what we today would call New Age ideas, left in disgrace. It seemed as if every major instrument of God in the church had been defeated or neutralized.[7]

But God is not only the God of His remnant church. He is equally interested in a perishing world. And His Spirit would respond to anyone seeking to make a decided change in their lives. So the greatest global revival witnessed in 200 years—"the most remarkable ever known"[8]—broke out in Wales in 1904.

The Last Worldwide Revival

The Welsh Revival was the global climax of a worldwide awakening, emphasizing what became known as "the Spirit-filled life," or the "triumphant life," with an emphasis on sanctification. This Holiness Movement resulted from sincere Christians growing weary of legalistic, dry, intellectual religion, much like what Seventh-day Adventists were experiencing in the 1870s and 1880s. A most influential promoter of this movement was the so-called Keswick Convention—annual Bible conferences that met for decades in England, continuing well into the twentieth century. They were founded "to promote practical holiness." The equivalent in America was the Northfield Bible Conferences, under the auspices of Dwight L. Moody.

In 1902, participants at a Keswick Convention formed a prayer circle and pledged themselves to pray for revival around the world.[9] In 1904, the revival began with a college student by the name of Evan Roberts. The clarion call of the revival became: "Bend the church and save the world." Like the previous revival of 1857–1859, it distinguished itself as mostly a lay movement. With simplicity and the deep unction of the Spirit, Roberts and others went from town to town throughout Wales, with the same basic, direct message: 1) You must confess any known sin to God and make right any wrong done to others, 2) You must put away any doubtful habit, 3) You must obey the Spirit promptly, and 4) You must confess your faith in Christ publicly.[10] And in response, people, mysteriously, would break down in repentance then and there.

The Spirit of God took hold of Wales by storm. In five months, half a million people became Christians. Taverns went bankrupt for lack of patronage. Unwed pregnancies practically disappeared. Judges were given white gloves: not a case to try—no robberies, no burglaries, no rapes, no murders, no embezzlements. Crime had simply stopped. District councils held emergency meetings to decide what to do with so many police with nothing to do! Some got creative; instead of patrolling football (soccer) games or the pubs at night, they began singing in the churches. So many coal miners turned their lives over to Jesus and stopped using foul language that the horses used in the mines slowed down production, not knowing what was now being said to them![11]

The revival spread to all English-speaking countries, including African colonies, and to Northern and Central Europe, India, Japan, China, Korea, Indonesia, and Latin America. Its impact may have exceeded any known previous awakening in history. In Wales, one of every ten citizens was converted. In Japan, the number of Christians doubled by 1910. In India, the Christian population grew by 70 percent in 1905–1906. Latin America experienced a 180 percent growth from 1903 to 1910. In the United States 35,000 new members were added to the Methodist Church each year; Southern Baptists saw an increase of 25 percent in just one year; and the Presbyterians called 1905 "the most remarkable year of evangelism."[12] Though not directly involved, even Seventh-day Adventists experienced unusual growth from the outpouring of the Spirit upon the world.[13] The revival had a most remarkable impact in the large cities, the very places where Ellen White kept urging Adventist leaders to concentrate their efforts.

Perhaps God was preparing the world so that His remnant people might offer the final warning in the power of the Spirit before His return. In 1904, Ellen White pled:

"Why do we not hunger and thirst for the gift of the Spirit, since this is the means by which we are to receive power? Why do we not talk of it, pray for it, preach concerning it?"

She urged that every minister should pray for the baptism of the Spirit; that "companies should be gathered together to ask" for help and wisdom to carry on God's commission in the world. "It is the privilege of every Christian, not only to look for, but to hasten the coming of our Lord Jesus Christ." She confirmed with confidence that God could finish the work very quickly.

"Quickly the last harvest would be ripened, and Christ would come to gather the precious grain. . . . [So,] plead for the Holy Spirit, God stands back of every promise He has made. With your Bibles in your hands, say: 'I have done as Thou hast said, I present Thy promise, "Ask, and it shall be given you; seek, and ye shall find; knock, and it shall be opened unto you."' Christ declares: 'What things soever ye desire, when ye pray, believe that ye receive them, and ye shall have them.' 'Whatsoever ye shall ask in My name, that will I do, that the Father may be glorified in the Son.' Matthew 7:7; Mark 11:24; 14:13."[14]

If God could do this in the world, with people whose knowledge of God, His character and plans, was considerably limited vis-à-vis that given to the remnant, what could He do with totally consecrated Seventh-day Adventists?

How Much Longer?

We must admit that the history of the Seventh-day Adventist Church is replete with missed opportunities to allow the special latter rain outpouring of the Holy Spirit to do such work in the heart as to prepare the way for total and complete global evangelization. This is not necessarily because the church had been in open rebellion before God. Many are faithful, conscientious believers. But we often get sidetracked, allowing "lesser things" to become more important than "the most urgent of all our needs." We have not generally, as a people, been willing to surrender all to Him so that character transformation may reflect Christ's character at a time when that character is to be tested.

In January of 1903, the servant of the Lord wrote something that every child of God should ponder carefully. She described a meeting at the 1901 General Conference session dealing with the subject of the outpouring of the Holy Spirit. There was fervent prayer, and "the meeting was marked by the presence of the Holy Spirit. The work went deep, and some present were weeping aloud." Leading brethren took the initiative to confess their wrongs and their ill feelings toward their colleagues. One repeated the message to the church of Laodicea and confessed his sinful condition, seeking forgiveness from others. "Those to whom he spoke sprang to their feet, making confession and asking forgiveness, and they fell upon one another's necks, weeping. The spirit of confession spread through the entire congregation." So powerful was this meeting, so overtaken by the Spirit of God, that Ellen White identified it as "a Pentecostal season." And, she added, "far into the night, until nearly morning, the work was carried on."

At that historic 1901 session, important work was done, such as the entire reorganization of the church. But the *greatest* work God sought to accomplish was total surrender to God and one another. Sadly, this was a vision that never materialized. The angel said to her: "This *might* have been." Ellen White concluded: "An agony of disappointment came over me as I realized that what I had witnessed was not a reality," even though "all heaven was waiting to be gracious" to them.[15]

The Adventists of the Millerite Movement missed preaching the third angel's message to a world that could have been ready to meet Jesus' return. The church of the late 1850s, as well as of the late nineteenth century, missed being ready for Christ's imminent return, because they did not heed the counsel of the True Witness calling Laodicea to repent. Many at the 1888 Minneapolis session missed a most propitious opportunity to truly understand how Christ's righteousness was the "third angel's message in verity." The message at the time meant the beginning of the loud cry of the third angel![16] Coolness to the message led to difficult years and leadership challenges that distracted from the cause, at the very time when God was readying the world with the greatest of all global revivals to date.

"We may have to remain here in this world because of insubordination many more years, as did the children of Israel," said Ellen White in 1901.[17]

The Seventh-day Adventist Church has been given the enormous privilege to understand these matters, to know the depth and breadth of the counsel of Jesus to us, His sad yet beloved Laodicean church. God has appealed for us to repent. He has shown us how, when subdued by the overwhelming love of Christ, we are to live with Christ within, by the power of the Spirit, to such an extent that the world will be compelled to see Jesus in His people.

The Holy Spirit is still at work in the church. He has never left us. He works today through scores of faithful believers, and He will continue to do so. But He wants to do more.

Christ waits patiently for His church to let Him in, to answer His appeal to Laodicea "to buy" faith refined by love, the righteousness of Christ, and the discernment of the Spirit, so that the loud cry of the latter rain may finish God's work with power and great glory. As Christ enters into the recesses of His people's hearts, the world will be convicted of sin, righteousness, and judgment (John 16:7, 8); and Christ will come to take us home.

Keep reading. Things are going to change in the church.

NOTES:

1. *1888 Materials*, 151, 152.

2. Arthur L. White, *Ellen G. White*, vol. 3, "The Lonely Years" (Hagerstown, MD: Review and Herald, 1984), 412, 413.

3. Duffield, 175.

4. White, vol. 3, 421.

5. *Ibid.*, 423.

6. *Review and Herald*, March 5, 1889, par. 10.

7. See White, vol. 5, "The Early Elmshaven Years" (Washington, D.C.: Review and Herald, 1981), 148–163, 223–235, 259–270, 280–306, 405–428. See also Schwartz, 262–272, 614–618.

8. Wesley Duewel, *Revival Fire* (Grand Rapids, MI: Zondervan, 1995), 210.

9. McDow and Reid, 276.

10. Collin Hansen and John Woodbridge, *A God-Sized Vision: Revival Stories That Stretch and Stir* (Grand Rapids, MI: Zondervan, 2010), 102.

11. J. Edwin Orr, *The Flaming Tongue: Evangelical Awakenings, 1900* (Chicago: Moody Publishers, 1975), 192, 193.

12. Duewel, 204–286; McDow and Reid, 282, 284, 296.

13. Statistics show that the Adventist Church in North America grew 2.1% in 1904 and 1.82% in 1906, whereas in the peak year of the revival, 1905, the church grew 5.55%. Similarly, whereas the average worldwide growth between 1901 and 1904 was 2.02% and between 1906 and 1910 was 3.66%, in the peak year of the revival the church grew by 6.84%, twice the average of following years and more than three times the rate of previous years, *General Conference Statistical Report*.

14. *Testimonies*, vol. 8, 22, 23.

15. *Ibid.*, 104–106.

16. *Review and Herald*, Nov. 22, 1892. See also *Selected Messages*, bk. 1, 363.

17. *Evangelism*, 696.

Questions for Reflection or Group Study

1. Why, do you think, do we tend to reject or ignore the very best God has to offer us?

2. Describe what happened when Ellen White and Elders Jones and Waggoner took the message of Christ Our Righteousness on the road? How do you think that could happen now?

3. Describe some of the tangible results of the Welsh Revival. What could be the equivalent in the Adventist Church?

4. Review the four-part message by Evan Roberts to the people in Wales. Why do you think that was the message of the Spirit then?

5. How can you explain God's moving upon churches and people who were not part of the remnant?

6. In 1903, Ellen White had a vision of a great revival that could have started at the 1901 General Conference session. Why didn't this happen?

7. What is it going to take to get us to give everything for "the most urgent of all our needs?"

8. When and how will we ever get to the point of confessing our wrongs and ill feelings toward one another, asking for forgiveness and forgiving others, no matter what they may have done to us?

9. What do you feel is the greatest need among us after reading this chapter? What can and should be your next step?

Person

CHAPTER SIX

Meeting the Holy Spirit

M ost literature on the Holy Spirit today, even among Seventh-day Adventists, focuses on the work and ministry of the Holy Spirit. But knowing His work without knowing His person poses inherent dangers for any Christian wanting a deeper experience with God. It implies that as long as things work the way we'd hope or expect the Spirit to lead, such work necessarily comes from Him. This thinking favors pragmatism over truth. Jesus warned us about mighty works in the last days that only the divine, presumably, can do, such as casting out demons, prophesying, or performing many miracles. But His sentence is as sobering as it is sad: "I never knew you" (Matthew 7:22, 23).

In view of this, I decided to add a brief chapter on the nature of the Holy Spirit.[1] If we don't know who He is, how could we recognize His work? Many Christians, including some Adventists, have simply decided that the Holy Spirit is some essence from God, a power tool in His hand, but not quite equal to God Himself. It makes a difference whether the Holy Spirit is God or not. Admittedly, we should be careful not to over-analyze the nature of the Spirit.[2] He simply has not revealed much about Himself, but what revelation we do have is worth reviewing. So I will try to answer three basic questions: 1) Is the Holy Spirit *God?* 2) Is the Holy Spirit a *person* in the Godhead? and 3) What is the *relationship* of the Spirit to the Godhead?

The Divine Spirit

We must admit that the direct scriptural evidence on whether the Spirit is God is scant. This, no doubt, is one key reason why so many sincere believers throughout the history of the Christian church have not been convinced of the divinity of the Holy Spirit. However, God has left enough evidence for us to understand basic truths.

The clearest of these may be the statement by Peter in Acts 5, where he asks deceiving Ananias why he had lied "to the Holy Spirit" regarding the sale of his land and then declared, "You have not lied to men, but to God" (Acts 5:3, 4). For Peter, "lying to the Holy Spirit" and "lying to God" were interchangeable expressions, his point being that Ananias was not *merely* lying to the apostles of the nascent New Testament church but to God Himself.

Another example of interchangeable expressions is the phrase Paul used in 1 Corinthians 3 and 6. In chapter 3:16, 17, he writes, "Do you not know that you are a temple of God, and that the Spirit of God dwells in you?" Three chapters later, he uses almost identical language: "Do you not know that your body is a temple of the Holy Spirit who is in you?" (1 Corinthians 6:19). Paul uses the *temple of God* or the *temple of the Holy Spirit* interchangeably.

"The Holy Spirit is not a mere spirit," said Martin Luther, "a creature, for example, or something apart from God and yet given to men by Him, or merely the work of God which He performs in our hearts—but that He is a Spirit who Himself is God in essence."[3]

Jesus also used the words *God* and *Holy Spirit* interchangeably. During the night encounter with Nicodemus, Christ made reference to how possible it was to be born *again*—a common reference to salvation—by the Spirit, even if the secret disciple considered it impossible, saying: "How can these things be?" (John 3:5–9). Later in His ministry, when another group of disciples gathered to inquire as to how it could be that people not expected to be saved could be saved, Jesus responded: "With men this is impossible, but with God all things are possible" (Matthew 19:23–26). Clearly, for Jesus, it was God who made salvation possible, even as it was the Spirit who caused men to be born again. This is because the Holy Spirit is the one with the ability to bring about conviction of sin, righteousness, and judgment (John 16:8–11).

In the book of Hebrews we find the only biblical reference to "the eternal Spirit" (Hebrews 9:14), whereas in the book of Deuteronomy we find the only biblical reference to "the eternal God" (Deuteronomy 33:27). We know that only God is eternal. We also know that only God can raise the dead to life.

> "Truly, truly I say to you, an hour is coming and now is, when the dead shall hear the voice of the Son of God; and those who hear shall live . . . all who are in the tombs shall hear His voice" (John 5:25, 28).

On what basis can Christ call the dead to life? He explains in the following verse: "Just as the Father has life in Himself, even so He gave to the Son also to have life in Himself" (v. 26). A few years later, Paul echoed Jesus' words, when he wrote, in Romans 8:11:

"But if the Spirit of Him who raised Jesus from the dead dwells in you, *He who raised Christ Jesus from the dead will also give life to your mortal bodies through His Spirit* who indwells you" (emphasis supplied).

The same Spirit who raised Jesus will raise you and me from the dead, because, like God, He too has life in Himself.

On the night of His betrayal, Christ announced the coming of the *parakletos,* often translated in English as *Comforter* or *Helper* (John 14:16, 17). Linguistically, this alludes to the "parallel" status the person introduced has with the One introducing Him. This is why Christ referred to the Holy Spirit as "another" Comforter, Christ Himself being the first one the disciples knew. The point to be made here is that Christ would *"ask [pray* in the King James Version] the Father" for the Spirit. A few minutes earlier Christ had referred to Himself and His Father as equals (vv. 9, 10). If the Comforter is equal—or parallel—to the Son, and the Son is equal—or one, with the Father—the Comforter, or Holy Spirit, is thus equal to the Father.

Three Divine Attributes of the Spirit

The Holy Spirit possesses attributes belonging only to God. He is *omnipresent,* making the psalmist exclaim: "Where can I go from Thy Spirit? Or where can I flee from Thy presence?" (Psalm 139:7). The Holy Spirit is *omniscient,* because, Paul says, "the Spirit searches all things, even the depths of God," for "the thoughts of God no one knows except the Spirit of God" (1 Corinthians 2:10, 11). And the Holy Spirit is *omnipotent,* since He distributes gifts "to each one individually *just as He wills"* (1 Corinthians 12:11, emphasis supplied).

Finally, a number of statements in Scripture mention all three members of the Godhead, making them equal in nature and rank, though not in function. The well-known baptismal formula that was part of the Great Commission states that Christ's followers must baptize new disciples "in the name of the Father, the Son, and the Holy Spirit" (Matthew 28:19). The formula highlights a *single* name, not three different ones, making each and all of them of the same substance or nature as the others. The apostolic blessing of 2 Corinthians 13:14 reveals the same triune God: "The grace of the Lord Jesus Christ, and the love of God, and the fellowship of the Holy Spirit, be with you all." And the spiritual gifts lesson by Paul makes the same point by speaking of "varieties of gifts but the same

Spirit," "varieties of ministries, and the same *Lord*," and "varieties of effects, but the same *God*" (1 Corinthians 12:4–6, emphasis supplied). In Peter's greeting, we find the triune Godhead linked together as before, yet giving hints of their various functions:

> "Peter, . . . to those who reside as aliens, scattered . . . , who are chosen according to the foreknowledge of God the Father, by the sanctifying work of the Spirit, that you may obey Jesus Christ and be sprinkled with His blood" (1 Peter 1:1, 2).

The Person of the Spirit

The personhood of the Holy Spirit was a concept with which early Adventist pioneers struggled. Along with anti-Trinitarian views, some thought of the Holy Spirit as less than a person. Long-time church editor and General Conference Secretary, Uriah Smith, for example, as late as 1891 described the Holy Spirit as "that divine, mysterious emanation through which they [the Father and the Son] carry forward their great and infinite work."[4] A year earlier, he had pictured the Spirit to be a "divine influence" and not a "person like the Father and the Son."[5] Even Ellen White, quoting the King James Version, kept referring to the Holy Spirit as an "it" in her writings. However, all that changed by 1898, when she used the personal pronoun "He" in reference to the Holy Spirit and called Him "the Third Person of the Godhead."[6]

At times, people have viewed the Holy Spirit as an "it," in part, because the neuter gender for Spirit, both in the original Greek—*pneuma*—and in English, have contributed to this concept. An example may be Romans 8:16, where the King James Version translates the text: "The Spirit *itself* . . ." (emphasis added). Since pronouns are to agree with their antecedents in person, number, and gender, you would expect the neuter pronoun to be used to represent the Holy Spirit. However, when John the Beloved recorded the words of Jesus, he used the masculine pronoun *ekeinos* ("he") when referring to the Holy Spirit. "When the Helper comes, . . . that is the Spirit of truth, . . . He will bear witness of Me" (John 15:26). "When He, the Spirit of truth comes, He will guide you into all truth" (John 16:13). "And I will ask the Father, and He will give you another Helper, that He may be with you forever" (John 14:16). Bible critics could point to the fact that Greek was not John's first language and that thus, he made a mistake. But either John made a *consistent* grammatical error, or he purposely called the Holy Spirit a "he." And since no similar "error" is made in the rest of John's gospel, he must have done it on purpose, to make the point that Jesus referred to a Person and not a thing.

The Bible also identifies, in the Holy Spirit, a number of attributes characteristic only of persons. For instance, the Holy Spirit wills. Paul and his companions were "forbidden by the Holy Spirit to speak the word in Asia; and when they had come to Mysia, they were trying to go into Bithynia, and the Spirit of Jesus did not permit them" (Acts 16:7, 8). In 1 Corinthians 12 we are told, after several gifts of the Spirit are mentioned, that "the same Spirit works all these things, distributing to each one individually just as He wills" (v. 11).

Also, the Holy Spirit is said to have a mind. Paul reminds us that "he who searches the hearts knows what the mind of the Spirit is" (Romans 8:27). Such mind, the Spirit uses to intercede on our behalf: "for we do not know how to pray as we should, but the Spirit Himself intercedes . . . with groanings too deep for words" (v. 26).

As only persons can, the Spirit gives instruction, as well. Paul writes to Timothy: "The Spirit explicitly says that in the latter days some will fall away from the faith, paying attention to deceitful spirits and doctrines of demons" (1 Timothy 4:1). Nehemiah reminisced about how God had given Israel His "good Spirit to instruct them" (Nehemiah 9:20). And Jesus promised His disciples that when facing danger or stress because of Him: "the Holy Spirit will teach you in that very hour what you ought to say" (Luke 12:12). In addition, no force can communicate verbally, as the Holy Spirit does. Only persons do. For example, the Spirit "says" to the churches what we find in Revelation 2 (vv. 7, 11, 17, 29) and 3 (vv. 6, 13, 22). And He answers the voice from heaven in Revelation 14:13. Finally, we are told that the "Spirit and the bride say, 'Come'" (Revelation 22:17), again suggesting qualities of personhood.

A further characteristic is the fact that the Holy Spirit is capable of feelings. Paul counsels the Ephesians to make sure not to "grieve the Holy Spirit of God" (Ephesians 4:30); and Isaiah recalls how Israel had so stubbornly "rebelled and grieved His Holy Spirit; therefore, He turned Himself to become their enemy" (Isaiah 63:10).

And the Spirit has influence. For Paul assures us that "no one can say 'Jesus is Lord,' except by the Holy Spirit" (1 Corinthians 12:3). Jesus promised that "when [the Spirit] comes, [He] will convict the world concerning sin, and righteousness, and judgment" (John 16:8).

Finally, only persons can love, and all three members of the Godhead love (see John 3:16 and 13:1). Paul appeals to the Romans: "Now I urge you, brethren, by our Lord Jesus Christ and by the love of the Spirit [to pray for me]" (Romans 15:30). And he had already told them, in Romans 5, that "hope does not disappoint, because the love of God has been poured out within our hearts *through the Holy Spirit*" (5:5, emphasis supplied).

The Relationship of the Holy Spirit to the Godhead

Even though the Spirit, in the New Testament, is regarded chiefly in relation to the church and the Christian life, the question of the Spirit's relation to God can be answered by Scripture. What we find is a voluntarily subservient role of the Spirit to the rest of the Trinity.

When Jesus announced the coming of the promised Comforter, He said, "'I will ask the Father, and He will give you another Helper . . . the Spirit of truth'" (John 14:16, 17). Though we clearly saw evidence that the Spirit has and exercises His will, we find in this text that it all depends on the two other members of the Trinity: the Son's request and the Father's provision. Through the Spirit, Christ would indwell His disciples: "In that day you shall know that I am in My Father, and you in Me, and I in you" (v. 20). Then Christ added that He will disclose Himself to them then (v. 21). In fact, the promise is that both Father and Son will come to make Their abode with them (v. 23), and even though no explicit mention is made about the Spirit being the Third Guest in their hearts, it is the Spirit who would aid the disciples to understand what He had just said. We find here a clearly subordinate role in the person of the Holy Spirit, even though He is another *parakletos*—another like the Son.

In no way should this be understood to mean that the Spirit is somehow a lesser God than Christ or the Father. This appears to be the Spirit's *role and function* in the Godhead, not His status or rank. In chapter 15, again the Spirit's subordinate role appears:

"When the Helper comes, whom I will send to you from the Father, that is the Spirit of truth, who proceeds from the Father, He will bear witness of Me" (John 15:26).

Finally, in chapter 16 we may find the most clear statements regarding this triune relationship:

"'When He, the Spirit of truth comes, He will guide you into all the truth; for He will not speak on His own initiative, but whatever He hears, He will speak; and He will disclose to you what is to come. He shall glorify Me; for He shall take of Mine, and shall disclose it to you. All things that the Father has are Mine; therefore I said, that He takes of Mine, and will disclose it to you'" (vv. 13–15).

Just as the Son reveals the Father's love and character, and just as the Son chooses not to take His own initiative but yields such prerogative to the Father (see John 5:30; 6:38), so does the Spirit in relationship to the Son. The danger here is to harbor a subconscious Arianism that sees the Father and the Son on one plane but the Holy Spirit on a lower, subservient plane because of His function in the plan of salvation, just as Arius' followers read statements in the Bible pointing to Christ's subservience to the Father and concluded He could not be fully divine. In fact, in this functional relationship, it appears as if the Father is the source, the Son the mediator, and the Spirit the one who applies what God designs to do.

The concept of a plural union within the Godhead that is interactive and mutually submissive is seen even in the passage Jews for generations have used to voice their monotheism—the Shema: "Hear, O Israel! The Lord our God, the Lord is one!" (Deuteronomy 6:4). The word 'echad, translated "one," means "one among others, the emphasis being on a particular one." According to Otto Christensen, "the possibility of there being others in this 'oneness' is inherent in the word." Moses could have used the word yachîd to indicate "one," as in "one alone." But the word he used results "from the unity of numerous persons."[7] The same word is used to describe the *submissive union* between the first pair: "Therefore a man shall leave his father and mother and be joined to his wife, and they shall become one flesh" (Genesis 2:24).

The Godhead, then, is a divine fellowship. Not a group of Gods but a union of three Persons who practice and express perfect love in perfect humility.

Why Understanding the Spirit's Nature Matters

Why does it matter to understand the Holy Spirit as a person in the Godhead? Our earlier treatment of the story of Ananias and Sapphira in Acts 5 gives us a clue: If we don't understand or refuse to understand that the Holy Spirit is a person in the Godhead, we will tend to treat Him as an "it" and incur our own destruction.

This is why the unpardonable sin is the one committed against the Holy Spirit (Matthew 12:31, 32). For us, the point of contact with God is through the Holy Spirit: "Where can I go from your Spirit? Or where can I flee from your presence?" (Psalm 139:7). The point of most immediate contact is not through the Father and not even through Jesus. Whereas Christ is the sinner's intercessor as our High Priest in heaven (Hebrews 7:17–8:2), the Spirit is our intercessor as *parakletos*—one like Him—on earth (Romans 8:26, 27), in our midst. Only through the ministry of the Holy Spirit can we access the efficacy of Christ's intercessory ministry. Without Him it would be impossible even to understand or accept Christ as our Savior and Lord.

If we treat the Holy Spirit as an "it"—a mere emanation or influence devoid of personality and will—we find it especially easy to ignore Him, to lend deaf ears to His voice and invitation to leave self behind and abandon it to the hands of a God, with whom all things are possible. Like the Pharisees of old, we are likely to reject the very One our hearts longed for and whom the Spirit reveals—the greatest object of our gratitude: Jesus Christ our Savior.

We can understand the Son's despair on the banks of the Mount of Olives that Sunday at dusk, when, looking to the temple, He knew that the time of probation for the leaders in Jerusalem that night would come to a close. They had rejected Christ the Messiah by rejecting the wooing of the Spirit to their hearts. With deepest emotion, Christ cried:

"O Jerusalem, Jerusalem, who kills the prophets and stones those who are sent to her! How often I wanted to gather your children together, the way a hen gathers her chicks under her wings, and you were unwilling. Behold, your house is left to you desolate!" (Matthew 23:37, 38).

A second reason it is important for us to understand that God the Spirit is a person is because, if we treat Him like a "feeling" or a mere "power" meant to warm our hearts when we sense the need for it, we will become unbelievers. In Revelation 16 we are introduced to the false trinity, an allegiance made up of the dragon, the beast, and the false prophet (Revelation 16:13, 14), with this last entity being the equivalent of the Third Person of the Trinity. Just as a prophet speaks for God; specifically, for the Holy Spirit—for "men moved by the Holy Spirit spoke from God" (2 Peter 1:21)—the false prophet pretends to do the same.

But whereas the Holy Spirit speaks through the Word of God, the false prophet does so by signs and the use of the supernatural. The Spirit of God is not a "cosmic vending machine, responding mechanically with power or blessing if only we insert enough coins of faith."[8] Those who will trust God only when able to see signs and wonders do not trust a Person but a "power" or a "sensation." They do not walk by faith, for "faith comes [only] by hearing, and hearing by the Word of Christ" (Romans 10:17). Faith does not come by miracles. Therefore, those who treat the Holy Spirit as a "power" to be called upon at will—instead of a Person to respond to by yielding our wills—will be deceived, perceiving a god of their own making rather than the God of the Bible. And a god of our making will in the end lead us to disappointment and unbelief for having been deceived.

A third reason that it matters for us to think of the Spirit as a Person in the Godhead is because a consideration of His utter humility, a trademark of his Person, will lead us to surrender and service. The Bible says, "'No one knows who the Son is except the Father, and who the Father is except the Son, and anyone to whom the Son wills to reveal him'" (Luke 10:22). Much more is said in the Bible about God the Father and God the Son than about God the Holy Spirit. Though the Holy Spirit is mentioned 88 times in the Old Testament and 325 times in the New Testament,[9] this amount is dwarfed by the thousands of references given about the other members of the Trinity. But it was the Spirit who inspired these biblical writers (2 Peter 1:21), yet He did so in typical divine humility. The Holy Spirit says very little about Himself.

That's the way love is, as revealed in the Person of the Spirit: He focuses on the Father and His relationship with the Son, more than on His own relationship with the Son or the Father. The Son was in the Father and the Father in Him, and the same can be said of His relationship with the Holy Spirit and that of the Holy Spirit with the Father. That the Spirit communicates so freely about the Father and the Son is an insight into the selfless love that exists in the Trinity, and in particular, the way the Spirit glorifies the Father and the Son. The Spirit voluntarily adopts a lower position of service because of His love for the Son and His desire to see Him glorified, in spite of the fact that He is the Person in the Godhead whose time of activity and preeminence is now. Obviously, for the Spirit, equality and submission are not mutually exclusive.

How God Differs From "gods"

The Christian God—three in one—is completely different from the gods in the Olympic pantheon or in the Nordic tales. The gods with the "small g" engaged in constant warfare with one another. They each had an individual will and plan and clearly were not of one purpose. They each had their pride and their turf to protect. Such gods remind us of the conflict and pride that existed among the disciples of Jesus before Calvary and Pentecost.

When the Spirit is allowed to work among those who wrangle and push for the preeminence and are suspicious of one another, however, a holy submissiveness takes over their hearts, which allows them to become of "one accord" (Acts 1:14; 2:1, KJV). The group then mirrors the Trinity in this respect. In fact, absolute humility may be the most distinct characteristic of the Triune God. How else could God handle His omnipotence, omniscience, omnipresence, and other attributes that only the God of the universe can have?

Jesus voiced this truth, when He said: "'Learn of Me, for I am *gentle* and *humble* in heart'" (Matthew 11:29, emphasis supplied). Humble in heart: that is, a matter of choice and will. God can do anything, but He chooses to restrain Himself, because He is love. As we contemplate the deep humility demonstrated for eternity by the Third Person of the Godhead, our pride and pettiness becomes dust.

A last reason why it matters that God the Spirit be a person is this: Only persons can choose to cooperate with one another, and we are invited to cooperate with the Spirit as He leads Christ's church. When the early church, led by the Spirit, faced their first major theological controversy (Acts 15:1–29), the church—"leading men among the brethren" (v. 22)—

convened at Jerusalem to deal with the matter. After the matter was decided, it is interesting to see how they described the decision: "It seemed good to the Holy Spirit *and to us* . . ." (v. 28, emphasis supplied). Such close association and cooperation can be achieved only through a trusting personal interaction. When Paul and his missionary associates wished to preach in Asia and twice were prevented from doing so by the Spirit, they ended up in Macedonia instead, "concluding that God [notice, the Spirit here is called God] had called [them] to preach [there]" (Acts 16:6–10).

Such open interaction can be achieved only among persons who love and respect one another. The Spirit is much more than an impression in Paul's mind. He is his constant Guide. When the glorified Jesus in Revelation addresses the churches in Asia through the Holy Spirit, He admonishes seven times to pay attention to "what the Spirit says to the churches" (Revelation 2:7, 11, 17, 29; 3:6, 13, 22). The warnings and counsels from the Spirit to the churches presuppose an established relationship. People can only have such relationships with persons they trust. To recognize the voice of the Spirit means believers have spent enough time listening to such voice. He is not just an ethereal heavenly ghost. The Holy Spirit speaks so we can actually listen.

This intimate relationship between God the Spirit and His people is seen in the last appeal from Revelation:

> "And the Spirit and the bride say, 'Come.' And let the one who hears say, 'Come.' And let the one who is thirsty come; let the one who wishes take the water of life without cost" (Revelation 22:17).

We note first what it does *not* say. It doesn't say "the Spirit and the church," or "the Spirit and the remnant of her seed." It says, "the Spirit and the bride." The picture is of a wedding. The attention is to be on the Heavenly Groom. His bride—the church—and the Heavenly Best Man—the Spirit—those who love the Groom most, cry out in unison: Come to feast on the riches of Christ! Come, come, come! So it will echo for eternity future, as it has for thousands of years now—the clarion call of the Spirit on behalf of the Son, for the sake of His own.

NOTES:

1. This chapter is based on my published article, "The Personhood of the Holy Spirit and Why It Matters," in *Journal of the Adventist Theological Society*, vol. 17, no. 1 (spring 2006), 11–32.

2. "It is not essential for us to be able to define just what the Holy Spirit is . . . . The nature of the Holy Spirit is a mystery. Men cannot explain it, because the Lord has not revealed it to them. . . . Regarding such

mysteries, which are too deep for human understanding, silence is golden." *The Acts of the Apostles*, 51, 52.

3. Martin Luther, "Sermon on John 15:26, 27," in *Luther's Works*, 24:297, cited in Arnold Valentin Wallenkampf, *New by the Spirit* (Mountain View, CA: Pacific Press, 1978), 14.

4. *General Conference Bulletin*, 146, 1891; *Review & Herald*, October 24, 1890, 664, cited in George R. Knight, *A Search for Identity: The Development of Seventh-day Adventist Beliefs* (Hagerstown, MD: Review and Herald, 2000), 18.

5. *Looking Unto Jesus* (Battle Creek, MI: Review and Herald, 1897), 10.

6. *The Desire of Ages*, 671.

7. Otto H. Christensen, *Getting Acquainted With God* (Washington, D.C.: Review and Herald, 1970), 69.

8. Donald T. Williams, *The Person and Work of the Holy Spirit* (Eugene, OR: Wift & Stock, 1994), 10.

9. The number varies according to the Bible version one uses and the scholars one consults.

Questions for Reflection or Group Study

1. What are some scriptural examples given in this chapter showing that the Holy Spirit is God?

2. What are the three attributes of the Holy Spirit which only belong to God?

3. What were Uriah Smith and Ellen White's concept of the Holy Spirit in the early part of our work? Is that concept still prevalent among some Adventists today? Why do you think that is?

4. What are some of the attributes, characteristic only of persons, given to the Holy Spirit in Scripture?

5. What do you see as the role and function of the Holy Spirit in the Godhead? How does He relate to the Father and the Son?

6. How does Arianism incorrectly see the Holy Spirit in relation to the Godhead?

7. How did Moses understand the Godhead, according to Deuteronomy 6:4?

8. Why is it important not to think of the Spirit as a mere influence, or as an "it"?

9. By trusting only in "signs and wonders" what are we saying about the Holy Spirit?

10. Why does the Holy Spirit say very little about Himself in Scripture?

11. How does Revelation 22 help us see that the Holy Spirit is a person?

12. In what ways do you see and understand the person of the Holy Spirit more clearly by reading this chapter?

CHAPTER SEVEN

The Gift of Jesus

W e were in the middle of a church board meeting, when some-one brought to us an urgent letter. The letter was from one of my members, who had become convinced in his mind that the church was Babylon, and he demanded that his name be stricken from the church records.

After I read portions from the letter, we were all speechless. Some began to tear up. How could this be? We all knew him. He was a qui-et, careful man and a faithful member with a sad face but a kind spirit. Alone since his wife left him, we knew he'd been attending a weekly or bi-weekly gathering of a few Adventists led by an influential man completely opposed to the church. We suspected those meetings were like poison to the soul, and after checking a bit more, we realized the damage. And our friend was the first victim.

"I'd like to volunteer to visit with him," said Mike, the Personal Min-istries leader. The strange thing is that he said it with a smile on his face, as if he knew something we didn't know. And visit he did. Every day— every day!—for six weeks. He spent between forty-five minutes and up to three hours with him each afternoon or evening. He asked our defect-ing brother to share with him this new "truth." He would listen and ask clarifying questions. By and by, Mike began, ever so gently and carefully, to share from the Word, God's teaching about the identity and character of the remnant church. Then, he would pray with him, for his growth in Christ, his witness on behalf of others, his health, and his life. He made a fast friend.

One Sabbath morning—I will never forget it—while we were having our customary 7:00 A.M. prayer time in one of the rooms at the church, in walked Mike and our confused brother, side by side. "Praise the Lord!" said Mike by way of introduction, with his trademark smile. "Praise Jesus!" echoed our newly reclaimed brother, never to doubt again what God thought of His beloved church, warts and all.

You may think, Wow! Visit each day for six weeks? With that dedication and intensity, all kinds of things could change in the church. And if you think that, I believe you would be right. You see, this was not an unusual and sporadic deed of kindness for Mike—he'd been at this for a while, since Jesus had taken center stage in his heart.

One time, as marriages began to fail and men separated from their wives, he invited them to live with him during their time of transition. One by one, the men came, until his four-bedroom house was full. He then moved out and rented a temporary apartment for himself, while still covering expenses at the house. He'd study the Word with them and pray with them, and especially, *for* them. He knew they were hurting and angry and confused about their futures. I distinctly remember one of the men. His wife had sought counseling and had told me things I wish I never knew about him. But after months went by, one by one again, each of these men saw their marriages heal—an amazing miracle, when you consider the challenges some of them faced. Mike had determined "to pray them back to their wives."

I could tell you a lot more about Mike, and perhaps someday he'll let me write his story. Do you think the Holy Spirit lived in this man's life? What do you think it takes to lead a life like that? Paul gives us the answer:

> "God willed to make known what is the riches of the glory of this mystery among the Gentiles, which is *Christ in you*, the hope of glory" (Colossians 1:27, emphasis added).

Christ and the Spirit

What does Paul mean by "Christ in you"? Is that really possible? Consider this statement: "It is through the Spirit that Christ dwells in us; and the Spirit of God, received into the heart by faith, is the beginning of the life eternal."[1] Did you read that? Through the Spirit Christ *dwells* in us. To dwell is to live or stay as a permanent resident. Can you fathom the thought of Jesus living *in* you? Consider this other statement:

> "Transformation of character is the testimony to the world of an indwelling Christ. The Spirit of God produces a new life in the soul, bringing the thoughts and desires into obedience to the will of Christ; and the inward man is renewed in the image of God."[2]

The abundant life that Jesus promised (John 10:10), and that everyone wishes they had, is nothing less and nothing other than Jesus *in* you through the Holy Spirit. When Jesus promised the Holy Spirit to His disciples, He was giving them Himself through the Comforter, and that is why it would be to their advantage that He leave (John 16:7). "When He comes," Jesus said in reference to the Spirit, "He will glorify Me, for He will take of Mine and will disclose it to you" (v. 14). Paul says that "if anyone does not have the Spirit of Christ, he does not belong to Him [Christ]" (Romans 8:9). And then he says, "If Christ is in you . . . the spirit is alive" (v. 10). It was "the Spirit of Christ within" the Old Testament prophets that led them to prophesy of "the grace that would come" (1 Peter 1:11, 10).

Is the "Spirit of Christ" a spirit emanating from Christ, or is He the Holy Spirit?

Isaiah had prophesied that the "Spirit of the Lord," the Third Person of the Godhead, would rest on the Messiah—"the spirit of wisdom and understanding, the spirit of counsel and might, the spirit of knowledge and of the fear of the Lord" (Isaiah 11:2). The Spirit is mentioned seven times in this passage. In the book of Revelation, seven spirits are mentioned in reference to the Lamb who was slain (Revelation 5:6). In the Bible, the number *seven* denotes completion, perfection. So Jesus was the One full of the Spirit, the supreme example of One with the totality of God's presence in His life, the One who daily received the baptism of the Spirit. And this is the reason Paul and Peter used the expression "the Spirit of Christ." Christ was so full of the Spirit, they were as one and the same, even though distinct Persons.

The Gift of God

When you consider the expression "the gift of God" in the New Testament, you find this beautiful truth. Is the gift of God the Holy Spirit, or is it salvation in Jesus? Let's review some examples.

The first is Jesus' encounter with the Samaritan woman:

> "Jesus answered and said to her, 'If you knew the gift of God, and who it is who says to you, "Give me to drink," you would have asked Him, and He would have given you living water'" (John 4:10).

Which gift is it here? The context indicated the gift of salvation.

Next is Peter's rebuke of Simon for trying to obtain the gift of the Holy Spirit with money. "But Peter said to him, 'May your silver perish with you, because you thought you could obtain the gift of God with money'" (Acts 8:20).

The third example is that immortal Pauline statement: "For the wages of sin is death; but the free gift of God is eternal life in Christ Jesus our Lord" (Romans 6:23).

The fourth example finds Paul advocating for the spiritual gift of celibacy in the Corinthian church:

"I wish that all men were even as I myself am. However, each man has his own gift from God, one in this manner, and the other in that" (1 Corinthians 7:7).

Next is one of the clearest statements on how we are saved:

"For by grace you have been saved through faith; and that not of yourselves, it is the gift of God; not as a result of works, so that no one may boast" (Ephesians 2:8, 9).

One last text—this time an admonition to timid Timothy:

"For this reason I remind you to kindle afresh the gift of God which is in you through the laying on of my hands. For God has not given us a spirit of timidity, but of power and love and discipline" (1 Timothy 1:6, 7).

Do you see it? Three times, "the gift of God" refers to the gift of Christ's salvation, and three times, to the gift or gifts of the Holy Spirit. The point is that with the Spirit comes everything we need in Jesus. Salvation and Spirit reception are intertwined.

"Only to those who wait humbly upon God, who watch for His guidance and grace, is the Spirit given. The power of God awaits their demand and reception. This promised blessing, claimed by faith, brings all other blessings in its train. It is given according to the riches of the grace of Christ, and He is ready to supply every soul according to the capacity to receive."[3]

This is why, when you receive the Holy Spirit, you receive salvation. The gift of the Spirit is the gift of salvation. "Wait," you ask, "weren't the disciples *saved* already, by the time they received the Spirit at Pentecost?" The answer to that is Yes and No.

Once, or Daily?

Salvation isn't something you experience just once in your life, just as it isn't something that cannot be reversed. When Christians say, "I was saved on such and such date," they are only referring to their first conscious acceptance of Jesus into their hearts. Some, unfortunately, believe in what is popularly known as "once saved, always saved" and actually do believe the one-time experience as sufficient. But the Bible tells us we must die "daily" to self (Romans 6:11; 1 Corinthians 15:31). If we must die daily to sin, it can only mean we resurrect daily to new life (Romans 6:5)! Years ago I heard Morris Venden say that the proper way to express personal salvation is to say, "I was saved, I am saved, and I will be saved." In other words, I was saved twenty centuries ago, because Jesus died then at the cross even for *me*. I am saved daily, as I respond by faith to the grace of God, and I will be saved when He comes in the clouds and my sinful nature will give way to an incorruptible one (1 Corinthians 15:51–54).

It is the same with the Spirit. We don't receive the Spirit just once in our lives but every day, as often and as frequently as we open our hearts to receive Him. We don't wait until we experience something supernatural, some electric shock or internal warmth or physical miracle, to know the Spirit has taken residence in our body temples. The Spirit comes by faith, or so Paul taught us (Galatians 3:2, 14). And faith is not something you see or feel but something you choose to believe is there because God said it's there.

The problem many have is wanting the gifts of the Spirit before they want the Spirit Himself. They desire the manifestations of the Spirit—the power, the miracles, the experiential moving of God—but they are not too sure they'd want the Spirit, unless He came with bells and whistles. They want the gifts but not the Giver.

Some years ago, I discovered something interesting while studying the subject of spiritual gifts. In Romans 12, we're told that "we have gifts that differ according to the grace given to us," and that's why we should use them "accordingly" (v. 6). In 1 Peter 4, we read that "as each one has received a special gift," we should "employ it in serving one another, as good stewards of the manifold grace of God" (v. 10). What is the common denominator in these texts? The grace of God. The Bible word for "grace" is *charis*, which the King James Version simply translates as "charity." This means that the gifts of the Spirit are gifts of grace, or *charismata*. That is, they are an expression of the Spirit, as prompted by the love of the Savior. Because grace is the favor of God for the sake of our salvation! "For by grace you have been saved . . . it is the gift of God; not as a result of works, so that no one may boast" (Ephesians 2:8, 9). The logical conclusion is that these spiritual gifts are the gifts of Jesus, who gives grace to all who receive it by faith!

The point is that spiritual gifts do not come from some cosmic warehouse, some inanimate heavenly power source—they come from Jesus, as part of His grace. So everyone who has experienced the grace of Jesus receives the gifts of Jesus. If you have Jesus, you have spiritual gifts. Ask for the Spirit in your life, to have Jesus in your heart. Receive Jesus in your heart, and you'll live the life of the Spirit.

The Electrifying Meaning of "Christ in You"

One of my favorite Ellen White statements on the Holy Spirit is the following:

"Pray that the mighty energies of the Holy Spirit, with all their quickening, recuperative, and transforming power, may fall like an electric shock on the palsy-stricken soul, causing every nerve to thrill with new life, restoring the whole man from his dead, earthly, sensual state to spiritual soundness. You will thus become partakers of the divine nature, having escaped the corruption that is in the world through lust; and in your souls will be reflected the image of Him by whose stripes you are healed."[4]

As thrilling and exciting as that statement is—"the mighty energies," "like an electric shock," "causing every nerve to thrill"—we must not miss the obvious: "you will thus become partakers of the divine nature . . . and in your souls will be reflected the image of [Christ]."

The whole idea about living in "the power of His resurrection" is that we must be "conformed to His death" (Philippians 3:10). Most Christians, including most Seventh-day Adventists I know—have missed the fact that what Jesus gives to us is not only pardon for sin but also power for a new life. But this power does not come from the death of Christ on the cross, it comes from the life of Christ at the throne room of God.

Let me explain. What Christ accomplished at the cross was the ransom for our souls. He was our Substitute. We should have died forever. Instead, He became sin on our behalf and died the second death for us (2 Corinthians 5:21). He paid there the penalty for our sin, giving Him the right to forgive us for our sin, something He will guarantee, as long as we confess our sin to Him (1 John 1:9). However, pardon for sin is not victory over sin. Pardon deals with the past, not with the present. If we were only to be forgiven time and again, we would never come to the point of reflecting the divine nature. God does not need to be forgiven time and again. True, "it has not appeared as yet what we will be," but the expectation is that "we will be like Him" (1 John 3:2).

Most people about now get nervous. They imagine this means we need to be perfect, in order "to be like Him." And our record of sin is so pervasive, consistent, and overwhelming that we naturally despair to think we will ever reach such a stage of victory. But we do not need to despair:

"Sin could be resisted and overcome only through the mighty agency of the Third Person of the Godhead, who would come with no modified energy, but in the fullness of divine power. It is the Spirit that makes effectual what has been wrought out by the world's Redeemer. It is by the Spirit that the heart is made pure. Through the Spirit the believer becomes a partaker of the divine nature. Christ has given His Spirit as a divine power to overcome all hereditary and cultivated tendencies to evil, and to impress His own character upon His church."[5]

How does this happen? The key is in the second work of Jesus for us,

His life in us. Just as we accept His death on the cross so our sins may be forgiven, it is our privilege to accept His very life in our heart so our sin may be overcome.[6] Here is Paul's marvelous summary:

"For if while we were enemies, we were reconciled to God through the death of His Son, much more, having been reconciled, we shall be saved by His life" (Romans 5:10).

What does Paul say will actually *save* us? Christ's *life*, not merely His death. Why? Because what Jesus came here to do first was to prove to the universe that what Lucifer proposed was a lie. The devil contended that no creature could fulfill the law of God and live a perfect life. After all, wasn't he the best example? Created perfect from the start, given marvelous gifts and abilities (Ezekiel 28:12–15, 17a), not even he was able to stay on the straight and narrow. And exhibit B? Adam and Eve. What then, can be expected of the rest of us? "It's a lost cause," Satan cried. "If you are a God of justice, as you say, you must annihilate everyone, just as you're planning to destroy me."

Yes, it all *appeared* to be a lost cause, especially after Adam and Eve surrendered to sin while perfect and living in a perfect environment. But Jesus would step in as the second Adam (1 Corinthians 15:45) to prove one can live without sin. In fact, the Son of God went much farther than the assumption of Satan. He came to a world with millennia of sin on its record and well practiced in it. Far from Eden was the manger of Bethlehem. But for more than thirty-three years, Jesus resisted sin unto death. He was baptized daily with the Spirit of God. Daily, He spent hours in communion with His Father, to breathe the atmosphere of heaven that would allow Him to walk without stumbling in a world not only steeped in sin but bent to make Him fall.[7] This was His victory! Not the cross alone—but a sinless life, in spite of constant attacks!

When Jesus died at the cross, the devil "had nothing" in Him (John 14:30). No one took His life, either. He gave it of Himself (John 10:17, 18; 19:30).[8] And the reason He did was to pay the penalty of *our* sin. He was God's substitutionary sacrifice on our behalf. His death for us, then, gave Him the right to grant us His perfect life. So what Jesus gives us is *both* His death and His life!

Again, His life *in* us through the Spirit is what will make possible victory over sin. This truth is everywhere in Scripture:

"I have been crucified with Christ; and it is *no longer I who live*, but *Christ lives in me*; and the life which I now live in the flesh *I live by faith in the Son of God*, who loved me and gave Himself up for me" (Galatians 2:20, emphasis supplied).

"Set your mind on the things above, not on the things that are on earth." Why, Paul? "For you have died and *your life is hidden with Christ* in God. When *Christ, who is your life*, is revealed [at the second coming], then you also will be revealed with Him in glory" (Colossians 3:2–4, emphasis supplied).

"For to me, *to live is Christ*, and to die is gain" (Philippians 1:21, emphasis supplied).

"I am the door," Jesus said, "if anyone enters *through Me*, he shall be saved. . . . I came *that [you] might have life*, and might have it abundantly" (John 10:9, 10, emphasis supplied).

The life of Christ in us through the Spirit *will*, most certainly will, gain the victory over sin in our lives. Remember, both "hereditary and cultivated" tendencies will be conquered—sin as a condition, as well as sin as a habit. This is not perfectionism. Perfectionism would mean doing any or all of this in my strength. My life is not what accomplishes it—Jesus' life does, as long as He lives in me via the Spirit.

He in Me, and I in Him

But Christ may not only live *in me* through the Holy Spirit. His accomplishment at the cross for the entire sinful world also meant I was included in His sacrifice. I was there, "in Him," as it were. Theologians call this the "in Christ" motif, so often referenced by Paul. An easy verse to understand would be when Paul spoke to the idolatrous Athenians about the Unknown God:

"For in Him we live, and move, and have our being," he said (Acts 17:28). That is, we live because God is alive—our lives depend on Him. However, it was Jesus Himself who led the way for this concept, on the night He introduced the Spirit to His disciples:

"I am the vine, you are the branches; *He who abides in Me and I in him*, he bears much fruit, for apart from Me you can do nothing" (John 15:5, emphasis supplied).

Ephesians 1 is full of this concept. "He chose us in Him, before the foundation of the world" (v. 4); "in Him we have redemption through His blood" (v. 7); "in Him also we have obtained an inheritance, having been predestined according to His purpose (v. 11); "you were sealed in Him with the Holy Spirit of promise" (v. 13). It's everywhere. Finally, Paul could say to the Colossians: "In Him you have been made complete" (Colossians 2:10).

The apostle John brings this idea down to basics:

"By this we know that we are in Him: . . . to walk in the same manner as He walked" (1 John 2:5, 6). "Now, little children," concludes John, "abide in Him," for "whoever abides in Him does not sin" (1 John 2:28; 3:6, KJV).

"By this we know that we abide in Him and He in us, because He has given us of His Spirit" (1 John 4:13).

Picture it with me. Christ *in* us, the hope of glory, and we *in* Christ, buried and resurrected with Him. That means we're surrounded by Jesus, doesn't it? We are completely covered, inside and out. Should that make a difference in our lives? It should change everything about us.

Frank Phillips, a pastor and missionary whose teachings are surfacing now, a generation after his death,[9] used to tell of an experience he once heard from a young wife and mother, while at camp meeting. As I recall, she came to him for counsel. Her marriage was in shambles. Her husband was an unbeliever, irresponsible, drank too much, and cared nothing for the family. She had a little girl and a boy five months old. They had tried counseling, but nothing helped. Tired, she was ready to throw in the towel.

"Are you willing to do whatever is necessary to save your marriage?" asked the pastor. She paused for a moment, thinking she already had.

"Yes, I think I am," she replied.

"Then, take the statement on this card with you. Read it, think about it, and pray over it. And if you choose to follow through with it, God will heal your marriage."

The pastor prayed with her, and she left. The card contained a statement from the little book *Thoughts From the Mount of Blessing:*

> "The Father's presence encircled Christ, and nothing befell Him but that which infinite love permitted for the blessing of the world. Here was His source of comfort, and it is for us. He who is imbued with the Spirit of Christ abides in Christ. The blow that is aimed at him falls upon the Saviour, who surrounds him with His presence. Whatever comes to him comes from Christ. He has no need to resist evil, for Christ is his defense. Nothing can touch him except by our Lord's permission, and 'all things' that are permitted 'work together for good to them that love God.' Romans 8:28."[10]

You will probably need to read it again. First of all, the Father *encircled* Christ, the same concept we've visualized Christ doing in our lives. He is *in* us, and we are *in* Him. In other words, we're completely surrounded with Jesus. Next, nothing happened to Christ but what His Father allowed for the blessing of the world. This was not only *His* source of comfort but also must be *ours*. That is why we need not resist evil. Christ didn't. Nothing can touch us except by our Lord's permission, and whatever evil does reach us will work together for good. OK—easier said than done, right?

The woman read it, prayed over it, and made the decision she would live by what it said. If a miserable home life was her lot, she would not only accept it, she would embrace it, knowing that Christ had already filtered that on her behalf. Did she make it?

The first three months after she began to thank God for those things that she'd naturally despise or wish would not be there, her marriage and husband seemed to grow worse, not better. In a crucible that called her daily to be on her knees long and often, she chose to acknowledge that Jesus was at work, when it seemed ever so clear that Satan was in control. But she kept at it, believing that she was surrounded by Jesus and that He had the power to filter anything touching her life. Suddenly, things began to change. Her husband stopped drinking, he held on to a job, became interested in the family, and helped with the kids. He even began to do things for her he'd never done before. He would spend time just with her *every* evening: a walk, a ride, a trip to the ice cream store. She could not believe what was happening to him. Oh, how he had changed!

Thanking God for this development became much easier than before. She felt things couldn't be better. Then one night, while her mother-in-law watched the children, they went on a nice ride together. The grand-mother put the now-eleven-month-old baby to sleep and sat down to take a nap, leaving her medicine uncapped, over on the counter. The boy woke up and managed to crawl out of his crib. He reached grandmother's pills and swallowed every one of them. After a few minutes, he lay dy-ing on the floor. When the grandmother woke up and saw what hap-pened due to her neglect, she literally froze to her chair. She couldn't even scream for help, being in total shock.

When the parents arrived, they grabbed the toddler and rushed him to the hospital. But he died only an hour later. How could this possibly be? From bliss to utter tragedy in one hour. The husband couldn't take it, and he disappeared. The in-laws also wanted to die. The woman, alone and desperate, cried to God: "How can I accept this as if coming from You, God? Where were You at the time? This is the work of the devil, just when things were going so well!" So she let go of the conviction that God was in control of her life. But she noticed that this made things worse. After three weeks, she was depressed, alone, and broken-hearted.

One afternoon, she saw someone from church pulling up in her drive-way to visit her. Every visit was the same thing: People commiserated with her loss, but that only helped keep the focus on the tragedy.

As she headed to the door, the Spirit impressed her: "Did you not prom-ise Me you would take everything that happened to you as if coming from My hand?" Convicted, she wept, "Yes, Lord, I did. Please forgive me. I don't understand, and this hurts so much, but I surrender even the death of my boy to You. I choose to believe You were there when it happened and al-lowed it in Your infinite wisdom." This entire encounter lasted just seconds.

Opening the door, she put her hand up and said, "Please, don't say any-thing. I need to surrender all to Jesus right now. Would you kneel and pray with me so I can do that?" Three weeks after the baby's death, her husband returned. He had gone to hell and back. He told her he was sorry he'd left in their hour of greatest need but that he realized he needed desperately to know God the way she did. He was done with his life, he told her, and wanted to turn it over to Christ. Days later, the in-laws came for a visit. They acknowledged that many years ago, they had once been Adventists but had left the church. They didn't raise their boy in the faith. But they saw that she seemed to know God personally—that she was the most Christlike person they'd ever known—and they needed her help to come back to God.

The young woman may not know why her baby died or why it happened under such tragic circumstances. But she knows she will see him when Jesus comes again. And she now knows her husband and whole family will be there, as well.

"Christ in me, the hope of glory." This is the work of the Spirit in our lives. This is life abundant. This is what the whole world needs: Jesus in me through His Spirit.

NOTES:

1. *The Desire of Ages*, 388.

2. *Patriarchs and Prophets*, 233.

3. *The Desire of Ages*, 672.

4. *Testimonies*, vol. 5, 267.

5. *The Desire of Ages*, 671.

6. An important difference exists between "sins" and "sin." Human beings are sinful by nature—they are born in sin, their proclivity is to sin, their natural tendency is to rush to it and move away from God. That is called sin—sin as a condition of our lives. Sins, however, are the result of being sinful. We commit sins because we are men and women of sin, under "the law of sin and death." God can forgive us of our sins, but the only remedy to our sin [singular], our state of being, is a new life. Pardon won't do. Only becoming new creations will. That is why we *must* be born again.

7. See *The Ministry of Healing*, 51–58, to review the devotional experience of Jesus with His Father.

8. John 19:30 says, "He bowed His head and gave up the spirit [breath]." In death, a person would die; that's why His head would drop. Here we find that Jesus dropped His head first, then expired. The verb is correct, He "gave up" His spirit. He gave up His life.

9. For example, his wonderful book *His Robe of Mine* (Berrien Springs, MI: Justified Walk Ministries, 2003). Check website for other sources: www.justifiedwalk.com.

10. *Thoughts From the Mount of Blessing*, 71.

Questions for Reflection or Group Study

1. What impresses you about the story of Mike?

2. What is "Christ in you, the hope of glory"? What does the expression mean?

3. When does eternal life begin? Why then?

4. Why does the Bible, at times, use the expression the "Spirit of Christ"?

5. In what way is the gift of the Spirit the gift of salvation?

6. How have we been saved, are saved, and will be saved?

7. What is your reaction to the statement: "Everyone who has experienced the grace of Jesus receives the gifts of Jesus?"

8. If accepting Jesus' death on the cross covers our sins, what brings about victory over sin in our life?

9. What actually saves us—Jesus' death, or Jesus' life? Explain.

10. What is the difference between victory over all sin and perfectionism?

11. How can we come to the place where we really believe and accept that everything that comes to us is filtered by Christ's love, as seen in the story of the young woman?

12. After reading this chapter, what is the greatest desire of your heart?

CHAPTER EIGHT

Witnessing By Fruit and Gift

Have you ever been a witness in a trial? First, they make you state that you will tell the truth and nothing but the truth. Then you are to answer questions only on the basis of what you heard and what you saw, never on inference, opinion, or hearsay. If you deviate from this norm, guess what happens?

"Objection, your honor! Hearsay."

When Jesus promised His disciples the gift of the Spirit, He gave them the reason they would need Him: "You will receive power . . . and you will be My witnesses" (Acts 1:8). Power to witness. Since a witness is someone who can give first-hand report of the facts, witnessing has little to do with ability but a lot to do with availability. Witnessing is listed nowhere in the New Testament as one of many spiritual gifts. Not something God grants to specific individuals to do His work, it is rather something everyone who has honestly followed Jesus is capable of doing. Witnessing, in short, is the privilege of the converted, not the talented.

Everyone witnesses: the girl who was just received a proposal from her handsome suitor, the fan who saw his team win the Super Bowl, the student who flunked the chemistry exam. If it is real to us, we will let it be known, one way or the other. If it is bad news, it will seep out through our body language, tone of voice, or in mere irritation, even if we are determined no one will find out about it. If it is good news, our smiles alone will give us away and invite conversation, because witnessing is the outward expression of something inwardly significant. When Christians say . . . "I can't witness—I don't have the gift!" . . . all they are really saying is, "I don't know Jesus enough to say or show anything about Him." It's that simple. Sad, but painfully true.

The Bible word for "witness" is *martys*, from which we get the English "martyr." That doesn't sound right, does it? Hold on. *Martyria*, in Greek, is the *content* of the witness. In English, we have one word for both concepts: the *witness* who *bears witness*. This ambiguity is actually helpful, to understand the full range of meaning—it is impossible to separate the meaning of the witness as a *person* from the *content* of the witness. And that's why the ultimate witnesses are the martyrs. Because they could not say No to what they had seen and heard in Jesus Christ, even under the threat of death. Their experience was that real.

The Manifestations of the Spirit

When the disciples prayed for the endowment of the Spirit in the Upper Room, they came to the point of full surrender, as never before. The result was an ardent desire to witness for their Master and Savior.

> "One interest prevailed; one subject of emulation swallowed up all others. The ambition of the believers was to reveal the likeness of Christ's character and to labor for the enlargement of His kingdom."[1]

Please note that it says *one* interest, yet it identifies two of them: revealing Christ's character and reaching out to expand God's kingdom. This is the proverbial two sides of one coin. When we receive the Spirit, it will be seen by the lives we live and in the burden we have for the lost.

This is why the New Testament identifies just two overall manifestations of the Spirit: the fruit and the gifts. But these are never to be in isolation from each other—they are twins that go together, everywhere we go. A man with spiritual gifts should bear evidence of the fruit of the Spirit in his life. A woman revealing the loveliness of Jesus won't stand aloof from sharing, on behalf of the lost, Christ's character; His kingdom. Sometimes people speak about living a Christlike life in contradistinction from sharing Christ with others, as if an exemplary Christian life exonerates them from sharing Jesus or getting involved in outreach. That is a false dichotomy. One comes with the other, or none come at all.

The apostle Paul spoke to the Galatians about the fruit of the Spirit. The Galatians had a problem: they were hypocrites (Galatians 2:11–14). Judaizers had persuaded some in the church to keep portions of the Jewish law in order to have favor before God.

"You foolish Galatians," Paul exploded, "who has bewitched you . . . did you receive the Spirit by the works of the Law, or by hearing with faith?" (Galatians 3:1, 2).

Then he reminded them that Christ had redeemed them from the curse of the Law (v. 13), that they now lived by faith (vv. 22–24), and that their baptism meant being clothed with Christ (v. 27). Next, he told those who sought to be justified by law that they were "severed from Christ" but that those living by the Spirit were "waiting for the hope of righteousness," urging them to "walk by the Spirit" so they would not "carry out the desire of the flesh." Finally, Paul contrasted the results of legalism and self-righteousness with those of walking by the Spirit. He said:

"The fruit of the Spirit is love, joy, peace, patience, kindness, goodness, faithfulness, gentleness, self-control; against such things there is no law" (Galatians 5:4, 5, 16, 22, 23).

The fruit of the Spirit is a miracle fruit: one fruit with nine flavors. It really is *love* revealed in manifold ways, much like a rainbow that is seen in several colors, thanks to the light of the sun. Any time you or I reveal genuine love or joy or inner peace or self-control, we mirror the very characteristics of Jesus our Lord. But that happens because He, like the sun shining on water droplets, is the One shining through us.

Paul makes one more important point. In Galatians 6, the apostle points out that you can reap the fruit of the Spirit only if that is the kind of seed you have been sowing—spiritual seed. If you sow seeds of corruption and decay, should you expect the fruit of the Spirit?

"The experience of many of us, I fear, is that we consistently sow seeds of decay and then in prayer ask God somehow to cause fruits of the Spirit to appear. That, says Paul (Galatians 6:7, 8), is an impossibility."[2]

How We Bear Fruit

Jesus made it abundantly clear that His intention for us is to bear *much* fruit, not just meager fruit. But He knows that this is a process that takes time. He spoke about it the night He announced the coming of the Comforter. Take your Bible if it's nearby, and turn to John 15.

"I am the true Vine, and My Father is the vine-dresser. Every branch in Me that *does not* bear fruit, He takes away; and every branch that *bears* fruit, He prunes it so that it may *bear more* fruit. . . . He who abides in Me and I in him, he *bears much* fruit, for apart from Me you can do nothing" (John 15:1, 2, 5, emphasis supplied).

Did you notice the stages in the text? First, there is no bearing of fruit. That gives way to bearing at least some fruit, to bearing more fruit, and finally, much fruit. "My Father is glorified by this, that you bear *much fruit*, and so prove to be My disciples" (v. 8). Jesus won't be satisfied until we bear *much* fruit, not just some.

How does He take a disciple from bearing *no* fruit to bearing *some* fruit? Verse two says "He takes [the branch] away." Now, that may appear confusing. Is Jesus saying He'll cut the branch off in order for it to bear fruit? That doesn't make sense, does it? For a branch that is cut off from the vine to bear fruit is impossible. Jesus even said that: "Without Me you can do nothing." The original word translated "take away" can also be translated "take up." And that is exactly what vintners do with branches that droop low to the ground. They bend them upward and tie them to higher branches or to sticks, so they can get better exposure to rain and sunlight—and this also avoids extraneous tendrils reaching down to draw nourishment directly from the ground instead of from the vine.

But the Heavenly Vine-dresser is not done yet. Once we begin bearing *some* fruit for His glory, He sets about preparing us to bear *more* fruit. How does He do that? The Bible says He *prunes* the branch (v. 2), freeing it of unnecessary foliage, shoots, and leaves, cutting here and there for the best possible exposure to sunlight, moisture, and air. This He does very carefully. "The Vine-dresser is never closer to the vine, taking more thought about its long-term health and productivity, than when He has the knife in His hand."[3] Have you ever wondered why difficult, even tragic things happen in your life? Why cancer takes a loved one, or financial collapse afflicts a family, or grievous injustices show up at your door? God is not the author of pain and misery, but He may use either or both for the sake of better health.

"Many who sincerely consecrate their lives to God's service are surprised and disappointed to find themselves, as never before, confronted by obstacles and beset by trials and perplexities. They pray for Christlikeness of character, for a fitness for the Lord's work, and they are placed in circumstances that seem to call forth all the evil of their nature. . . . [They question,] 'If God is leading us, why do all these things come upon us?'

"It is because God is leading them that these things come upon them. Trials and obstacles are the Lord's chosen methods of discipline and His appointed conditions of success. . . . He sees that some have powers and susceptibilities which, rightly directed, might be used in the advancement of His work. In His providence He brings these persons into different positions and varied circumstances that they may discover in their character the defects which have been concealed from their own knowledge. He gives them opportunity to correct these defects and to fit themselves for His service. Often He permits the fires of affliction to assail them that they may be purified."[4]

Our loving Savior won't give up on us, even if we blame Him for the discomfort and pain we may be experiencing. As long as we remain attached to the Vine, He'll be at work in us to bear more fruit. But how does He lead us to His ultimate objective of bearing *much* fruit? He invites us "to abide in Him" (v. 5).

Abide in Christ

Something is different now. In the first two transitions—from no fruit to some fruit, and then from some fruit to more fruit—God took the initiative. The Lord does not usually ask us whether or not we'd like to be "bent" out of our natural comfort zones, or "cut" away from our cherished idols, indolence, and selfishness. He just does it. If you wish to really shine with all His glory and be laden with much fruit that belies the source of your life, then you must choose to "abide in Him."

What does that mean? The word *abide* is not part of our everyday language today. It means "to remain," "to stay," "to endure." In this context, it means "to hang on." Yes, what Jesus is saying is that to yield much fruit for His glory, we must hang on to Him for dear life. Just as a branch hangs on to the vine, even when facing fierce wind or rain, we must hang on to Jesus when the storms of life overwhelm us. The entire exercise makes us stronger *in* Him.

But for those analytical minds who wonder why a verb such as "abide" would be used in connection with a branch—which should be a natural appendage to the vine—the answer is simpler than you thought. The truth is that as human beings, we are *not* naturally attached to Jesus. Our sinful natures make us reject Life and choose death instead. We look at Jesus and say: *I want to be a part of Him*—then we mysteriously walk away! We never chose Him, really. He chose us. "You did not choose Me," Christ said, "but I chose you, and appointed you that you would go and bear much fruit" (v. 16). Paul reminds us that we as branches have been "grafted in" (Romans 11:17–24). We were not born of Christ to begin with. Visualize this: a farmer grafting a wild branch onto a healthy vine. What does he have to do to that vine? Cut it—hurt it—so he can insert the wild branch *into* the vine. Isn't that what the cross is about? Didn't our adoption into Christ's life cause Him pain? Absolutely. But He loved us to the end (John 13:1) and wouldn't have it any other way.

Here is the point: We must hang on now. Hang on as Jacob did with the Angel (Genesis 32:26). We must *not* let Him go. For even though this

104 • ADVENTISM'S GREATEST NEED

is the only way to have life, our natural tendency will be to leave. Don't leave. Don't walk away. Abide in Him until you, as the branch, so identify with the Vine that it will be impossible ever to leave again!

The Gifts of the Spirit

Reflecting the character of Christ and bearing fruit that can tell which tree we belong to is one side of the witnessing coin. The other is using the gifts of the Spirit "for the advancement of His kingdom."

Four major chapters, or sections, in the New Testament teach about and list spiritual gifts: Romans 12, 1 Corinthians 12–14, Ephesians 4, and 1 Peter 4. References to additional gifts are found elsewhere (1 Corinthians 13:3; 7:7, 32–34; Ephesians 3:1, 7), but in each of the main references, the root foundation of the fruit of the Spirit—love—is alluded to in connection with the gifts. After listing prophecy, service, teaching, exhortation, giving, leadership and mercy, Paul tells the Romans to "let love be without hypocrisy" (12:6–9). These, after all, are gifts of grace; that is, gifts of love. To the Corinthians, Paul devoted a whole chapter about love, in the middle of his teaching about gifts, concluding that "love never fails" because even though gifts may come and go, faith, hope, and love abide, and "the greatest of these is love" (1 Corinthians 13:8, 13).

To the Ephesians, the apostle is writing to a more mature church about those gifted to lead them: apostles, prophets, evangelists, and pastor-teachers. The objective of such gifting by God is to lead them "to the unity of the faith, and of the knowledge of the Son of God"—to spiritual maturity that would eventually reflect "the fullness of Christ" (4:13). As a result, they would be stable, not easily "carried by every wind of doctrine," and would "speak the truth in love," while growing up in all aspects into the Head, Jesus Christ. (v. 14). Last, Peter urges the followers of Jesus to use their gifts, "serving one another as good stewards of the manifold grace of God" (1 Peter 4:10) but introduces his admonition with: "Above all, keep fervent in your love for one another, because love covers a multitude of sins" (v. 8).

I mentioned already that the gifts of the Spirit were gifts of grace—*charismata*—coming from Jesus yet distributed by the Spirit. So the grace of Jesus secured the right to give us the gifts (Ephesians 4:7, 8), but it is the Spirit of Jesus who manages such rights on earth. Paul says, "The same Spirit works all these things, distributing [the gifts] to each one individually just as He wills" (1 Corinthians 12:11). Gifts are given, then, according to grace and according to the Spirit. I found it interesting that both sources—grace and Spirit—are inexhaustible in the economy of God. For "when sin abounded grace abounded *all the more*"

(Romans 5:20, emphasis supplied), being that Christ's grace "is sufficient" for us (2 Corinthians 12:9). Regarding the Spirit, John the Baptist assured us that He is given "without measure" (John 3:34).

The Multiple Purpose of the Gifts

The New Testament also teaches the multiple purposes of spiritual gifts: for the sake of church unity and spiritual maturity (Romans 12:3–5, 9–16; 1 Corinthians 12:4–7; 1 Corinthians 12:31 – 14:40; Ephesians 4:13–16), to carry on the ministry of the church (Ephesians 4:11, 12), and for the glory of God (1 Peter 4:10, 11). Some might be surprised to see major purposes of spiritual gifts as being church unity and the spiritual growth of the body, but there is a logic to it. Jesus had told His disciples, "Love one another, even as I have loved you, . . . by this all men will know that you are My disciples, if you have love for one another" (John 13:34, 35). If we as the church want to make an impact in the world, it won't be through our resources, institutions, or even our fool-proof doctrines. It will be because the love of God has taken over our lives in such a way that family member, neighbor, friend, and stranger will see in us such Christ-like love for each other that they will conclude that is simply not of this world.

Often we spend time in spiritual gifts seminars focusing on particular gifts and on whether or not we have them. The inventory approach to learning about the gifts is very limited in its ability to get the big picture. What we need is Jesus, all of Him, every day. His presence through the Spirit will fill us to the brim, and He will spill out in a variety of manifestations or gifts (the New Testament does not give us an exhaustive list), each calculated to make an impact on the soul of another for the glory of God.

A little girl and her grandmother were in church one morning. The girl kept working on her drawing, apparently oblivious to what the preacher was saying. But she was listening. She pulled on her grandmother's sleeve and asked: "Grandma, did the preacher say God lives in us?"

"Yes, honey. He does."

She kept drawing, until moments later, when another question needed an urgent answer.

"Grandma, did the preacher just say God is bigger than us?"

"Of course, precious. God is bigger than us."

"If He is bigger than us, and He lives in us, shouldn't some of Him show through?"

Indeed, He should. Is your experience with Jesus so real and genuine that it is impossible for Him not to "show through" in your life? That is witnessing. That is what the Holy Spirit, manifested through fruit and gifts, can do through God's people and for God's work.

"The promise of the Holy Spirit . . . belongs as much to us as it did to them [the early church], and yet how rarely it is presented before the people, and its reception spoken of in the church. In consequence of this silence upon this most important theme, what promise do we know less about by its *practical fulfillment* than this rich promise of the gift of the Holy Spirit, whereby *efficiency* is to be given to all our spiritual labor?"[5]

A Christlike Life and Christlike Ministry

Back in 1921, a missionary couple named David and Svea Flood went with their 2-year-old son from Sweden to the heart of Africa, to what was then called the Belgian Congo.

They met up with another young Scandinavian couple, the Ericksons, and the four of them sought God for direction. In those days of great sacrifice, they felt the Lord leading them to set out from the main mission station and take the gospel to a remote area.

At the village of N'dolera they were rebuffed by the chief, who would not let them enter his town, for fear of alienating the local gods. The two couples opted to go half a mile up the slope and build their own mud huts. They prayed for a spiritual breakthrough, but there was none. The only contact with the villagers was a young boy, who was allowed to sell them chickens and eggs twice a week. Svea Flood, a tiny woman only four feet, eight inches tall, decided that if this was the only African she could talk to, she would try to lead him to Jesus.

Day after day, she told the boy about Jesus and the God of heaven.

Meanwhile, malaria continued to strike one member of the little band after another. In time, the Ericksons decided they'd had enough and returned to the central mission station. David and Svea Flood remained near N'dolera to go on alone. Then, of all things, Svea found herself pregnant in the middle of the primitive wilderness. She gave birth to a little girl, whom they named Aina. The delivery, however, was exhausting, and Svea Flood was already weak from bouts of malaria. She died seventeen days later.

Something inside David Flood snapped. He dug a crude grave, buried his 27-year-old wife, then took his children back down the mountain to the mission station.

Giving his children to the Ericksons, he snarled, "I'm going back to Sweden . . . God has ruined my life." Eight months later, both of the Ericksons were stricken with a mysterious malady and died within days of each other. The little girl was then given to some American missionaries, who adjusted her Swedish name to "Aggie" and eventually brought her back to the United States at age 3.

How could so much go so wrong, when all they wanted was to serve God in faith? But God had worked through His servant Svea. Her daughter Aggie grew up in South Dakota. As a young woman, she met and married a young pastor, who in time became president of a Christian college. One day, a Swedish religious magazine appeared in her mailbox. She had no idea who had sent it, and of course, she couldn't read the language. But as she turned the pages, suddenly a photo stopped her cold. There, in a primitive setting, was a grave with a white cross, and on the cross were the words SVEA FLOOD. Aggie jumped into her car and went straight to see a college faculty member who, she knew, could translate the article.

"What does this say?" she demanded. The instructor summarized the story about missionaries in N'dolera long ago, the death of Aggie's young mother, the contact with the African boy, and the fact that many Christians were living in the area now.

A few years later, Aggie and her husband were attending a high-level evangelism conference in London, England, when a report was given from the Republic of Congo. The superintendent of the national church spoke eloquently of the gospel's spread in his nation. Aggie could not help going to ask him afterward if he had ever heard of David and Svea Flood. And what she heard brought tears of joy and thankfulness to her eyes.

"It was Svea Flood who led me to Jesus Christ," he smiled. "I was the boy who brought food to your parents before you were born." Svea Flood's love and Christlikeness and her earnest desire to bless the boy made an eternal impression on him. He accepted Jesus as His Lord and Savior. After he grew up, he persuaded the chief to let him build a school in the village. He led all his students to Christ. Then the children led their parents to Christ, and eventually even the chief became a Christian. Today, 600 Christian believers live in that one village—and over 100,000 in the country![6]

A Christlike life and a Christlike ministry. This is why the Spirit gives us gifts—and we can then bear fruit of His power and grace. This is the reason for His ministry in our lives—for the sake of the world. The world will be convicted of righteousness, Jesus declared, for I will send the Helper "to you" (John 16:7, 8).

NOTES:

1. *The Acts of the Apostles*, 48.

2. Jan Paulsen, *When the Spirit Descends* (Washington, D.C.: Review and Herald, 1977), 131.

3. Tom Wright, *John for Everyone*, vol. 2 (Louisville, KY: Westminster John Knox, 2004), 71.

4. *The Ministry of Healing*, 470, 471.

5. *Testimonies to Ministers*, 174.

6. Story adapted from Jim Cymbala and Dean Merrill, *Fresh Power* (Grand Rapids, MI: Zondervan, 2003), 115.

Questions for Reflection or Group Study

1. Explain what witnessing is, from the introduction of this chapter.

2. In what ways do the words *witness* and *martyr* interplay with each other?

3. What are the two overall manifestations of the Holy Spirit? Why would that be "two sides of the same coin"?

4. How can a branch produce fruit by "taking it away"? What does "take away" mean in John 15?

5. When would you say that God, as the Vine-dresser is the closest to us? Think and share examples from your own life.

6. How does Jesus lead us to His ultimate objective of bearing much fruit? What does it mean to abide?

7. If the gifts are given from the inexhaustible sources of grace and the Spirit, what does this imply regarding the kind and number of gifts a Christian can have?

8. What are the multiple purposes of spiritual gifts? Why do you think a primary purpose is church unity?

9. How do you see that spiritual gifts inventories are limited? What do you think might be helpful for the church, in addition to learning which gifts each may have?

10. What would the Spirit want to tell you through the story of Svea Flood?

Praxis

CHAPTER NINE

Baptized With the Spirit

Charles G. Finney is one of the most iconic figures in American religious history. Reared in central New York State, he was first a teacher, then a law clerk, and finally, one of the most influential evangelists of all time. His conversion experience is remarkable.

At the age of 26, he was "almost as ignorant of religion as a heathen." He had a Bible and went to church, because that's what everyone else did in 1818. But he didn't get the sermons. He couldn't understand the meaning of regeneration, or sanctification, or even faith. And he did not believe in prayer much, because he saw little by way of clear answers. He did, however, realize he was a sinner in need of salvation—something he concluded was "of infinite importance."[1]

One Sunday night, he decided to settle the question of his salvation. He read his Bible for two whole days. By Tuesday night, he became anxious for lack of tangible results and thought he might die and be lost forever. Early the next morning, as he set out for his law clerk's office, "an inward voice" confronted him: "What are you waiting for? Did you not promise to give your heart to God? And what are you trying to do? Are you endeavoring to work out a righteousness of your own?"[2]

Just at this point, Finney's mind opened like a thousand windows to the sunlight, and he was able to see "the reality and the fullness of the atonement" and that salvation was "an offer to be accepted." Then the question was forcefully pressed upon his mind: "Will you accept it now, today?"

"Yes," he replied, "I will accept it today, or I will die in the attempt."[3] So instead of going to the office, he walked away to a wooded area of town in order to pray. But to his great chagrin, he could not pray! He was more concerned about someone listening to him pray than about praying.

Immediately, this scripture came to mind:

"Then shall ye call upon me, and ye shall go and pray unto me, and I will hearken unto you. And ye shall seek me, and find me, when ye shall search for me with all your heart" (Jeremiah 29:12, 13).

In Finney's own words:

"I instantly seized hold of this with my heart. I had intellectually believed the Bible before, but never had the truth been in my mind that faith was a voluntary trust instead of an intellectual state. . . . Somehow I knew that that was a passage of scripture, though I do not think I had ever read it. . . . I cried to him, 'Lord, I take Thee at Thy word.'"[4]

That evening, back in the office, he again became deeply convicted, wanting to pour out his whole soul to God.

"It seemed as if I met the Lord Jesus Christ face to face. It seemed to me that I saw Him as I would see any other man. He said nothing, but looked at me in such a manner as to break me right down at this feet. . . . I fell down at this feet and poured out my soul to him. I wept aloud like a child and made such confessions as I could with my choked words."

This encounter lasted for a while.

"But as I turned and was about to take a seat by the fire, I received a mighty baptism of the Holy Spirit. . . . [He] descended upon me in a manner that seemed to go through me, body and soul. I could feel the impression, like a wave of electricity, going through and through me. Indeed it seemed to come in waves of liquid love, . . . It seemed like the very breath of God [fanning] me, like immense wings.

"No words can express the wonderful love that was spread abroad in my heart. I wept aloud with joy and love. I literally bellowed out the unspeakable overflow of my heart. These waves came over me, and over me, and over me, one after the other, until I remember crying out, 'I shall die if these waves continue to pass over me.' I said, 'Lord, I cannot bear any more,' yet I had no fear of death."

Later that evening, a church member found Finney weeping loudly. He asked if something was wrong—or if he was in pain. Finney answered,

"No, but so happy that I cannot live."[5] When he woke up the next morning, he recalled:

> "The baptism that I had received . . . returned upon me in the same manner. . . . I wept aloud with joy, and remained for sometime too much overwhelmed with the baptism of the Spirit to do anything but pour out my soul to God. . . . In this state I was taught the doctrine of justification by faith as a present experience. . . . My cup ran over with blessing and with love."[6]

Finney became a powerful evangelist, literally, overnight. So efficient was his ministry that he "could not remember one whom [he] spoke with, who was not soon after converted." That evening, as he sat to have dinner with a young man who distilled whiskey for a living, he began praying for the food, and the young man suddenly fled to his room and came out the next morning, converted. "The Word of God had wonderful power, every day," Finney wrote in his memoirs, "and I was surprised to find that a few words spoken to an individual would stick in his heart like an arrow."[7] For the next thirty years, he went up and down a myriad towns in New York State, preaching and praying and converting record numbers of people. Stories exist of people giving their hearts to Christ the moment the train in which the evangelist traveled went by the station.

Finney's experience is viewed by many today as Exhibit A of what an honest-to-goodness baptism of the Holy Spirit is all about—a powerful second blessing for those already Christian. Others simply view this as Finney's true and first conversion. How are we to interpret it? The baptism of the Holy Spirit remains one of the most controversial subjects in theology today.

What exactly is the baptism of the Spirit? First, let's contemplate a bit of history.

Spirit Baptism in Historical Context

The first in Christian history to emphasize the manifestations of the baptism of the Spirit were the second-century Montanists. Montanus was a converted pagan priest who considered the church spiritually dead and called it back to the golden days of the early church of Pentecost. He wished to see the church of signs and wonders and sought to expand the inspiration of the Holy Spirit beyond the canon of Scripture. Referring to himself as "the Mouthpiece of the Holy Spirit," he gathered a group of followers, founded a commune, and began to prophesy about the corruption of church leaders and of the coming of the Lord. He and his two women prophets would fall into trances and spiritual frenzies and speak for God in the first person. This phenomenon helped spur the church to settle on to the concept of "apostolic succession." In order to discern between self-proclaimed charismatic leaders and those whom the church could trust, they chose bishops who could trace their ordination pedigree back to the early apostles.[8]

The Christological and Trinitarian controversies of the next few centuries made the work and person of the Holy Spirit take a back seat to these other theological discussions. Not until the nineteenth century did a focus on the Holy Spirit rise again with any serious significance.

Hyper-Calvinism—the emphasis on the sovereignty of God to the point that those saved are predestined to be so, even against their wills—met a serious challenge from John Wesley and other Arminians, who believed that the Bible taught free choice in matters of individual salvation. Wesley emphasized the *sanctification* of the believer, against the over-emphasis by the Reformed tradition (Calvinists) of forensic *justification*. In other words, to be saved, one does not only need to be legally justified by grace—something that gives us acceptance in Christ (Romans 5:1)—but also sanctified by grace. He or she needs to allow Christ to dwell in the heart by faith, as a witness that Christ is actually and truly saving the person He has justified. This is the whole concept taught by Paul as "Christ in you, the hope of glory" (Colossians 1:27).

With the new emphasis on sanctification, the Holiness Movement was born in America. Many groups and churches placed a greater-than-ever emphasis on the work Christ would do *in* us—the temple of the Holy Spirit—and not just *for* us—forensic righteousness. Eventually, this focus on the evidence of the Spirit's work in the life led to the birth of classical Pentecostalism.[9]

The founder of the modern Pentecostal Movement was Charles Fox Parham, a Holiness preacher who sought the "latter rain" outpouring of the Holy Spirit as a greater personal manifestation of God's power. He became convinced that the manifestation of the baptism of the Holy Spirit would be *glossolalia* (speaking in tongues), challenging the students of his Bible school to seek for such an experience. One of them, Agnes Ozman, experienced glossolalia on January 1, 1901, and that date has since been considered the birth of the movement.[10]

This phenomenon grew with amazing speed. By 1906, the movement was making mainstream press headlines in Los Angeles, with the Azusa Street Revival. By 1930, dozens of Pentecostal denominations were born. This First Wave of Pentecostalism, as it is called, gave way to the second, in 1960—the Neo-Charismatic Movement. That is, leaders and members from typically mainline churches—Episcopal, Lutheran, Methodist, Congregational—began to experience a "renewal" in corporate and personal worship that included speaking in tongues, healings, and other "manifestations of the Spirit." By the early 1980s, the Third Wave arrived. This latest wave affected traditional Evangelical churches—churches that had always had a strong emphasis on God's Word but which now became open to the same type of manifestations accepted in classical Pentecostal churches.

The Pentecostal-Charismatic Movement is the fastest-growing movement in Christianity today. In barely over 100 years, it has galvanized over 600 million adherents worldwide—almost a third of all of Christianity—a growth rate not even seen with the early church of the first century.

Three Views on Spirit Baptism

For centuries, the concept of the baptism of the Holy Spirit was clear in Protestant churches. It taught that such "baptism" is, basically, conversion to Christ. A person is baptized with the Spirit as he or she surrenders to the love of Jesus. Never was it seen as anything other than a concurrent experience with salvation. When followers accept Christ as their Savior, they accept the fullness of the Spirit in their lives. This baptism, then, is the only baptism the New Testament teaches (Ephesians 4:5; 1 Corinthians 12:13). The baptism of water is only the external symbolism of the internal transformation taking place in the new believer. These are not two distinct baptisms but one.

When John Wesley came along, he put a greater emphasis on the need for the "witness" of the Spirit in one's life (Romans 8:13–16). That put a spotlight on *sanctification* as a necessary and complementary experience in the Christian's life. However, Wesley never taught that the baptism of the Spirit was a second work of grace in the life of the believer. He simply highlighted the need for sanctification. But as often happens with theological developments, some of the Methodist leaders after Wesley began to call sanctification "the baptism of the Spirit." This emphasis was picked up and expanded by the Holiness Movement, with its roots in Methodism, and the table was set for an additional "conversion" experience.

Whereas the post-Wesleyan and Holiness groups emphasized sanctification—sometimes calling it "instant sanctification," leading some to yearn for something instantaneous and supernatural—the Pentecostal Movement that followed placed the emphasis on power. That is why the baptism of the Holy Spirit, for these groups, can only be identified as a work of supernatural power—speaking in tongues, prophesying, performing miracles, etc.

You see the progression, don't you? Three centuries ago, the baptism of the Spirit was conversion. One hundred and fifty years ago, the baptism of the Spirit was sanctification, or instant sanctification—a second work of grace on behalf of the believer. One hundred years ago, the baptism of the Spirit became viewed not only as a second work of grace but as a work of power; that is, as a supernatural manifestation that sets the believer apart from others who haven't experienced it.

What is the truth? What does the Bible say?

The Evidence From the New Testament

Whether or not the baptism of the Spirit is a second work of grace is more important than what first meets the eye. Theologians call it a matter of *ordo-salutis*, or the proper order of God's activity on behalf of our salvation. And the implications of believing one way or the other have far-reaching consequences, especially for the way we view the times of the end. So let's explore the biblical evidence.

Just a few examples are on record, in the New Testament, of people being baptized with or by the Spirit, most of them in the book of Acts. The one exception is the baptism of Jesus.

> "Now when all the people were baptized, Jesus was also baptized, and while He was praying, heaven was opened, and the Holy Spirit descended like a dove, and a voice came out of heaven, 'You are My beloved Son, in You I am well-pleased'" (Luke 3:21, 22).

Even though Jesus did not need to be baptized for the repentance of any sin in Him, He did it "to fulfill all righteousness" (Matthew 3:13–15). Clearly, His baptism by water and by the Spirit are concurrent experiences, not one coming years after the other. Since Christ is our Example, this is significant for understanding the timing and purpose of the baptism of the Spirit.

The next case is the disciples on the Day of Pentecost. On that day, "they were all filled with the Holy Spirit and began to speak with other tongues, as the Holy Spirit was giving them utterance" (Acts 2:4). Peter calls this infilling "the promise of the Holy Spirit" (Acts 3:33), and Jesus called this promise the "baptism" of the Spirit (Acts 1:4, 5). So infilling and baptism are used indistinctively in this instance. This is one of the texts Charismatics use to indicate *sequence* versus *concurrence*. They believe that baptism came to 120 already committed Christians, showing that the fullness of the Spirit can only be expected some time *after* one's conversion.

The third example is found two chapters later. Again, a group of disciples was praying for boldness to preach God's Word, and "they were all filled with the Holy Spirit and began to speak the word of God with boldness" (Acts 4:31). Basically, this presents the same argument as the previous case, with the possible exception that *infilling* here may not be synonymous with baptism; that is, it is not a start but a continuation of the previous experience.

The next case tells the story of the conversion of the Samaritans. Philip breaks Jewish protocol and shares Jesus with people seen as too far gone to be saved. His preaching is accompanied by healing miracles and the casting out of demons (Acts 8:5–7). And the Samaritans "believed Philip" and "were being baptized" (v. 12). Now, here is where it gets interesting. Nothing is said about them receiving the Holy Spirit at that point. So their baptism was by water only. In fact, they did not receive the Spirit until Peter and John came down from Jerusalem and, laying their hands on them, prayed "that they might receive the Holy Spirit" (vv. 14–17). This is the strongest argument used by second-blessing theologians to identify the baptism of the Spirit as a second work of grace. And it certainly appears that conclusion may be right. But we'll come back to this soon.

The fifth case is the result of Paul's encounter with Jesus on the road to Damascus. After Paul was blind for three days, thinking about what God had attempted to show him through His faithful church, Ananias is sent to Paul to heal him and fill him with the Spirit (Acts 9:17). And as soon as he regained his sight, Paul was baptized (v. 18). Here is a reference to water baptism for someone who needed to repent from his sins, die to self, and start a new life. Follow carefully here. Paul was baptized with water because he was converted—he became a follower of Jesus. And as he regained his sight, he was filled with the Holy Spirit. So basically, these are concurrent experiences.

The same thing happens in the next chapter, where we find Cornelius and his household accepting Peter's message about the gospel of Jesus.

"While Peter was still speaking these words, the Holy Spirit fell upon all those who were listening to the message. All . . . who came with Peter were amazed, because the gift of the Holy Spirit had been poured out on the Gentiles also" (Acts 10:44, 45).

What is happening here? For the first time in the experience of the early church, except in the Ethiopian eunuch's case, Gentiles accept Jesus as their Savior, and this results in the automatic outpouring of the Spirit on them! This clear evidence of God's favor is what convinced the disciples that these Gentiles ought to also undergo the public rite of water baptism (v. 47).

The last clear case of the reception of the Spirit takes place in Ephesus in Asia Minor. When Paul arrives, he meets twelve disciples, and right off asks them if they had received the Holy Spirit when they believed. They said, "No, we have not even heard whether there is a Holy Spirit" (Acts 19:2). Astonished, the apostle asks them about what type of baptism they could have experienced, to which they responded, "John's baptism" (v. 3). Paul explained that this was only a baptism of repentance, pointing to

Jesus (v. 4). Evidently, he then told them about what Jesus *did*, and not only what He *would do* (which is what John the Baptist would have taught), and they were rebaptized then, and "the Holy Spirit came upon them" (vv. 5, 6). This incident may present the clearest evidence for the fact that water baptism was considered insufficient or inadequate, since the real baptism is the one by the Holy Spirit!

When, Then, Are We Baptized With the Spirit?

According to the New Testament, in some cases it appears that the Holy Spirit baptism is *subsequent* to conversion, while in others, that it is *concurrent* with conversion or water baptism.

We must realize that Bible narratives may be more tricky to interpret correctly than clear explanations or direct Bible teaching. This is something that Protestant interpretation has always kept in mind, while Charismatic hermeneutics (methods of interpretation) has placed a greater emphasis on the narratives. The Holy Spirit has designed the New Testament in such a way that it is replete with doctrinal teaching, and that's why well over half of it consists of instruction given by Paul, Peter, John, James, and Jude. They present direct teaching, much as the prophets of the Old Testament gave direct messages from God to Israel and Judah.

The intent of God may be clear by listening to what Peter said to his audience on the Day of Pentecost. When, under conviction of sin, they asked what they should do, Peter answered, "Repent, and each of you be baptized in the name of Jesus Christ for the forgiveness of your sins . . ." (Acts 2:38a). Let's pause for a moment. What baptism is Peter referring to? The baptism by water, since water baptism is known in the Bible as "the baptism of repentance" (Acts 19:4; 1:5; Mark 1:4). But Peter doesn't stop there. He goes on to say, ". . . and you will receive the gift of the Holy Spirit. For the promise is for you and your children and for all who are far off [the Gentiles]" (vv. 38b, 39). Since we already know that "the promise" refers to Spirit baptism, and it also refers here to "the gift of the Holy Spirit," Peter is clearly saying that for those who repent and are baptized by water, the reception of the gift of the Spirit is part of the package! No inference is found anywhere there, that this gift should come years or decades after their repentance. The teaching is plain: with repentance comes the gift of the Spirit.

Paul makes it even more clear. The New Testament chapter with the greatest number of references to the Holy Spirit is Romans 8. The entire chapter is worth reading carefully. He says: "If anyone does not have the Spirit of Christ, he does not belong to Him" (v. 9). Quite clear, isn't it? If the Spirit is not in us, we don't belong to Jesus. In other words, if we have not accepted Jesus, the Spirit does not abide in us, because it is the Holy Spirit who brings Jesus in! It is impossible, then, to separate the coming or baptism of the Spirit, from conversion. If you have given yourself to Jesus, it is because the Holy Spirit has baptized you! Andrew Murray put it this way:

"Two diverse things cannot at once and the same time occupy the very same place. Your own life and the life of God cannot fill the heart at the same time. Your life hinders the entrance of the life of God. When your own life is cast out, the life of God will fill you. So long as *I myself* am still something, *Jesus himself* cannot be everything. My life must be expelled; then the Spirit of Jesus will flow in."[11]

The Samaritan Puzzle

What about the Samaritans? Did they not receive the baptism of the Spirit *after* they were baptized by water? Yes, they did. But there were other things that influenced that order of events. That's why context is important if we are to draw accurate lessons from Bible narratives.

Remember how, when Jesus articulated the Great Commission in Acts 1, He told them to be witnesses to Jerusalemites, Judeans, Samaritans, and even to Gentiles? None of these people belonged to the Galilean culture of the early disciples, and it would normally be a struggle for them to obey Jesus' command. In the case of the Samaritans, there might be a reason why the outpouring of the Spirit was delayed, and the reason might be because of the disciples, not the Samaritans. Note that none of the Twelve were the ones Jesus could use to minister to them. As Galilean Jews, they were still too prejudiced to reach out to them. So God used Philip, a Hellenistic Jew, to accomplish the task.

Once the apostles in Jerusalem heard that *Samaritans* had received the gospel and were baptized (Acts 8:14), they sent Peter and John to them. Well, was sending John a good idea? The last encounter John had experienced with Samaritans was only weeks before Christ's death. At that time, the Samaritans refused to give Jesus and His disciples lodging, due to their intense prejudice. John, the beloved disciple, thought the best thing then would be for *fire* to descend from heaven and burn these people up (Luke 9:51–56)! But in a twist of divine irony, the Lord now sent John to minister to Samaritans, because their hearts had been opened, and instead of praying for consuming fire, John was to pray for the fire of the Spirit to descend on them. That may be the reason for the delay.

Why the Confusion?

Now, there may still be some confusion about this. Why would we find so many statements by Ellen White urging the people of God to be baptized with the Spirit, if they already walk with Christ?

Part of the confusion may be due to the use of the terms. *Baptism* implies initiation into the Christian life. It symbolizes death to self, submersion under water as a type of burial of the old self, and resurrection with new life (Romans 6:3–5). The rite of baptism, then, is symbolic of the new birth. This is why re-baptisms should be rare, the constant reminder being our participation in the rite of footwashing instead (John 13:8, 13–15). However, *infillings* should be daily and constant, like breathing again every few moments. The fact you breathed once when you came out of your mother's womb does not mean that was all the breath you ever needed. It only meant you had started. If you don't keep breathing, you will die.

In my study, I have found over thirty different expressions in the New Testament, as well as in the Spirit of Prophecy, that refer to the same work of the Spirit. Nouns such as *baptism, reception, gift, filling, endowment, anointing,* etc., all refer to the same thing. And Ellen White often uses these expressions interchangeably, in a non-technical way. Look at the following statement and see how many different expressions referring to the Holy Spirit she uses in just a small paragraph!

"Today you are to have your vessel purified, that it may be ready for the heavenly dew, ready for the showers of the latter rain; for the latter rain will come, and the blessing of God will fill every soul that is purified from every defilement. It is our work today to yield our souls to Christ, that we may be fitted for the time of refreshing from the presence of the Lord—fitted for the baptism of the Holy Spirit."[12]

Here, she used five different expressions to say the same thing. "The heavenly dew" and "the latter rain" are analogous to the outpouring of the Holy Spirit. Methodists often referred to "the blessing of God" as code for the baptism of the Spirit, and we must not forget that Ellen White was raised Methodist. "The time of refreshing" is taken right out of Peter's second sermon (Acts 3:19), which echoed the same Pentecost message as his first (Acts 2:38, 39). And of course, "the baptism of the Holy Spirit."

When Ellen White wrote of Christ that "daily He received a fresh baptism of the Holy Spirit,"[13] she could have used a more technically precise word such as *infilling,* instead of *baptism.* For she does not mean to say that Christ was *baptized* over and over but that He was *filled* over and over with the Spirit. However, even here she qualified it, by saying "a fresh baptism."

Here is the point. The baptism of the Holy Spirit is given to us upon surrender of our lives to Christ. And He comes into our lives every time we surrender, not just once, but as many times as we yield to the love of Christ. So settle it in your mind that this is a work of faith. You receive

Him by faith (Galatians 3:2, 14; Acts 19:2), and every time you trust your Savior, He abides with you yet again.

When Wrong Theology Misleads

Why is this important? Because expecting a supernatural influx of the Spirit sometime later in the Christian life is an appealing, romantic idea but is void of truth. It leads people to seek a certain *experience* or *feeling* that may or may not come. And that's dangerous. That is the exact mind-set of the Charismatic or Pentecostal. Unfortunately, well-meaning people are teaching this even in our church today, and books are being published with this error in them.[14]

The Bible teaches *one* baptism, not two. And the point of the Spirit's entrance into our lives does not come in two steps. *Because* the Spirit has taken possession of our lives, we become Christians. That is why we even have a desire to follow Jesus where He leads! Believing in second-blessing theology, or the Spirit's supposed second work of grace, makes Christianity of none effect. The Christian is a Christian because he or she chose to trust God's Word and believe what the Spirit has said Christ has done and will do for us. Christians live by faith, not by sight. *We* don't need to wait for proof that what God promised, He will actually carry out.

Paul deals with this in Romans 6. After explaining in the previous three chapters how Christ saves us from sin by grace, he asks the logical question: "Are we to continue in sin that grace may increase?" (v. 1). Of course not! That would defeat the whole idea of being saved by grace. Then he clarifies the baptism analogy: Just as Christ died, was buried, and resurrected, our Christian baptism mirrors Christ's experience. We too have to die to self—leave it behind, as if buried—and then we'll come up to a new life (vv. 3–5). "Now," he says, "if we have died with Christ, we believe that we shall also live with Him" (v. 8). In other words, if we believe Christ's death is on our behalf, we must also believe His resurrected life is on our behalf! And then, the clincher: *"Even so consider yourselves to be dead to sin, but alive to God in Christ Jesus"* (v. 11, emphasis supplied).

Many times I don't *feel* I'm dead to sin and alive to God, do you? That's why the apostle says to "consider" it to be so—to "reckon" it, as the King James Version translates it. To live the Christian life is a matter of faith, not sight. Accordingly, the baptism of the Holy Spirit needs to be accepted by faith, and we need not wait for some other Christian experience to know we've been baptized.

Waiting for a supposed "real" experience in the future is counting on one's own sensory interpretation of the facts instead of on God's own description of the facts. The sincere Christian who believes in the *second* blessing is waiting for something God has already provided, making God a liar by still waiting for it.

But why, you may ask, are so many Christians and churches "dead"? Don't they need the baptism of the Spirit to come alive, such as seen in the prophecy of the dead, dry bones? (Ezekiel 37). True. But the fact that they are "dead" does not mean that the Spirit's initial work in their hearts was insufficient. It simply means they have stopped receiving the Spirit, whom they once received. The baptism of the Spirit can only be real, as long as it is a *recurring* infilling of the Spirit—time and time again. The reason for that is because we tend to be "leaky" vessels, as Ellen White calls it.[15] Our sinful nature always pulls us away from God. And leaky vessels, in order to remain full, must be filled time and again.

NOTES:

1. Helen Wessel, ed. *The Autobiography of Charles G. Finney* (Minneapolis, MN: Bethany House, 1977), 8, 10.

2. *Ibid.*, 15.

3. *Ibid.*

4. *Ibid.*, 17, 18.

5. *Ibid.*, 21, 22.

6. *Ibid.*, 24, 25.

7. *Ibid.*, 29, 31, 32.

8. Roger E. Olson, *The Story of Christian Theology: Twenty Centuries of Tradition and Reform* (Downers Grove, IL: InterVarsity Press, 1999), 31, 32.

9. Two good sources to examine the origins of the Holiness Movement and its subsequent aftermath, the Pentecostal Movement, are Melvin E. Dieter, *The Holiness Revival of the Nineteenth Century*, 2nd ed. (Lanham, MD: The Scarecrow Press, 1986), and Donald W. Dayton, *Theological Roots of Pentecostalism* (Peabody, MA: Hendrickson, 1987, 2000).

10. J. R. Goff Jr., "Parham, Charles Fox" in *The New International Dictionary of Pentecostal and Charismatic Movements*, rev. and exp., Stanley M. Burgess, ed. (Grand Rapids, MI: Zondervan, 2002, 2003), 955, 956.

11. *The Full Blessing of Pentecost* (New York: Fleming H. Revell, 1908), 65ff.

12. *Review & Herald*, March 22, 1892; also in *Evangelism*, 702.

13. *Christ's Object Lessons*, 139.

14.   Dennis Smith, *40 Days: Prayers and Devotions to Prepare for the Second Coming* (Hagerstown, MD: Review and Herald, 2009), 9. In the first chapter, entitled "Two Works of the Holy Spirit," Smith writes that the first work of the Holy Spirit leads a person to water baptism, while the second "is to fill the Christian with His presence so he or she can truly live the Christian life and do the works of God. This is the baptism of the Holy Spirit, and this work of the Spirit is not for the unbeliever—only the believer in Jesus Christ."

The revised New King James Version edition of the book (2010) tried to make this point less obvious (p. 11), but without success. This is Charismatic theology and does not correspond with the teaching of Scripture.

On page 13, Smith also claims that "Ellen White understood that Christians do not automatically receive the baptism of the Holy Spirit at conversion or when baptized in water," because "if Christians automatically had the baptism of the Holy Spirit [at conversion], Mrs. White would not admonish us to receive it."

Ellen White admonished the church to seek and pray for such baptism many times. That is correct. But she meant it as our need for successive *infillings* of the Spirit and not because we had not received Him at conversion. The fact that Smith is (in this author's opinion) wrong on this point does not take away from the many valuable points made in the book about how to be ready for Christ's coming.

15.   *Mind, Character, and Personality*, vol. 1, 102; *The Ellen G. White 1888 Materials*, 1350.

Questions for Reflection or Group Study

1. How does the story of the baptism of the Holy Spirit in Finney's life affect you?

2. What corrective to hyper-Calvinism was brought about by John Wesley and other Arminians regarding the work of the Spirit? Why would that be important?

3. What is wrong with the concept of "instant sanctification"? What is the problem with the typical Pentecostal emphasis on "power" by the Holy Spirit?

4. Why do we need to be cautious when interpreting biblical narratives, compared to biblical explanation or direct Bible teachings?

5. According to the New Testament, when are we baptized with the Spirit? Why is that so?

6. What could be the reason for the delay of the baptism of the Holy Spirit in the Samaritans who gave their lives to Jesus?

7. Why does Ellen White urge that we be baptized with the Holy Spirit, if we have already been baptized when we gave our lives to Jesus?

8. What are some different expressions used for the baptism and filling of the Holy Spirit? What does this mean to you?

9. Why is it so important to clearly understand when the baptism of the Holy Spirit takes place?

10. Why does believing in the second-blessing theology or the Spirit's supposed second work of grace, make Christianity of none effect?

11. How does Romans 6 help us understand the baptism of the Holy Spirit?

12. How do you plan to implement the teachings found in this chapter in your life?

CHAPTER TEN

Experiencing the Power

Intrigued by miraculous healing, Dr. Eion Giller, the pastor of an Adventist church in the Southwest, decided to attend well-known televangelist Benny Hinn's healing crusade. To his great joy, it was there that his daughter was born again, and his baby granddaughter was healed from seizures and other neurological damage. At another of Hinn's services, on October 22, 1994, pastor Giller received "a baptism of fire."

"Fire rolled through my body for two and a half hours. I could not focus on the worship, the preaching, nor the healings. I was immersed in fire, lost to everything around me. Pastor Hinn even spoke a word of knowledge about the fire on someone in the congregation. . . . I remember trying to walk down the aisle, quietly sobbing, when Pastor Hinn called for those who had been healed or who had fire all through their bodies to come forward. I could scarcely walk. My wife had to hold me up."

In the spring of 1996, while present at the Airport Vineyard Christian Fellowship near Toronto, Giller was singled out from a crowd of 2,500 as one who had become "a prophet of the Lord." Later that year, while attending the House of Prayer Conference filled with Charismatic leaders, one of the speakers prophesied that Giller would receive "new truth for this hour." Two days later, during a moving service, Giller sensed the word from the Lord that came to him while seated on the balcony:

"This is a wedding [between Charismatics and evangelicals]. . . . Every wedding is made by a third party. You are the third party. . . . Since early this century, the adversary has focused on keeping the Spirit and the Truth separate. These days are over. I am putting the Spirit and the Truth together in My Church. The Evangelicals with the Gospel are to join with the Charismatics in the Spirit. I seek worshippers who will worship Me in Spirit and in truth. Go down and announce this marriage to this church, this city and this nation."

Eion Giller did as he was told, and the church erupted with praise and hallelujahs. As he left the meeting that night, the Lord, he said, "spent forty minutes giving me specific details about the role He wants the Seventh-day Adventist Church and its leadership to play in the forthcoming marriage." When he complained that this would never work—that it would be resisted because the Adventist Church would never agree to such a plan—the Lord assured him the marriage would take place.[1]

What do you make of such an experience? Do questions arise in your mind? Is the Seventh-day Adventist Church to unite with Charismatics and Evangelicals to form a church based on "spirit and truth"?

The Charismatic Phenomenon

Pastor Giller is not the first, nor is he likely to be the last Seventh-day Adventist sincerely deceived by signs and wonders. More are likely to leave the church, as he did, in search of a more "powerful" experience.

Modern revival fires have been igniting all over the world for a century now. From the Azusa Street revival to the so-called Toronto Blessing, sincere, honest, God-seeking Christians have hungered for more of the supernatural presence of the Spirit in their lives. From the Pentecostal to the neo-Charismatic to the current Third Wave Movement, millions have replaced Scripture with the Spirit—at least some sort of spirit.

> "Christianity is undergoing a paradigm shift of major proportions—a shift from faith to feelings, from fact to fantasy, and from reason to esoteric revelation. . . . Sardonic laughter, spasmodic jerks, signs and wonders, super apostles and prophets, and people being 'slain in the spirit' are pointed to as empirical evidence of the power and presence of the Holy Spirit. The form and function of the church is being so radically rearranged that even the secular world has taken note."[2]

This movement is the last and biggest in religious history, drawing rich and poor, educated and uneducated, North, South, East, and West into a natural ecumenism that will not need any agreement on dogma to achieve oneness. Supernatural experience will suffice. Even today's sociologists, anthropologists, and other academics assume that a Charismatic global culture will unite the world.[3] But although it is thoroughly international, the movement is foreign to God's Spirit.

It's the name it and claim it, blab it and grab it, confess it and possess it scheme to get everyone excited about being excited. Crowds rush to Charismatic services for "Holy Spirit parties," where Christians get "thoroughly blasted" while, they say, "Jesus picks up the tab."[4] Men and women, irrespective of religious background, ethnicity, age, or educational level, find themselves barking like dogs, chirping like birds, oinking like pigs, or pinned to the floor for hours on "Holy Ghost glue." And the "holy laughter" may last for hours. People are so "drunk" with the spirit that they are literally unable to drive home or walk straight for up to two days! John Arnott, the pastor responsible for the now-famous Toronto Blessing that began on January 20, 1994, was, for a long time, resistant to such phenomena. "I had no desire," he admitted, "for Christians to fall down, roll around and laugh." He expected that with the coming of the Spirit, the Lord would "save the lost, heal the sick, and expand the kingdom."[5] But as he preached salvation messages, the Lord rebuked him, telling him that His plan was "just to love up on my church for a while."[6]

Along with Greek-Armenian Benny Hinn, Canadian John Arnott, and German Reinhard Bonkke, South African Rodney Howard-Brown is one of the heavyweights in Charismatic circles. He is known as "the Holy Ghost bartender." Typical of his services is this admonition:

> "'This is the day, this is the hour,' saith the Lord, 'that I am moving in this earth. This is the day that I'll cause you to step over into the realm of the supernatural. . . . The drops of rain are beginning to fall to the glory of God. . . . I'm going to break the mold,' saith the Lord . . . . Rise up this day in great boldness. Rise up this day and be filled afresh with the new wine of the Holy Ghost. . . . To drink, to drink, to drink, to drink, to drink, to drink, to drink, to drink, to drink [tongues]. We drink . . . [tongues, laughter]. O yea, yea, yea, yea, yea, we don't worry about what other people say. No, it doesn't matter what they think. Ha, ha, ha, ho, ooooh [tongues]."[7]

Certainly, it is God's will for His people to be filled with the Spirit. Paul even likens the experience to being "drunk" with the Spirit:

> "Be careful how you walk, not as unwise men but as wise, making the most of your time, . . . So then do not be foolish, but understand what the will of the Lord is. And do not get drunk with wine, for that is dissipation, but be filled with the Spirit" (Ephesians 5:15–18).

His point is that just as a drunk cannot stay drunk unless he drinks again, we should make the most of our time and be filled with the Spirit, in order to walk wisely, in the Spirit.

Ellen White writes that we could "have pentecostal seasons even now," if people would earnestly pray and believe God's promises.[8] *How* is the Spirit to come into the life of the believer? What does the Bible teach?

How the Spirit Comes

The same references brought up in the last chapter will be reviewed again—this time, in order to see *form*, not timing. Following is a chart comparing each New Testament experience of the arrival of the Spirit in believers' lives.

Text	People Imbued	Setting	Supernatural Phenomena, if Any	Laying on of Hands?
Luke 3:21, 22	Jesus	Praying after water baptism	Spirit descended as a dove, and the Father spoke audibly	No
Acts 2:1-4	The 120 in Upper Room	Praying for the Holy Spirit	Tongues as of fire, noise as rushing wind, and tongues-speaking	No
Acts 4:31–33	Leading apostles in Jerusalem	Praying for courage, boldness	The place where they were praying shook	No
Acts 8:14–19	Samaritan converts	Peter and John praying/laying hands on new converts	Unspecified, although some supernatural manifestation may have taken place, since Simon, a former magician, longed to have the same power	Yes
Acts 9:17, 18	Paul	Ananias laying hands on Paul after his conversion	Paul was healed from blindness: "there fell from his eyes something like scales"	Yes
Acts 10:44–46	Cornelius and his household	Peter speaking of Jesus to the group who'd asked for this	Speaking in tongues, something that amazed Peter's company	No
Acts 19:1–6	Ephesian believers	Paul teaches them about Jesus, and they were rebaptized	Speaking in tongues and prophesying	Yes

We should note several things. First, there is no direct correlation between the reception of the Spirit and the laying on of hands. In only three of the seven experiences reviewed did laying on hands happen, and frankly, it is difficult to see a consistent common denominator for the three. Even if you consider the fact that Peter, John, and Ananias all faced a former enemy, that would be clearly true of Peter with Cornelius, as well, yet no laying on of hands is part of that experience. This doesn't mean the laying on of hands is insignificant. It follows Old Testament practice, symbolic of blessing, such as Jacob's blessing on his sons (Genesis 48:14), or Moses' empowerment of Joshua (Numbers 27:23), but the laying on of hands does not carry any sort of "sacramental" power.

Next, speaking in tongues is not a universal outcome of Spirit reception. Again, in only three of the seven cases is this true. No tongues phenomenon appear in the case of Jesus, the Jerusalem leadership, the Samaritans, or Paul's experience. The traditional Pentecostal assumption that Spirit baptism leads to speaking in tongues simply does not stand up to scriptural scrutiny.

However, there *is* one thing that all these experiences demonstrate: Something demonstrably supernatural takes place when the Spirit is poured out. And this is one of the arguments presented by Charismatics to argue in favor of signs and wonders as a mark of the believer's favor with God. Should we, then, expect something supernatural in our lives before we can know the Spirit has come?

The Great Commission Landmarks

All these experiences were recorded by Luke. The physician disciple writes for the sake of inquiring Gentiles; particularly, to someone called Theophilus, meaning "lover of God." And his objective in Acts is to highlight the mighty works of the Holy Spirit (Acts 1:1–8).[9] Just as the prophets of the Old Testament gave messages from God, now the apostles spoke, as moved by the Holy Spirit. Just as Jehovah performed mighty miracles on behalf of the Israelite community, the church of God would demonstrate the power of God through signs and wonders. The important thing for Luke in Acts is to show how what Jesus promised regarding the Spirit came to pass in His followers.

However, the fact that every recorded incident of the Spirit's outpouring is connected with something supernatural does not imply that the supernatural is always present or perceived. For instance, we know from Acts 6 that seven other men were also "full of the Spirit," but we are not told when or how this happened (vv. 3, 5–7). The same was true with Barnabas (Acts 11:22, 24). Besides, the demonstration of the Spirit does not automatically imply miracles, since the fruits of the Spirit are traits of Christlike character. Perhaps the fact that miraculous manifestations took place in the seven narratives we explored have less to do with some sort of a "Pentecost-inducing formula" and more with the specific plans of God.

In Acts 1, Jesus gives the Great Commission in the context of ethnic and geographic challenges: first Jerusalem, then Judea, next Samaria, and last the Gentile world (Acts 1:8). We must remember that the first disciples were uneducated Galileans, and their speech and ways would give them away in Jerusalem, as well as in the towns of Judea. Jesus knew this would be His followers' greatest challenge—to reach those they normally would shun. And it is demonstrated by the fact that it took years for them to reach the Samaritans, and when they did, it was through one of the seven "deacons" and not the twelve apostles.

Even Paul, the consummate man of the Spirit, failed at first to be obedient to Jesus. Called to reach the Gentiles (Acts 26:16–18), he delayed over a decade actually to do so! You may remember that as soon as he was converted, Saul sought to preach in the Damascus synagogues to the *Jews* (Acts 9:20–22)! That did not succeed. So he went to Arabia to study and think for three years, before returning to Damascus again (Galatians 1:17).[10] Once back, he again tried his hand among the Jews instead of the Gentiles. The attempt went so badly he had to escape, lowered in a basket over the city wall (Acts 9:23–25). What's next, Saul? The Bible says he went to Jerusalem then to meet with the apostles (vv. 26, 27). However, he couldn't help himself and ended up preaching to the Hellenistic Jews, who also wanted to kill him. These were Greek-born Jews, but still Jews, not true Gentiles! As a result, the brethren figured it would be best to ship poor Saul over to his home town of Tarsus (vv. 28–30). While living there, apparently, the would-be apostle witnessed in the regions around Tarsus, such as Syria and Cilicia (Galatians 1:21, 23).[11]

If Saul had worked among the Gentiles in demonstration of the Spirit, Luke probably would have included it in his account, but the fact that nothing is said would lead to the conclusion that Saul's ministry there had not met with success. Finally, more than a decade after his conversion, the Lord had to move on the members of the Antioch church to take the gospel "to the Greeks [Gentiles] also," and "a large number" believed (Acts 11:20, 21). This was such an amazing development that the leaders in Jerusalem heard about it and sent Barnabas to check it out. When he confirmed that God was at work among Gentiles, he must have remembered Saul's conversion story and the fact God had set him apart for Gentile work. Barnabas decided to fetch him from a no-win situation in Tarsus and bring him to work with the Gentiles (vv. 22–26). Finally, Saul overcame his natural apprehension and became obedient to the Lord. The next time Luke mentions Saul is when he becomes Paul, in the context of Gentile mission work, as confirmation that God truly changed his heart. From that time on he is never Saul anymore (Acts 13:1, 2, 9).

The same could be said about Peter's reluctance to share the gospel with Gentiles or Samaritans. The point here is that each of the Great Commission objectives—Jerusalem, Judea, Samaria, and the Gentiles—were landmarks for empowered though still culturally prejudiced apostles to conquer. And conquering their fear and prejudice is related to the miraculous way with which the Spirit is imparted.

In Jerusalem dwelt the disciples' *religious* adversaries, including Saul, at the time. Their decision to minister to *them* was confirmed by a miraculous manifestation of the Spirit on the Day of Pentecost (Acts 2), and then when accepting Saul as a brother (Acts 9). In Judea lived the disciples' *cultural* adversaries, including the Roman military. When the disciples asked God to preach with boldness, in spite of these circumstances—and when Peter went to Caesarea to minister to a Roman centurion and his Jewish household, in spite of serious misgivings—then the Spirit confirmed their faith with miracles (Acts 4 and 10). Samaria constituted the apostles' *ethnic* adversaries. When they agreed to pray for them, the Spirit manifested Himself (Acts 8). Finally, when Paul went to polytheistic Ephesus to reach out to the Gentiles, considered by Jews as lost masses beyond salvation, again the Spirit manifested Himself in miraculous power (Acts 19).

This point is most poignant in the case of Jesus. The Son of God gave up everything to leave the courts of heaven and become a lowly man, to come to live and die among us (Philippians 2:7, 8). His baptism signified the anointing of His public, "official" ministry among men and women (Acts 10:38). So it was that God then signified His surrender and commitment to the human race with a supernatural anointing of the Spirit of God (Luke 3).

What's Normative?

So what is normative about receiving the Spirit into your life? Perhaps this is the wrong question. Neither the Bible nor the Spirit of Prophecy provides us with a formula. Therefore, unlike Pentecostals and Charismatics who yearn for something tangible, we need to look for what the Bible offers. And the offer of the Spirit is a Christlike life—the fruit of the Spirit—and Christlike ministry—the gifts of the Spirit. These dramatic experiences in Acts may have more to do with other items in God's agenda. It is His choice as to how He will pour His Spirit among us. What we must do is look for the *results* of the Spirit's indwelling and not the drama or lack of it in the outpouring.

Miraculous manifestations may also have to do with the personalities or situations of individuals. Paul was often tried and persecuted for His commitment to the gospel of Jesus, both by people inside as well as outside of the church. Perhaps Jesus gave him such a tangible demonstration of His presence at his conversion so that he'd never forget, at the most trying moments, how real what he had seen and heard was.

In late 1842 or early 1843, before she was given the gift of prophecy, Ellen Harmon was a teenager with a great heart toward God. After a powerful spiritual experience, although an introvert, she began sharing her faith in Christ at every possible opportunity. Eventually, some people became annoyed at her constant sharing, and she, ever sensitive to others around, withheld her testimony so as not to offend anyone. She felt, however, that she was not "perfectly free in the Lord." Soon after, at a prayer meeting, she was "much blessed, and again lost [her] strength." A skeptic present said "he had no faith that it was the Spirit of God," causing her to be overwhelmed, and he "selected one who was considered a man of God, a devoted humble Christian, and said, 'If this is genuine, why does it not come upon Bro. R., and he lose his strength?' Bro. R. was immediately prostrated, and as soon as he could give utterance to his feelings, declared that it was of God."[12]

Obviously, one cannot manipulate or even anticipate the movings of the Spirit. Charismatics seek for signs, while non-Charismatics tend to disavow signs. Both err by not letting the Holy Spirit be sovereign in these matters.

The Experience of Ellen White

The personal experience of Ellen White—Ellen Harmon at the time—should be instructive for us. Struggling for months after her baptism, with feelings of joy and discouragement for what she considered to be lack of progress in her Christian walk, she finally went to see Elder Levi Stockman, who told her to simply trust in Jesus, "for He will not withhold His love from any true seeker."[13] Later that evening, the shy girl of barely 15, while at a prayer and small-group spiritual meeting—the typical Methodist Class Meeting—decided to trust Jesus with her whole heart, and she started to pray in public for the first time. As soon as she began, she received a mighty baptism of the Spirit. This, she would never forget:

"In that moment the promises of God appeared to me like so many precious pearls that were to be received only for the asking. As I prayed, the burden and agony of soul that I had so long endured, left me, and the blessing of the Lord descended upon me like the gentle dew. I praised God from the depths of my heart. Everything seemed shut out from me but Jesus and His glory, and I lost consciousness of what was passing around me. The Spirit of God rested upon me with such power that I was unable to go home that night."

And what did the experience do for her?

"Faith now took possession of my heart. I felt an inexpressible love for God, and had the witness of His Spirit that my sins were pardoned. My views of the Father were changed. I now looked upon Him as a kind and tender parent, rather than a stern tyrant compelling men to a blind obedience. My heart went out toward Him in a deep and fervent love. Obedience to His will seemed a joy; it was a pleasure to be in His service.[14]

For six months after this, "not a shadow clouded [her] mind," and her whole burden was "to do the will of God" and keep Jesus continually in sight. She was "surprised" and "enraptured" by how clearly she saw the atonement and work of Christ. She "loved to meditate and pray." Young Ellen would seek every opportunity to testify of Jesus' love, for she "was so happy." Her "heart was so thankful to God for the blessing He had given" her that she "longed to have others participate in this sacred joy," and she used every opportunity to help her "young friends into the light." She determined to work on their behalf until they yielded to Jesus. Her burden was so intense that she spent "several entire nights" in prayer for them, until, finally, "everyone was converted to God."[15]

The Value of the Real Experience

To miss the entire tenor of this experience is impossible. Yes, she became unable to walk home that night, and she felt the blessing of God descend on her "like the gentle dew." But that is as far as similarities with contemporary Charismatic experience go. The results of her Spirit baptism were, in fact, a greater love for Jesus, a greater appreciation for His grace and His atoning work, and a clear burden for the lost—Christlike life and Christlike ministry. And she was only 15.

In her late sixties, after many experiences with the Holy Spirit, she wrote the following about Him:

"The Holy Spirit of God alone can create a healthy enthusiasm. Let God work, and let the human agent walk softly before Him, watching, waiting, praying, looking unto Jesus every moment, led and controlled by the precious Spirit, which is light and life."[16]

Many Seventh-day Adventists today genuinely long for more of God in their lives. I was following an Adventist blog the other day, reading comments going back four years. Many of those writing were young adults, and oh, how they longed for religion to become real to them! Nothing is wrong with this desire. Jesus came to give us *abundant* life, not a mere existence. But as important, even critical, as our need is to search earnestly for the Spirit of God in our lives, our homes, and our churches, this needs to be from God's perspective and not our own. The fullness of the Spirit will not be given to those who want "power," or desire "fire" in their bellies, or wish they could be "wowed" by the sheer presence of God. The fullness of God will come to those who seek Him in hopes He will actually change them to be like Him and to empower them to be instruments, in *His* hands, to accomplish *His* mission in the world.

If this is your desire and your determination, the experience will follow. God is always good on His promises.

NOTES:

1. Eion Giller's personal written testimony obtained from the Biblical Research Institute, August 2007.

2. Hank Hanegraaff, *Counterfeit Revival*, expanded and updated ed. (Nashville, TN: W Publishing Group, 2001), 9.

3. See Karla Poewe, ed. *Charismatic Christianity As a Global Culture* (Columbia, SC: University of South Carolina Press, 1994).

4. John Arnott, *The Father's Blessing* (Orlando, FL: Creation House, 1995), 209, 210.

5. *Ibid.*, 206.

6. John Arnott and Guy Chevreau, pastors' meeting, Toronto Airport Vineyard Church, 19 October 1994, audiotape, in Hanegraaff, 53.

7. Cited in Hanegraaff, 27, 28.

8. *Signs of the Times*, February 10, 1890, par. 7.

9. See, for instance, Matthias Wenk, *Community-Forming Power: The Socio-Ethical Role of the Spirit in Luke-Acts* (Sheffield, England: Sheffield Academic Press, 2000).

10. See also *The Acts of the Apostles*, 125.

11. *Ibid.*, 153.

12. *Spiritual Gifts*, vol. 2, 26, 27.

13. *Life Sketches*, 37.

14. Arthur White, *Ellen G. White: The Early Years*, vol.1 (Hagerstown, MD: Review and Herald, 1985), 39; *Life Sketches*, 38.

15. *Life Sketches*, 39–42.

16. Letter 68, 1894 in *Selected Messages*, bk. 2, 16, 17.

Questions for Reflection or Group Study

1. What are some of the false manifestations of the Holy Spirit evident today?

2. Who are some of today's most influential Charismatic leaders? Why would they be so influential?

3. What would lead a Seventh-day Adventist to get caught up in this experience, regardless of what the Bible says?

4. What does it mean that of the seven cases in the NT showing the outpouring of the Spirit, only some include tongues-speaking, and in only some there is the laying on of hands?

5. What is normative when it comes to the reception of the Spirit in one's life? What should we look for?

6. In what way do both Charismatics and non-Charismatics err, when it comes to signs and wonders?

7. What key instruction did Elder Levi Stockman give Ellen Harmon in regard to feelings of discouragement? How does that apply to our time today?

8. Describe young Ellen's experience of receiving the Spirit of God. Why do you think this is not repeated time and again for every Seventh-day Adventist today?

9. How determined was Ellen in her burden for her friends salvation? What would it take for us to have the same burden?

10. Why would the fullness of the Spirit not come to those who merely want "power," or desire "fire" in their bellies, or wish they could be "wowed" by the sheer presence of God?

CHAPTER ELEVEN

Conditions for the Endowment of the Spirit

When our son Christoffer was barely a teen, he came with me to Ghana to conduct some evangelistic meetings. We were the first school involved with *ShareHim*, so we took along a dozen of Southern Adventist University's best and brightest to simultaneously preach the Word throughout the city and environs of Kumasi. The Spirit of God blessed our meetings beyond our expectation, leading over 900 souls to surrender and baptism and to joining the remnant church.

On our last Sabbath afternoon, a mass baptism was organized at Lake Bosomtwi. Hundreds and thousands came in cars, buses, bikes, and on foot from all over those hills. Twenty-five pastors baptized people for over six hours straight—3,188 souls! Just like on the Day of Pentecost.

But the battle between good and evil was very real in that place. One young woman was possessed by an evil spirit just as her turn for baptism came. She stiffened and became very rigid, unable to talk or move. The pastors, it was clear, had seen this before. While people prayed, six of them tried to submerge her under water. After some time, they did, and back up came a joyous, free woman in Christ.

While there, I learned about the black magic commonly used by street children for play or for profit. I learned too about the tendency of many

Christians to communicate with the dead when facing difficulties. We met an ex-fetish priestess, now a servant of the Lord, who told us that most of her clients during the day had been Christians seeking healing—and that most during the night had been Christian pastors seeking power, even though they knew perfectly from whence it came.

West Africa, though long under the shadow of spiritualism, is surprisingly similar to the Christian West. Nearly 80 percent of the population in Ghana today claims Christianity, though most don't follow Christ but his enemy, when it really matters. Here at home also, most Christians are not really Christians. If Christians are those who follow Christ as their Master and Lord, few who claim His name actually do.[1] If we had to peg the dominant god for the Christian West, we could say it's entertainment, or leisure, or work, or money—take your pick. Secularism pervades the decisions of most Christians—even church-going Christians—even Seventh-day Adventist Church–going Christians. Think about it. Would you say most Christians spend *more* time with Jesus than anyone or anything else on a given day? Is Jesus the center of most Christians' affections? Do they gravitate to Him time and again, morning, noon, and night? Christianity is not monasticism, nor is it isolation from the world. But real Christians, from heaven's point of view, are light and salt (Matthew 5:13–16), not fun and games.

I say this to frame this chapter, perhaps one of the most important in the book. Here is where we'll begin discovering where we are in relation to the fullness and supremacy of the Spirit in our lives. This is real life. The Bible points to conditions and hindrances to the Spirit's abiding in us, and if we take what it says seriously, our lives can become everything God always wanted and we always suspected.

So let's begin. I have narrowed this to seven major conditions, although there could be more.

Repentance

"Now when they heard this, they were pierced to the heart, and said to Peter and the rest of the apostles, 'Brethren, what shall we do?' Peter said to them, 'Repent, and each of you be baptized in the name of Jesus Christ for the forgiveness of your sins; and you will receive the gift of the Holy Spirit" (Acts 2:37, 38).

This is condition number one, without which it would make little difference whether any other conditions were met. But it's important to understand the scope of this repentance. In the Bible, the use of this word implies "a radical, moral turn of the whole person from sin and to God."[2] This is not simply changing our minds about the direction we're going—a common understanding by many Christians. This is a radical departure from who we are and what we do. This repentance is not the 8-year-old boy kneeling with his mother before going to bed, praying, "And forgive me for all my sins," without any real notion of what they are. The context from Peter's sermon is clear: They needed to repent from crucifying the Savior (vv. 22, 23)! This is repentance from unbelief in what Jesus is capable of doing—the reason for Jesus' preaching: "Repent, and believe in the gospel" (Mark 1:15). This is the type of repentance I alluded to in chapter 1: a complete flooring of who we are, in view of who Jesus is, of His long-suffering toward us, and His great love in spite of our great sin.

The Bible warns us about people repenting too late, wishing they could repent but being unable to do so.

"For sorrow that is according to the will of God produces a repentance without regret, leading to salvation, but the sorrow of the world produces death" (2 Corinthians 7:10).

What is "the sorrow of the world"? This sorrow is that of those who have compelling evidence that they have made a total mess of their lives and who now view the dire consequences of it—such as going to jail or losing their family. This "repentance" does not change the heart but fills it with fear for what's coming upon them. Esau and Saul exercised this repentance, but peace and forgiveness never came to them (Hebrews 12:16, 17).[3] They had rejected the very Holy Spirit who could change their hearts.

The Bible tells us what will produce repentance leading to life: exposure to God's character of love and goodness.

"Or do you think lightly of the riches of His kindness and tolerance and patience, not knowing that the kindness of God leads you to repentance?" (Romans 2:4).

This is why it is simply imperative that we look for Jesus every day. We must sit at His feet and contemplate His love and goodness toward us. This and only this will bring about genuine repentance—the kind leading a person to surrender all and then some; the kind that makes one abandon himself into the arms of God, knowing full well he deserves not a whit of what Christ did for them. They are compelled to genuinely repent and are absolutely reduced to nothing, before such Love.

Twenty years ago, I placed on the inside cover of my study Bible this quote: "He who beholds the Saviour's matchless love will be elevated in thought, purified in heart, transformed in character. He will go forth to be a light to the world, to reflect in some degree this mysterious love."[4] Below that note is my prayer, expressing my earnest desire to partake of this wonderful experience.

Have you repented from crucifying the Lord of glory? Have you owned the fact that you kept the Savior there every time you willed to sin to please yourself? Have you come to the point in your life where you want nothing more to do with self and instead desire Christ, His honor, His happiness, more than anything in the world? If so, the infilling of the Spirit is not far behind.

Implicit Trust

"We would receive the promise of the Spirit through faith" (Galatians 3:14).

In America, at least, belief and trust are sometimes differentiated. While trust is seen as a moving forward based on certain convictions, belief is often viewed as intellectual assent. Someone may need to go to Walmart at midnight, believing the store should be open at that time. But her faith in that belief can only become trust once she gets in her car and drives there. The driving proves her trust—she is doing something about it.

In the Bible, faith is always trust, never mere intellectual assent. When our daughter was 3 years old, we were walking on a trail, and I decided to put her up, facing away from me, on a tree stump as high as my shoulders. Then I said, with my arms forward, "Stefani, put your arms out, don't look behind you, and fall back without bending your knees—and Daddy will catch you!" She did it without a moment's hesitation. She liked it so much she kept climbing back up the stump to do it again! That is trust.

And that's a condition for the reception of God's Spirit into our lives. So often people look for signs and wonders, for something powerful and supernatural that would indicate the Spirit has finally arrived. But we are to trust that God will send the Spirit because He promised, not because we can "feel" Him. One of the most important statements I've ever read on this topic is the following. Read it slowly and with care. As you read, remember that "the blessing" was a typical Methodist expression of the nineteenth century, akin to the outpouring of the Spirit in one's life. Ellen White wrote this early in her life, when her Methodist roots were still seen in her writings.

"Feeling is not faith; the two are distinct. Faith is ours to exercise, but joyful feeling and the blessing are God's to give. . . . True faith lays hold of and claims the promised blessing before it is realized and felt. We must send up our petitions in faith within the second veil and let our faith take hold of the promised blessing and claim it as ours. We are then to believe that we receive the blessing, because our faith has hold of it, and according to the Word it is ours. . . . Here is faith, naked faith, to believe that we receive the blessing, even before we realize it. When the promised blessing is realized and enjoyed, faith is swallowed up. But many suppose they have much faith when sharing largely of the Holy Spirit and that they cannot have faith unless they feel the power of the Spirit. Such confound faith with the blessing that comes through faith. The very time to exercise faith is when we feel destitute of the Spirit."[5]

As you meet the various conditions in Scripture, claim the promise of the Spirit in your life. Thank Jesus for giving you His Spirit and for heaven's willingness that you be filled to overflowing with His love, His power, and His grace. Then get up from your knees, telling yourself that this day, the Spirit of Jesus is in control of your life, not because you feel it, but because He said so.

Obedience

"And we are witnesses of these things; and so is the Holy Spirit, whom God has given to those who obey Him" (Acts 5:32).

In the Bible, faith and obedience go hand in hand. If you trust God with all your heart, you will obey His commands because you trust Him. If you obey Jesus from your heart, that happens because you've come to know Him enough that you trust Him. "If anyone loves Me," said Jesus, "he will keep My word" (John 14:23).

> "But whoever keeps His word, in him the love of God has truly been perfected. By this we know that we are in Him: the one who says he abides in Him ought himself to walk in the same manner as He walked" (1 John 2:5, 6).

This obedience is not pharisaic legalism, in order to earn the right to be saved or be blessed. This comes from the heart, as a genuine desire to please God. I once heard Mark Finley preach a sermon pointing to the fact that God sees a lot of pain, sin, sorrow, and disappointment. All this brings heaviness to His heart. But who is the one who will bring a smile to *His* face?

Dwight L. Moody was converted in Chicago as a late teen and led for many years the largest Sunday School in the nation. He was an excellent businessman and had made considerable money over the years. But now his struggle was whether or not to give *all* to the Lord. On a trip to Ireland, he heard British evangelist Henry Varley say, "The world has yet to see what God will do with, and for, and through, and in, and by, the man who is fully consecrated to Him." Moody thought for just a moment and then pledged: "By the grace of God, I will be that man." He became the most effective American evangelist of the last half of the nineteenth century.

The Holy Spirit will be given to those who obey Him.

A Burden to Share

"If you then, being evil, know how to give good gifts to your children, how much more will your heavenly Father give the Holy Spirit to those who ask Him?" (Luke 11:13).

This Luke 11 reference is a fascinating story, and it contains our conditions four and five for the reception of the Spirit. The disciples found Jesus "praying aloud" one morning, and they "were deeply moved."[6] Never had mortal ears heard such mighty petitioning before the Father. Even though they had known to pray for some time, to them it was as if they had never learned how, so they asked Jesus, "Teach us to pray" (Luke 11:1). Christ repeated portions of the Lord's Prayer and then illustrated the seriousness and intensity of the task with a story: A man arrives at his friend's at midnight. His host, having no bread, asks the neighbor for three loaves. Will the neighbor give him what he asks, or will he rebuff him? The neighbor said to come back in the morning, because "the door has already been shut and my children and I are in bed" (v. 7).

The homes of "the people of the land" in those days were basic, one-room dwellings on two levels. They had one entrance and one window, small enough that robbers or predatory animals could not get in at night. On the lower level, cooking took place, and small animals spent the night. On the second level, not much above the first, the family slept all on one large mat. Bolting the door was not a simple affair, since they laid a heavy bar through rings across the entrance. Getting up meant disrupting the entire household, waking the family, and riling the animals. Even though hospitality protocol was nearly sacred in that culture, this was too much to ask of the neighbor.

The point that can't be missed, however, is that the bread was not for himself—it was for someone else who needed it. The man's bold petitioning originated from his desire to satisfy the hunger of his traveling friend. Likewise, "The Holy Spirit will come to all who are begging for the bread of life to give to their neighbors."[7]

This may be an excellent gauge to evaluate our desire to be filled with the Spirit. Why do we want Him in our lives? Some want the Spirit to *feel* something wonderful or otherworldly in their lives. Some wish the gift of the Spirit, in order to become spiritual giants of some sort. But it isn't until you ask for the Spirit to flood your life because of your burden to bless others, that a motive to which God can respond is finally found. If I have little interest in the salvation of others, if I have no burden for them to know my Savior and grow in Him, the coming of the Spirit into my life will not make any sense. The Holy Spirit is all about leading people to Christ. How could I have the Spirit, while ignoring others' greatest of all needs?

Evan Roberts, the man God used as a catalyst to start the great Welsh Revival of 1904, expressed such a burden this way:

"I was filled with compassion for those who must bend at the judgment, and I wept . . . the salvation of the human soul was solemnly impressed upon me. I felt ablaze with a desire to go through the length and breadth of Wales to tell of the Savior, and had it been possible, I was willing to pay God for doing so."[8]

That's a burden for the lost!

Persistent Intercession

The fifth condition is also found in the story illustrating how to pray for the Holy Spirit. In fact, this is the main point Jesus sought to get across.

"I tell you, even though [the neighbor] will not get up and give him anything because he is his friend, yet because of his persistence he will get up and give him as much as he needs. So I say to you, ask, and it will be given to you; . . . for everyone who asks, receives. . . . If you then, being evil, know how to give good gifts to your children, how much more will your heavenly Father give the Holy Spirit to those who ask Him?" (Luke 11:8–10, 13).

The word translated "persistence" or "importunity" is milder than the original New Testament word. It should read "shamelessness," or "gall." God, of course, is *not* at all reluctant to give us the Spirit. The question is, are we so eager to have Him that not only will we not take No for an answer, but we will not leave His presence until the door is open? If even an irritated person responds to boldness, we can be bold with the Gracious One.

Corrie ten Boom was a Dutch Christian Holocaust survivor who helped Jews escape the Nazis during World War II. Her gripping story was immortalized in the book *The Hiding Place*. After the war, she kept busy in various ministries, including helping fellow Dutch citizen, Brother Andrew, of *God's Smuggler* fame, smuggle Bibles and Christian literature beyond communism's Iron Curtain. At times, it seemed impossible to get the job done, due to government restrictions, suspicions, and a myriad of whistle-blowers. Their lives were in constant danger. But their burden was getting God's Word into the hands of those who knew nothing of the God of heaven.

When every door seemed shut, Brother Andrew, Corrie ten Boom, and other leaders would get together to "pray without ceasing" (1 Thessalonians 5:17), convinced the Lord would break through the situation. Witnesses tell of Corrie's boldness before the Lord: "Lort, you must do something!" she'd pray in her thick Dutch accent. "There is no time to waste." Then, like a lawyer before a court, she would quote God's Word back to Him, finding the exact passage, and arguing that on the basis of His Word, He needed to respond! With her Bible up in the air, she would cry, "Here, Lort, read it Yourself!"

This is no disrespect before a holy God. This is confidence in a holy God. "Let us draw near with confidence to the throne of grace, so that we may receive mercy and find grace to help in time of need" (Hebrews 4:16), because God is immensely pleased when we put our entire weight of trust in Him (11:6).

Martyn Lloyd-Jones, famous Westminster Chapel preacher and author of yesteryear, writing on the burden of prayer by many whom God used for Christian revivals, said:

> "You will find this same holy boldness, . . . this putting the case to God, pleading His own promises. Oh, that is the whole secret of prayer, I sometimes think. . . . Do not leave alone. Pester Him, as it were, with His own promises. Tell Him what He said He is going to do. Quote the Scripture to Him. . . . It pleases Him. . . . God is our Father, and He loves us, and He likes to hear us pleading His own promises, quoting His own words to Him, and saying, 'In light of this, can You refrain?' It delights the heart of God."[9]

Ellen White had as much or more to say on the subject, as we will see. If you genuinely desire to be filled with God to overflowing, ask and keep on asking, until this happens. And then continue asking for the inexhaustible riches of heaven. God never runs out of grace. He does not need persuasion on our part for Him to grant us everything He already promised; we need to keep praying in order to realize for ourselves how important this actually is for our lives. Our hearts need persuasion by insistence.

Honor the Body Temple

> "Or do you not know that your body is a temple of the Holy Spirit who is in you, whom you have from God, and that you are not your own? For you have been bought with a price: therefore glorify God in your body" (1 Corinthians 6:19, 20).

Throughout history, various philosophies and ideas led religious, or otherwise respected people, to consider the human body as solely for pleasure. The Epicureans, for instance, alive and well in the time of the apostles (Acts 17:18), believed the greatest good was the prudent pursuit of pleasure and the absence of pain. Although this idea appears harmless, and they did preach against excesses, the focus was on what made a person feel good. The philosophy's extreme was some form of hedonism, which taught, unabashedly, that the pursuit of the highest pleasure for the body was the highest good. Hedonists gave themselves to sexual pleasure, for that reason.

Today, in the name of individual human rights, people—especially in Western societies—feel very protective of their right to do whatever they wish with their bodies. Thus no one is to criticize co-habitation, extra-marital sex, or even the most hideous and wicked types of freedom of expression readily accessible on the Internet. Pleasure rules. This attitude is also fueled by a belief in dualism—the idea that the physical realm is distinct and separate from the spiritual. But research has clearly established that whatever happens to our bodies deeply affects our minds and spirits.[10]

The Bible clearly teaches that our bodies are the temple, the residence, of the Holy Spirit; thus, we need to glorify God with our bodies if we want the Spirit to abide there. This is also part of the Adventist message to the world: "Fear God, and give glory to Him" (Revelation 14:7). Glorifying God means to honor Him in what "we eat or drink or whatever [we] do" (1 Corinthians 10:31). The Holy Spirit even affects our bodies physically.

"The Holy Spirit . . . will renew every organ of the body, that God's servants may work acceptably and successfully. Vitality increases under the influence of the Spirit's action."[11]

If we want the Holy Spirit, if we wish to make room for God in our lives, we simply cannot treat our bodies any way we wish. "For if you are living according to the flesh," Paul reminds us, "you must die; but if by the Spirit, you are putting to death the deeds of the body, you will live" (Romans 8:13). We cannot eat what and when we please, use and abuse our bodies, or work until we drop, without that affecting our ability to perceive the love and will of God for our lives. If we prosper in health, our souls will prosper (1 John 3:2).

A little-known Bible text teaches that in the last days, "there will be mockers, following after their own ungodly lusts," who will be "devoid of the Spirit" (Jude 19). The apostle James sternly warns his readers:

"You adulteresses, do you not know that friendship with the world is hostility toward God? . . . Or do you think that the Scripture speaks to no purpose: He jealously desires the Spirit which He has made to dwell in us" (James 4:4, 5).

In other words, God is a jealous God (Deuteronomy 6:14, 15), and He is not pleased when His Spirit, who is meant to dwell in us, is displaced by the world in us. This is equivalent to committing spiritual adultery.

"When men and women are truly converted, they will conscientiously regard the laws of life that God has established in their being, thus seeking to avoid physical, mental, and moral feebleness. Obedience to these laws must be made a matter of personal duty . . . . We must answer to God for our habits and practices. Therefore the question for us is not, 'What will the world say?' but, 'How shall I, claiming to be a Christian, treat the habitation God has given me? . . . Let all examine their own practices to see if they are not indulging in that which is a positive injury to them. Let them dispense with every unhealthful gratification in eating and drinking. . . . Let them bring their daily practice into harmony with nature's laws; and by doing as well as believing, an atmosphere may be created about both soul and body that will be a savor of life unto life."[12]

A Desire for Christ to Abide in the Heart

"We know by this that He abides in us, by the Spirit whom He has given us" (1 John 3:24).

This last point is almost too obvious to consider, but it won't hurt to go over it again. If the ministry of the Spirit is to glorify Jesus (John 16:14) "by revealing His grace," then "the very image of God is to be reproduced" in us.[13] If we have no desire for Christ to abide in our body temple, then nothing else about the Christian life makes any sense. Christ in the life is what really matters. This is why He is ministering for us in the heavenly sanctuary and why the Spirit ministers to us here on earth. But if you find that your heart does not want Christ in you right now, yet you would *like* to want to, do not despair. God has always known of our reluctance to accept Him wholeheartedly. Go to your knees time and again and simply ask Him to *give* you a desire to have Jesus in your life on a permanent basis. Do so until it happens. You have not seen miracles, until you've seen what God can do with this sincere request from the heart.

In chapter 2, I quoted from *Christ's Object Lessons*, page 384, about the Holy Spirit being "the implanting of Christ's nature" in us, which, in turn, gives us "unselfish love" for others. That love, however, is not generated "by *trying* to love others," but only "by the love of Christ in the heart."

Many years ago, while I was pastoring in California, a wreck of a woman once came to our church. Like oil on water, she instantly repelled people. A former Adventist, she chain-smoked, swore like a sailor, was a practicing lesbian, and was demon-possessed to boot. She looked twenty years older than her biological age, had no friends, and kept moving from place to place, because no one ever opened their doors to her. I was young and didn't know any better than to listen to her and try to see if God's Word could break through to that poor soul. Eventually, I became her only friend.

In those days, the Lord was doing very important spiritual work in my heart and in my wife's, and we were growing to love Him and seek His face with relish. One day, the church office got a call from this sister, asking the pastor or someone to come to her home—it was urgent.

On arriving, the place was very dark—one or two candles barely flickering. She asked me not to turn on the lights. A voice came out from her—a guttural, basso, hellish voice that made my hair stand on end. That was no human voice. This was not my first experience encountering evil spirits, but it was no less nerve-wracking. I knew better than to pronounce some "scriptural incantation," recognizing that many factors are at work in cases like these. She said little, while she smoked in the dark. I could not see her face, for which I was actually thankful. Not knowing exactly what to do, I opened God's Word and read a few passages, which she mocked with disdain. I asked questions, but she did not answer. Then, after some time passed, I offered a simple, earnest prayer for forgiveness from sin, deliverance from evil, and the grace and peace of our Lord in her heart.

The visit ended without major incident. Until I reached my van, that is. As soon as I got in, the floodgates opened wide. I cried like a baby for this poor, wretched soul, a prisoner of Satan, who deep down wanted out and didn't know how. I told the Lord I'd be willing to trade my life for hers. For thirty-plus years it had been my privilege to know Him, and He had been so gracious and kind and patient with me, but this woman was worse than dead. I begged Jesus to give her the same joy I'd had—even if it meant my life—and to flood her with His love.

Except for one time when the life of Alex, our son, was threatened as a baby, I had never willingly yielded my life on behalf of another. You have to understand that selfishness, self-centeredness, had been my god for the bulk of my life. And the love I had for that woman that day was not natural with me. It was "the love of Christ in the heart." Paul reminds us: "The love of God has been poured out within our hearts through the Holy Spirit who was given to us" (Romans 5:5).

That was a Spirit moment. Shortly after this incident, she disappeared, and we never heard from her again. But perhaps one day soon, when we all stand on the sea of glass, a woman, whom we'll hardly recognize, will approach and say: "Jesus delivered me from sin and death, and I am here today because I wouldn't want to be anywhere else, ever."

NOTES:

1. Eddie Gibbs is only one of many thinkers and researchers who have demonstrated this point. See his *In Name Only: Tackling the Problem of Nominal Christianity* (Pasadena, CA: Fuller Seminary Press, 2000).

2. William D. Mounce, ed., "Repent, Repentance," in *Mounce's Complete Expository Dictionary of Old and New Testament Words* (Grand Rapids, MI: Zondervan, 2006), 580, 581.

3. In reference to Saul, this is what Ellen White has to say: "[Samuel said:] 'Because thou hast rejected the word of the Lord, He hath also rejected thee from being king.'

    "As the king heard this fearful sentence he cried out, 'I have sinned: for I have transgressed the commandment of the Lord, and thy words: because I feared the people, and obeyed their voice.' Terrified by the denunciation of the prophet, Saul acknowledged his guilt, which he had before stubbornly denied; but he still persisted in casting blame upon the people, declaring that he had sinned through fear of them.

    "It was not sorrow for sin, but fear of its penalty, that actuated the king of Israel as he entreated Samuel, 'I pray thee, pardon my sin, and turn again with me, that I may worship the Lord.' If Saul had had true repentance, he would have made public confession of his sin; but it was his chief anxiety to maintain his authority and retain the allegiance of the people. He desired the honor of Samuel's presence in order to strengthen his own influence with the nation." *Patriarchs and Prophets*, 631.

4. *The Desire of Ages*, 661.

5. *Early Writings*, 72.

6. *Christ's Object Lessons*, 140.

7. *Testimonies*, vol. 6, 90.

8. Cited in Brian H. Edwards, *Revival! A People Saturated With God* (Darlington, UK: Evangelical Press, 1997), 152.

9. *Revival* (Wheaton, IL: Crossway Books, 1987), 81.

10. Neil Nedley, MD, David DeRose, MD, ed. *Proof Positive: How to Reliably Combat Disease and Achieve Optimal Health Through Nutrition and Lifestyle* (Ardmore, OK: Neil Nedley, MD, 1999), 1–9.

11. *Review and Herald*, January 14, 1902, par. 8; also in *Medical Ministry*, 12.

12. *Testimonies*, vol. 6, 369–371.

13. *The Desire of Ages*, 671.

Questions for Reflection or Group Study

1. If you were to be honest concerning your life, what is really dominant—Christ, entertainment, leisure, work, or money?

2. How would you define repentance according to this chapter, and what does that imply?

3. According to 2 Corinthians 7:10, there is "the sorrow of the world [that] produces death." What does that mean? Is that possible for church members?

4. Read again the longer statement by Ellen White on feelings versus faith. What does this tell you about the reception of the Holy Spirit in your life?

5. How does obedience differ from faith? How is it like faith?

6. What did you learn from the story of the man asking for bread at midnight? How similar is his experience to yours? Why?

7. How is being persistent more for our good than for persuading God?

8. Why is it important to keep our bodies healthy and strong, in relationship with the Spirit? Is this even more relevant today than in the days of Paul?

9. What will it take to love the unlovable?

10. Of the seven conditions for the Holy Spirit filling your life, which one do you need to focus on the most?

CHAPTER TWELVE

Driving Away the Spirit

For each of the conditions in the previous chapter, the opposite should be considered as a detriment to the indwelling of the Spirit in your life. Since *implicit trust* is a condition, *unbelief* would then be a clear detriment. "How often they reveled against Him in the wilderness and grieved Him in the desert!" complains the psalmist regarding his people Israel (Psalm 78:40). "They rebelled and grieved His Holy Spirit," adds the prophet (Isaiah 63:10). Two million of them perished in the wilderness due to their unbelief, when it had become so clear that God's Spirit was leading them.

Grieving the Spirit is only a step away from the unpardonable sin. Jesus said that "any sin and blasphemy shall be forgiven people, but blasphemy against the Spirit shall not be forgiven" (Matthew 12:31). Why could any offense, or blasphemy, against the Son of God be forgiven, while sinning against the Spirit has its limits? In the Bible, *blasphemy* is defined as taking the place of God (John 10:33; Mark 2:7). And this we do when we will no longer listen to the gentle whisper of the Spirit. In fact, we irretrievably break the first commandment. God's Spirit is constantly at work on our behalf. What Jesus has done and is doing for us is actually carried out by the Holy Spirit. But when we keep ignoring His "teaching, reproof, correction, and training" (2 Timothy 3:15), the compelling force of the Spirit wanes until it disappears.

When our young family moved from California to Tennessee, we stayed in a university apartment for a while, next to the campus. At about 5:15 A.M., the train would blare by, less than a mile away, and in the stillness of the night, that was very loud. Being a light sleeper and not accustomed to the nocturnal ruckus, I'd wake up every time this happened, fearing I'd never be able to sleep past it in our new home.

Well, you guessed it. Within about a week, I no longer heard the train whistle. The trains kept coming as usual, but my ear had decided not to listen to it anymore. This is like the unpardonable sin. It has nothing to do with God ceasing to speak to us. Instead, it has everything to do with our no longer listening to Him. Is there anything in your life you know you must surrender to God—that you must change or give up? Don't delay in doing so. Do so while it is clear that you must surrender it. In time, you may consider doing it, but it will then be too late. Nothing in you will prompt you anymore.

The Bible as well as the Spirit of Prophecy highlight several issues with the potential of driving the Spirit away from our lives. But I'd like to pinpoint some which may not always be considered. Please read the following carefully, and prayerfully talk with Jesus about each item.

Secondary Concerns

"Let Christians put away all dissension and give themselves to God for the saving of the lost. Let them ask in faith for the promised blessing [of the Spirit], and it will come. . . . [But] the promise of the Spirit is a matter little thought of; and the result is only what might be expected—spiritual drought, spiritual darkness, spiritual declension and death. Minor matters occupy the attention, and the divine power which is necessary for the growth and prosperity of the church, and which would bring all other blessings in its train, is lacking, though offered in its infinite plenitude."[1]

"Minor matters occupy the attention." In an age designed for effectiveness, we spend more time than ever on secondary things. Whether in surfing the Internet, or checking up on our social networks, or texting on the phone, technology has become one of our greatest demons to tame. Fewer people read, and many of the ones who still do don't do it to learn anything but to be entertained. Most, however, watch something, either on TV, on their laptops, or even on their iPods. We do these things because we can, not because we must. Endless distraction is the newest, most powerfully effective weapon for today's generation. And because we major in minors, we never graduate to new levels of spiritual growth.

The admonition does not apply only to technology and entertainment, it applies to life values and priorities. What do we talk about with friends? Where does our mind go when in neutral? What do we find ourselves doing with our discretionary time? Many Christians, if they were to do an objective analysis of their use of time, would find that it translates into living very inconsequential lives, if not lives which should cause them concern. Much potential, across the age spectrum, is misused, if not wasted today. Satan is succeeding in making a mockery of the human race, including Christians, by leading them to set their sights so low they don't know if the bar exists anymore, much less how high it is.

I speak to myself first in this respect. I have wasted years of my life doing stuff that didn't need to be done, or worse, that shouldn't have been engaged in to begin with. If you are young, don't let that happen to you. God forgives, but the time gone cannot be redeemed.

"Our time belongs to God. Every moment is His, and we are under the most solemn obligation to improve it to His glory. Of no talent He has given will He require a more strict account than of our time."[2]

Would you be ready to give an account of your time? These are sobering words for trifling times.

Pride and Self-Reliance

"When I kept silent about my sin, my body wasted away through my groaning all day long." "Do not cast me away from your presence and do not take your Holy Spirit from me" (Psalm 32:3; 51:11).

King David felt annoyed by any insinuation that his sin with Bathsheba was so bad. The king of the most powerful nation on earth at the time, he already had many wives and concubines, so what was one more added to the harem? But deep inside, he knew. He knew that cultural allowances did not excuse adultery, and even less, murder (2 Samuel 11). But those were the results of a greater sin—pride and self-sufficiency. Pride is always the last to surrender.

"The people of God have accustomed themselves to think that they must rely upon their own efforts, that little help is to be received from heaven; and the result is that they have little light to communicate to other souls who are dying in error and darkness. The church has long been contented with little of the blessing of God; they have not felt the need of reaching up to the exalted privileges purchased for them at infinite cost . . . and they are disqualified for the work the Lord would have them to do. They are not able to present the great and glorious truths of God's Holy Word that would convict and convert souls through the agency of the Holy Spirit. The power of God awaits their demand and reception. A harvest of joy will be reaped by those who sow the holy seeds of truth."[3]

Apparently, there is an inverse correlation between our pride and unconfessed sin—and our soul-winning effectiveness. The more we hold on to our sin, the less we are able to evangelize people to Christ effectively. David himself had learned that. Right after he asked God not to take the

Spirit from him because of his sin, he wrote, "Restore to me the joy of Your salvation. . . . Then I will teach transgressors Your ways, and sinners will be converted to You" (Psalm 51:12, 13). Could it be that we make such meager strides in our mission objectives at home, in part, because much unconfessed sin still exists in the life of Christ's followers? Remember David. For nearly a year, he justified his actions without surrendering to God, and he "wasted away." Release, freedom, and efficiency was ultimately his, but only after he committed all to God, even his cherished sin.

A Retaliatory and Critical Spirit

"An indwelling Saviour is revealed by the words. But the Holy Spirit does not abide in the heart of him who is peevish if others do not agree with his ideas and plans. From the lips of such a man there come scathing remarks, which grieve the Spirit away, and develop attributes that are satanic rather than divine."[4]

"When trials arise that seem unexplainable, we should not allow our peace to be spoiled. However unjustly we may be treated, let not passion arise. By indulging a spirit of retaliation we injure ourselves. We destroy our own confidence in God, and grieve the Holy Spirit."[5]

This first quote is in the context of church work and church leadership. To fall into the trap of becoming critical of others' actions or attitudes is relatively easy. Ellen White counsels us to restrain our negative thoughts and feelings toward others; otherwise, we "are brought under the influence of evil angels and invite their presence and their control."[6] Most of us would never think of being under the influence or control of evil angels, but when we complain and criticize, that's exactly whose power we come under.

We must understand that the devil is both clever and very efficient in leading us to fall. He knows what works, and more to the point, he knows what works with *you*. He leads us to sin, first, by taking our eyes off Jesus. Then he makes us fall into sin. Next, he makes us wallow in it. Even after we sin and recognize it, feeling guilty, the power of sin holds sway as long as we keep looking at the sin, whether ours or anyone else's. It keeps us looking down, at the problem, instead of away to Jesus, the only solution. My good friend Jack Blanco says we need to take a quick look at our sin and a long, long, long, loooong, look at Jesus—in that proportion.

Let's say you are in a church board meeting, or talking with a member, or planning church work, and someone says something you consider really dumb, or misguided, or hurtful, or frustratingly naïve. You have a

choice: You can respond by focusing on the deed, which is clearly negative, and respond or think or talk in kind. Or, you can look away. Even
though you may be correct, or your comment may be more enlightening
than the previous one, *if* it is focused on the wrongfulness of the other,
it will remain at the same sinful level. The Holy Spirit is nowhere to be
found in such an environment. Instead, you could silently pray for the
Holy Spirit, then turn your gaze upward instead of sideways, and see the
thing from God's perspective and not your own. In so doing, the would-
be criticism turns into a helpful addition—something that even sinners
are able to recognize as the intervention of God. And that is where the
Spirit lives.

"For the one who sows to his own flesh will from the flesh reap
corruption, but the one who sows to the Spirit will from the Spirit
reap eternal life" (Galatians 6:8).

Intense Amusements

"Many have turned away from God's plan to follow human inventions to the detriment of spiritual life. Amusements are doing more
to counteract the working of the Holy Spirit than anything else, and
the Lord is grieved."[7]

This hindrance to the Holy Spirit is more frighteningly relevant today than when it was first written. Think of it: "human inventions" that
deter from spiritual life and "amusements" that counteract the work of
the Spirit more than anything else! She published this in 1913, when
amusements and human inventions could refer to attending the theater,
playing cards, or even to a game of chess. How mild and innocent are
those things compared to today's violent video games, R-rated movies,
meaningless, sex-filled television programs, and the wrongful use of the
Internet! Even secular society has recognized our downward societal spi-
ral in our thirst for vacuous amusements. Neil Postman's classic on the
subject, *Amusing Ourselves to Death*,[8] was written a quarter of a century
ago, when the PC was barely born, DVDs did not exist, and the Internet
was still years away.

God's messenger says these things are "a detriment of spiritual life."
This whole subject comes close to home. Ever since I was a boy, I have
been fascinated with moving pictures. My parents did not buy a television until I was older. In the meantime, I could be found perched outside
a neighbor's closed window watching the black-and-white screen inside.
It didn't even matter that I could not hear a thing! Such pathetic behavior
multiplies in severity with the endless availability of movies and other
entertainment right at your laptop fingertips today.

And it's not just TV or movies anymore. Perhaps one of the most tragic developments is the universalization of pornography, fueled by the three A's of the Internet: accessibility, affordability, and anonymity.[9] Research is showing that Christians have as much of a problem with pornography as non-Christians do. And what's even more disturbing is the fact that Christian pastors don't fall far behind.

But even if all that was available to view today was as innocent as an episode of *Leave it to Beaver*, the question remains: Does it promote or does it deter from your spiritual life? I remember excusing my TV-watching habits as a pastor, because I came home tired at night, the kids often in bed already, and my wife yawning her way there. "It is time to decompress," I would tell myself. And on came the TV to watch the 11 o'clock news—which, in the words of my good friend Mike, is nothing but the "devil's daily parade"—followed by a comic talk-show and even something else after that. Was I decompressed after two hours of TV? I was actually more tired than before, filled with secular images in my head and less likely to wake up early in the morning to spend time with my Savior. What a tragedy!

We fail to recognize that over a hundred years ago, psychologists had already concluded that nothing we ever see or hear or feel is ever gone from our brains. The fact that we cannot recall it at will does not mean it has disappeared. "Nothing we ever do is, in strict scientific literalness, wiped out."[10]

Job "made a covenant" with his eyes, not to lust after "a young woman" (Job 31:1). "Flee immorality," Paul shouts, knowing the deathtrap it represents (1 Corinthians 6:18). Nothing is more calculated to become as addictive as immorality. As the mind warps, it wants more and more just to maintain stimulation, until it becomes like a runaway truck, unable to stop. If this is an issue for you, you must stop immediately. Eliminate the sources, stay away from the places of temptation, and you may even want and need to seek professional help. Regardless of how you find help, no help will *be* help until you "fix your eyes on Jesus" (Hebrews 12:2). And I mean "fix"! *Rivet* your eyes on Him. Look for Him in His Word, turn your face to Him day by day and moment by moment. The more you do this, the weaker the pull of the lust of the world on you. This really is the only solution. The only One.

You may think I'm making too much of this. What I know is the power amusements of this nature can have on my own soul. I'm never better off for having exposed myself to these things, as apparently mild and harmless as they may appear. No, I'm only farther out to sea. C. S. Lewis conveyed the subtle and clever ways Satan uses to lead his prey to the slaughter:

"It does not matter how small the sins are provided their cumulative effect is to edge the man away from the Light and out into the Nothing. Murder is no better than cards if cards can do the trick. Indeed, the safest road to Hell is the gradual one—the gentle slope, soft underfoot, without sudden turnings, without milestones, without signposts."[11]

Remember the psalmist's pledge: "I will set no worthless thing before my eyes" (Psalm 101:3). Do that—and you will live.

NOTES:

1. *Testimonies,* vol. 8, 21.

2. *Christ's Object Lessons,* 342.

3. *Testimonies to Ministers,* 175.

4. *Review and Herald,* April 9, 1901, par. 6.

5. *Christ's Object Lessons,* 171, 172.

6. *Testimonies,* vol. 5, 310.

7. *Counsels to Parents, Teachers, and Students,* 281.

8. (New York: Penguin, 1985, 2005). Postman's book is considered a communications classic, presenting a withering critique of television's degrading influence on American society. The sequel was *Technopoly: The Surrender of Culture to Technology* (New York: Vintage Books, 1993).

9. See, for instance, William M. Struthers, *Wired for Intimacy: How Pornography Hijacks the Male Brain* (Downers Grove, IL: IVP Books, 2009).

10. William James, *The Principles of Psychology,* 83, in Roland Hegstad, *The Mind Manipulators* (Washington, D.C.: Review and Herald, 1974), 13ff.

11. *The Screwtape Letters* (New York: Time, Inc., 1963), 61, 62.

Questions for Reflection or Group Study

1. Can you think of something in your life that could lead you to commit the unpardonable sin against the Holy Spirit?

2. Why do you think the Bible uses the expression *to grieve* the Holy Spirit? What does it mean?

3. What are some secondary concerns or minor matters that you have allowed into your life that affect your relationship with Jesus?

4. How have you seen that pride, self-sufficiency, or unconfessed sin have held back your ability to share Jesus with others?

5. Why are we so reluctant to repent and ask for forgiveness?

6. Why is criticism so dangerous?

7. What is a good approach to take when something negative is expressed?

8. Do you engage in entertainment that keeps you from growing in Jesus?

9. What are the three "A's" that have fueled the universalization of pornography? Do you think this is a problem in the church today?

10. What are some steps one can take in overcoming those activities that draw us away from the life Jesus longs for us to live?

CHAPTER THIRTEEN

Asking in One Accord

In some parts of the world, bargaining for a gift or a product becomes an art. You look at the item in question and hold it in your hand, all the while fully knowing the owner or vendor has his eyes glued to you. Before you lay it down, he's bound to make you an offer, usually at least twice what the product is remotely worth—let's say 200 (in units of the local currency). Now the game is on.

You say, "Nah . . . I'm not sure," and move away from it, looking at—but not touching—other stuff.

"You like?" is often the next question. "I give to you for good price."

"Maybe," you reply with a show of ennui.

"OK, I give to you for 150. Very low price."

You come back to the item and look at it again. "I . . . don't think so."

"What do you want to pay?" he asks, and before you answer, he does: "OK, OK—125. No more."

"Well, I think it's worth 80."

"80! Nooo, this is quality product!" he says, trying to substantiate his point.

"Your colleague down the block was willing to let it go for 100."

"100, huh. Hmm . . . OK. I give to you for 100. I will not make money."

If you have any experience with these things, you know that's usually far from the truth. Chances are that the item in question cost about a fourth or less of his original asking price, giving him plenty of cushion to work with. In some areas of the world, it is a matter of pride to get the sale, once you get far enough into it. Also understood is that assuming the owner's kindness is appreciated. Treating him with disdain will turn things sour. So now it's your turn to ask.

"Look, I'd like to get this for my sister," you say, "but I can only pay 80. I know this is less than what you'd like, but could you let it go for 80?"

Pause. Then, a big smile. "Sure, sure! For *you*, I sell for 80." And the transaction is complete.

Asking God

Westerners sometimes feel uncomfortable with all this give and take. They would rather be told a fair price, up or down, so they can make up their mind. But that keeps buyer and seller at arm's length. In some of the places where bargaining is the norm, the process is like a dance with someone you're getting to know.

Asking is a big theme in the Bible, because we have a big God in the Bible. "Ask," Jesus encouraged the thousands listening to the Sermon on the Mount, "and it will be given to you; seek, and you will find; knock, and it will be opened to you" (Matthew 7:7). To Solomon, God appeared in a dream, encouraging him to "Ask what I shall give you" (2 Chronicles 1:7). The apostle James reminded us:

"If any of you lack wisdom, let him ask of God, who gives to all generously, and without reproach, and it will be given to him. But let him ask in faith," he adds, "without any doubting" (James 1:5, 6).

Christ again: "If two of you agree on earth about anything that they may ask, it shall be done for them by my Father who is in heaven" (Matthew 18:19).

When you think of them, these are amazing statements! The God of heaven pledges Himself to acquiesce to your asking! Of course, it's not as simple as that, for we should ask according to His will (1 John 5:14)—but almost. And regarding the Holy Spirit, the promises are even more astounding. Elisha was bold enough to ask for a *double* portion of Elijah's spirit (2 Kings 2:9). Evidently, this actually happened, because a lot more is told about Elisha's ministry than Elijah's, including double the miracles. The prophet Zechariah urges believers to "Ask rain from the LORD at the time of the spring rain [KJV, "latter rain"] " and promises to "pour out . . . the Spirit of grace and supplication" that will cause revival (Zechariah 10:1; 12:10–12).

Why Ask for the Holy Spirit?

To the disciples in the Upper Room, Christ promised the Holy Spirit:

"Whatsoever you shall ask in my name, that I will do, so that the Father may be glorified in the Son. If you ask Me anything in my name, I will do it" (John 14:13, 14).

Seven times in one night Jesus encouraged His followers to "ask" in His name! The other five are in John 15:7, 16, and John 16:23, 24, and 26.

The reason this is important is because people have sometimes wondered why we should ask, or pray, for the Holy Spirit (Luke 11:13), when He is at work in our lives anyway! Others look at it from a historical perspective and say, "If the Spirit came at Pentecost, the church already has Him. Why ask for Him again?"

Why ask God for *anything* again? If we ask Him for our *daily* bread, should we be asking for it *every* day? Doesn't He already know we need bread daily? Or when our loved one is very sick, do we ask Him once and then forget it? We can't forget that our praying to God is not to keep Him updated but to keep us *connected*. And the more we ask, the more we may develop a burden for what we ask. And when it comes to the outpouring of the Spirit in our lives, we should be asking earnestly and constantly!

"We are not willing enough to trouble the Lord with our petitions, and to ask Him for the gift of the Holy Spirit. *The Lord wants us to trouble Him in this matter*. He wants us to press our petitions to the throne."[1] Did you hear the urgency, the intensity? "It is not because of any restriction on the part of God that the riches of His grace do not flow earthward to men. If the fulfillment of the promise is not seen as it might be, it is because the promise is *not appreciated as it should be*. If all were willing, all would be filled with the Spirit."[2]

Matthew Henry, the great Bible commentator and historian of God's activity in the world, used to say that when God intends great mercy upon His people, "the first thing He does is set them a-praying." That's exactly what happened before Pentecost. Those 120 in the Upper Room, "all with one mind were continually devoting themselves to prayer" (Acts 1:14). The conditions for revival are very clear: 1) confession, 2) humiliation [surrender], 3) repentance, and 4) earnest prayer. And since the first three depend on the last one, "a revival need be expected only in answer to prayer."[3]

A Church That Prayed

At the last congregation I pastored some years ago, I saw, as never before, a church that took prayer seriously. The church was made up of educated Caucasians living in bedroom communities. Their recent new sanctuary sat 400 people, but barely 100 showed up on Sabbath mornings. When we first arrived there, I found that Adventists, in that metro area full of churches, liked this church, but for some reason, didn't care to be members there.

Even though I was a young pastor, I had no doubt about the three

Christian non-negotiables: Bible study, prayer, and witnessing. I also believed that it is "Not by might nor by power, but by My Spirit" (Zechariah 4:6) that God can change the situation. So I took *Bible* preaching more seriously than ever. I spent hours reading, comparing, exegeting, and poring over the text of Scripture, until God's message became clear. So much time was spent on this study that not enough time was spent on actual sermon-crafting. So very early on Sabbath mornings, I'd go and pray earnestly for God's Spirit to move in our midst and make up for my deficiencies. People started to come out of the woodwork: inactive members, transfers from other churches, friends of Adventists thirsting for something more in life, and lots of young adults. By the end of the first year, Sabbath attendance had tripled, and the church was changing.

Fifteen months into this adventure, I set out to do a series on prayer. My friend Dwight Nelson says we preachers preach what *we* need to hear. And he is absolutely right, of course. I needed to know more and grow more regarding prayer—so thus the series. A whole new world opened up for me. Prayer and communion with God became much more real and concrete. My relationship with Jesus grew much closer than ever before. I finally realized how most of us seem to live our lives three inches below the water-line: we know we're drowning but assume this is our lot in life, ignorant of the fact that just above us is a whole new world.

The Spirit of God moved on the church. People began to pray. We continued the mid-week prayer meeting, but now every Sabbath afternoon during daylight saving time, we'd gather for an hour to do nothing but pray. We prayed for the outpouring of the Spirit, prayed for our burdens, for our church, and for our community. During standard time, we met on Friday evenings. Then, after realizing that several of our church families were under severe satanic attack, I invited my elders to join me for prayer at five in the morning for special intercession. Yes, you read right—five in the morning, before people left for work. Seven of the ten elders came, and our prayer time was so blessed we decided to do it every week. Then, we added Fridays. And then Sabbath and Sunday mornings. By this time, deacons asked if they could join us. Then, other members did. And we expanded that time of morning prayer to every day of the week.

The church board began to pray. I was amazed at how God would take potentially conflicting issues and simply convict members of what to do, without much fuss. Leaders who'd never prayed like this before saw the power of prayer. No one would come late to the board, because the first thirty minutes was nothing but pleading and surrendering before God. And that had become real to us now. Evangelism also became more of a way of life for the church. We'd go door to door on Sabbath afternoons, and we transformed the fellowship hall into The Better

Living Center, where a dozen health-, finance-, and family-oriented seminars began to be offered to the community every year. We used Easter for evangelism, and every fall conducted a full-length evangelistic series. Each year, we baptized an average of forty people, all from the community, for we did not have a church school. And the church grew by leaps and bounds.

The Holy Spirit Takes Over

After the prayer revival of the second year, I decided it was time to do a sermon series on the Holy Spirit. Oh, what a blessing that was to me! And God used the series to bring more and more conviction upon hearts. By now, we had two worship services each Sabbath, the second often lasting past one o'clock. And as the church grew spiritually, giving increased. Offerings increased so that our church budget went up tenfold. Tithe increased so we could support up to ten full-time pastors, even though we only had one.

Church leaders decided it was time to plant another church just north of where we were, and after some intense praying, a few miracles, and knocking on over 3,500 doors to get acquainted and take a survey of needs, the new church was born. Twenty-five leaders trained for nine months to become church planting core members. But even though they represented only 7 percent of the membership, they provided 32 percent of the church income. Again, we prayed and turned it over to God, fully knowing that if we gave of our best, He would give of His best. And He came through: Our finances and leadership vacuum were easily and quickly replenished, and the beautiful new church plant is still thriving today after so many years.

God became concretely real in the lives of so many that a testimony time became part of our Sabbath service. Some attendees would drive two hours to get there, just to hear what God was doing in our midst. I seldom began preaching for the second service before noon. Small groups began to form, but these were *missionary* small groups—groups that would target people to pray for and to invite to the group and to the church. Some groups became Sabbath School ministry teams.

The leaders of these groups were remarkable men and women, most in their thirties and forties. On Tuesday evenings, I'd meet with them for *our* small group. What I experienced time and again during those gatherings, I will never forget: the intensity of Bible study, the powerful and real time for intercessory prayer, the synergistic insights going back and forth on the love and work of God, the singing, and the sheer joy of being in the presence of God! I had never experienced anything like that in group dynamics before. It seemed to all of us that heaven was very near.[4]

But not everything was perfect, as you can imagine. Especially because, whenever you choose to grow in Christ, the devil will set out to harass and annoy. Some families began to struggle: divorce, teenage drug use, illnesses. So it came time for corporate fasting and prayer. We encouraged participants to fast according to their experience and health, and we gave them materials to read and prepare. We'd do this from Friday afternoon through Sunday morning and divide that time into fifteen to seventeen sessions of ninety minutes each: singing, prayer request cards, prayer, a message, and twenty minutes of corporate prayer, before a fifteen-minute break. Imagine hundreds scattered across the sanctuary, hallways, and Sabbath School rooms praying together twenty of every ninety minutes for the Holy Spirit, during an entire weekend! People would register—up to 800 hundred for one of them—and stay for as many sessions as they wished. The people most affected were young adults and professionals. They had not experienced anything like this. Never had they spent so much time in the presence of God, and an intense weekend like this would be enough to produce radical changes in their lives. Some sold their sports cars and nice boats to downsize and live simpler lives. Others changed jobs, driven by personal outreach and ministry opportunities. In short, they put God first. God changed so many of them. The Spirit of God was really at work.

His work was evident in real results. Tithe quadrupled, and giving for evangelism rose a whopping 5,000 percent! The church membership tripled in size, and that's not counting the church plant. Three-fourths of the members were involved in some form of service or ministry. And we baptized almost 200 people in five years. This may not be unusual for some places in the world, but for us, in our circumstances, this was clearly the Spirit at work.

During those years, it was my privilege to witness the powerful moving of the Spirit in the lives of regular, cultural, Laodicean Adventists. We woke up as if from a dream. God became real. Faith became strong. Personal surrender and commitment became tangible. Never again have I been in a place where such intensity of devotion and search for God was so earnestly sought or concretely given.

People in that church still remember when God was at work in such powerful ways. But was this supposed to be an exception? Why doesn't this happen more often in churches all around North America? Could it happen in *your* church? Would you be part of it?

United Prayer

One reason this happened is because a critical mass of people were willing to embark on it *together*. They prayed together, they worked and planned together, they fasted together. Writing to brother and sister Farnsworth one day, Ellen White gave the following counsel:

"We are encouraged to pray for success, with the divine assurance that our prayers will be heard and answered. 'If two of you shall agree on earth as touching any thing that they shall ask, it shall be done for them of My Father which is in heaven. For where two or three are gathered together in My name, there am I in the midst of them' (Matthew 18:19, 20). . . . The promise is made on *condition that the united prayers of the church are offered*, and in answer to these prayers there may be expected *a power greater than that which comes in answer to private prayer*. The power given will be proportionate to the unity of the members and their love for God and for one another."[5]

Perhaps the reason revival begins with young adults is because they are more likely to do things together. On February 3, 1970, an otherwise routine Tuesday chapel service at Asbury College, a Wesleyan school near Lexington, Kentucky, was taken over by God's Spirit. The service began with Custer Reynolds, the academic dean, giving his personal testimony of Christ's love and forbearance and then inviting others to do the same. One by one, students came, giving testimonies of the love of God, until a long line of them wove all the way to the back of the auditorium. Some went directly to the altar, sobbing their repentance before God. The crowd began singing, "Just As I Am." Others knelt with friends and prayed. Still others wept quietly in sorrow for their sin.

The bell rang for classes to resume, but none of the 1,500 students packed into Hughes Auditorium wanted to leave. The college administration, recognizing the powerful and unusual moving of the Spirit in the student body, did not force the issue and allowed the "chapel" to continue. It went on the whole afternoon—orderly, soberly—and did not break at evening, going through the night. It continued the next day, and the next, and the next. The single service lasted 185 continuous hours—almost eight entire days![6]

By Thursday, reporters from every paper in middle America were on campus, wondering what this was all about. Students began driving to nearby colleges and churches to share the good news. They couldn't wait to share with others the love of Jesus. After the dust settled, and the phenomenon was analyzed with some care, the full impact of the student revival came out: over 2,000 witnessing teams had gone to share with others across the nation, and the revival had spread to at least 130 other colleges and universities, not to speak of hundreds of churches around the country. Even today, those who were there four decades ago recall those days as the turning point in their lives.

Zeal According to Knowledge

Sometimes it is hard for the Western mind to fathom the necessity of community in our search and work for God. But nothing is more consistent in the history of revival leading to reformation than the coming *together* for this work that the Holy Spirit is eager to do in our midst. I am convinced that here is a simple key. If we as a people were willing to come together, to pray, to meet as small groups, to organize into mission teams, all in order to seek the Holy Spirit, every stultified and petrified portion of the church would begin to jar loose.

> "Could there be a convocation of all the churches of earth, the object of their united cry should be for the Holy Spirit. When we have that, Christ our sufficiency is ever present. We shall have every want supplied. We shall have the mind of Christ."[7]

To pray for revival and reformation in the comfort of our living room, by our lonesome, is simply *not* the same—even if agreed to do it at the same time others pray—as when we take the effort to physically gather together and do so.

The Yoido Full Gospel Church in Seoul, South Korea, is the largest congregation in the world, with over one million members.[8] This is a Charismatic church, but two things they do right, that we don't tend to do even though we should: They are structured as small groups or ministry teams (otherwise, it would be impossible to be *one* church with so many members), and they take the prayer meeting seriously. So seriously, in fact, that hundreds, even thousands stream to the church at ten each evening to pray until sunrise.

Christ's disciples were told to "tarry" in Jerusalem until they received "power from on high" (Luke 24:49). They were to do this *together*. And because they were obedient, in spite of their differences, petty jealousies, and suspicions, God's Spirit was able, in merely ten days, to mold them into a living, loving community. Ellen White urged us:

> "Let all seek for the outpouring of the Holy Spirit. As with the disciples after the ascension of Christ, it may require several days of earnestly seeking God and putting away of sin. When God's people are worked by the Holy Spirit, they will manifest a zeal that is according to knowledge. . . . They will reflect the light that God has been giving for years. The spirit of criticism will be put away. Filled with the spirit of humility, they will be of one mind, united with one another and with Christ."[9]

The statement reminds me of one of the most successful Adventist pastors in the world. In the northeastern province of Jilin, China, Zu Xiu Hua is in charge of a district of more than 20,000 members. She personally started over 380 congregations! These are now led by hundreds of volunteers, whom she trains to give Bible studies, preach, and offer spiritual care on a regular basis.

The following story was told by General Conference leadership as they visited there recently. In one church where they worshiped, there were two halls, one on each floor, and both of them were filled to capacity. People were sitting in the stairways between them, straining to listen for every word coming out of the halls. "I saw those believers sitting in the hallway," remembers *Adventist Review* and *Adventist World* editor Bill Knott, "faces alight, singing hymns as though they were on the front row. And they were only within earshot of an old, decrepit loudspeaker. It was deeply moving to me to see how absolutely attractive the gospel is to them." When asked what she most likes to preach about, Pastor Zu Xiu Hua disarmingly says, "The cross—what else?" And when she was asked, "How do you account for this? What is the extraordinary appeal?" she replied, "The people come to the teachings, and they see our zeal and the Holy Spirit."[10]

The people see our zeal and the Holy Spirit. Even though the situation in China is very different than the one in the West, we cannot excuse our Laodicean condition, nor can we argue away the lack of God's Spirit in most of our churches. People are still people, and God is still God, whether in the Far East or wherever you live. Why not press together, systematically, with the members of the church, and determine together to remain asking God, in faith, to change the situation and to send the Holy Spirit, until this actually happens? If a few begin, God will show up at your door and change your world.

NOTES:

1. *Fundamentals of Christian Education*, 537 (emphasis supplied).

2. *The Acts of the Apostles*, 50 (emphasis supplied).

3. *Selected Messages*, bk. 1, 121.

4. At this time, I became acquainted with what Ellen White says about church work, in *Testimonies*, vol. 7, 18–22. She speaks there of the need for ministers to focus on training and reaching the lost versus appeasing the saints, of members being fully engaged in the ministry of the church, of the value of testimonies in church on Sabbath mornings, of the need to plant new churches, of trusting new converts with ministry, of the value of door-to-door work, of the need for missional small groups as the basis for outreach, and of the need of corporate prayer to plan for outreach.

I believe any church that decides to use these five pages as a template for church life and mission will greatly succeed.

5.   Letter 32, 1903, p. 5, "To Brother and Sister Farnsworth, January 28, 1903," in *Manuscript Releases*, vol. 9, 303 (emphasis supplied).

6.   Robert E. Coleman edited an inspiring eyewitness account of the revival, in *One Divine Moment: The Asbury Revival* (Old Tappan, NJ: Fleming H. Revell, 1970).

7.   Manuscript 8, 1892, p. 4, "Christ Our Sufficiency," November 25, 1892; also in *Manuscript Releases*, vol. 2, 24.

8.   See Karen Hurston, *Growing the World's Largest Church* (Springfield, MO: Gospel Publishing House, 1994). A number of reports have circulated regarding the founding pastor, now retired—Dr. David Yonggi Cho. The oral reports indicate that some time ago, Adventist pastors met with him, in part to learn about his church growth success, to which Cho retorted, showing them Ellen White's books *Evangelism* and *Gospel Workers:* "If you were to follow what your prophet says, you too would have success." I have not been able to ascertain the veracity of such reports. However, what Cho purportedly said is, nevertheless, true.

9.   *My Life Today*, 58.

10. Bill Knott and Jan Paulsen, "Finding Faith in China," in *Adventist World*, August 2009.

Questions for Reflection or Group Study

1. Do we sometimes have a problem when it comes to asking God for something?

2. How does Scripture picture God's willingness to give to us as we ask, and what are some of His promises?

3. Why ask God for anything, when He knows what we need?

4. Why do we need to keep asking for the Holy Spirit in our lives? How does the answer relate to the four conditions for revival mentioned by Ellen White?

5. What impressed you most about the story of "A Church That Prayed?" Why?

6. Why isn't personal, private prayer enough for the great outpouring of the Holy Spirit?

7. What do you see as the main ingredients of effective small groups that will allow the filling of the Holy Spirit?

8. What do you make of the statement: "The promise [of the Spirit's outpouring] is made on condition that the united prayers of the church are offered, [yielding] a power greater than that which comes in answer to private prayer"?

9. What would have to happen for one of our churches or institutions to experience something like the 185 continuous hours of seeking God in prayer, such as it happened at Asbury College?

10. What do you see as some of the keys to Spirit-filled living in China?

11. What should we do next to seek God together, to see the outpouring of the Spirit in our lives?

Power

CHAPTER FOURTEEN

The Latter Rain

E ver since I was a child, I've liked exploring new places. Oblivious to parental watchcare, I'd go far ahead or lag behind in my desire to see personally what was "out there." Not a few times, I gave my parents justified concern, because little Ronny was nowhere to be seen. Nothing seemed to frighten me, and the solo explorations of buildings, roads, and trees held a special attraction.

That was perhaps the root cause, when, many years later, I found myself charting my own course in the ancient city of Ephesus, in today's Turkey. With academic colleagues, I had walked Curetes Street—the main thoroughfare—stopping to observe the Hercules Gate, the Fountain of Trajan, the Baths of Varius, and even the ever-popular latrines. Yes, they had those in the first century, and they were public. We ogled and chatted excitedly before the Library of Celsus, one of the largest in the ancient world, built only a few decades after the first apostles were there. This was incredibly exciting to me, for we were witnessing what Paul saw when he first took the gospel to that great pagan city. But after we all gathered at the infamous theater—the same one where the Ephesians used to chant for two hours: "Great is Diana [or Artemis] of the Ephesians!" (Acts 19:23–32)—I decided to forgo lunch and explore on my own.

The road I had seen from the top of the theater was just too inviting to miss. This road once led to the port—the one Paul would have used to disembark for his new labors. But it was off limits to tourists. Well, after checking out a sixth-century Byzantine church, I decided to go across the fields, regardless of rattlesnakes. Lo and behold, I ended up on that long, ancient road to the port. I felt privileged indeed. As I walked the forbidden road, I found four pillars dedicated to the four gospel writers: Matthew, Mark, Luke, and John. This was remarkable, for earlier, I had seen the remains of the Temple of Diana, patron goddess of the Ephesians. All that was left of it was a single pillar, with a stork's nest on top of it! I thought to myself: Amazing! Here is one of the most pagan, cosmopolitan cities of the ancient world, thoroughly in the grip of Satan, and a single man by the name of Paul turned the town upside down. Centuries later, a temple known the world over as one of the seven ancient wonders of the world is gone, except for one pillar. But evidence of Christianity is all around.

The Challenge of Worldwide Evangelization

Have you ever wondered how we are ever going to be able to share the gospel with the entire world? The challenge is great. Half of the nearly seven billion people in the world have never even *heard* of Jesus or seen a Bible, let alone knowing anything of the third angel's message. We rejoice today because there is one Adventist for every 400 people or so, better than the every 519 in the year 2000. But the truth remains that places such as Indonesia, the Middle East, Northern Africa, and China remain formidable barriers to our message. China is a good example to help us keep things in perspective. The work there is among the most powerful and successful for us in all the world, with 400,000 believers today. Less than a dozen countries in the world can boast of so many Adventists. Yet the population is 1.3 billion citizens. That is one Adventist for every 3,250 Chinese, or only 0.03 percent of it!

The early church, however, had met just such improbable odds. At least one third of the world population today has some ties to Christianity. But when the apostles began, it was zilch. Today, it is politically correct, even if not practiced worldwide, to be tolerant in matters of religion. But then, even though polytheism was widely accepted in the Roman world, Christianity was the singular exception. Christians were viewed as a branch of Judaism, and the Jews had many enemies in the empire. But the ultimate offense was Christianity's exclusiveness—the message that there was only one God, and that God was our Savior, and that this Savior happened to die on a Roman cross to accomplish it. What? No wonder they thought it all foolishness (1 Corinthians 1:20–23)!

The common denominator of all pagan gods had always been *power.* The concept that a God who could have the power to create the world would let Himself be humiliated on a cross seemed just too far-fetched. A well-known, second-century grafitto found near Rome depicts a man—kneeling before Jesus hanging on the cross, naked—with a donkey's head. The mocking inscription below it reads, "Alexamenos worships his god."

Said New Testament scholar Gordon Fee:

"It is hard for those in the christianized West to appreciate how utterly mad the message of a God who got himself crucified by his enemies must have seemed to the first-century Greek or Roman. But it is precisely the depth of this scandal and folly we must appreciate if we are to understand . . . why it was well over a century before the cross appears among Christians as a symbol of their faith."[1]

Thirty years after Pentecost, Paul was able to declare that the gospel "was proclaimed in all creation under heaven" (Colossians 1:23). Even if he only meant the Roman world, that was the vast majority of people living at the time! How do you think they did that? No satellite communications, no Internet, not even radio or TV. No transatlantic air travel, no cell phones, not even books, such as we have today. How did they ever do it?

"Look, how they love one another, . . . and how they are ready to die for each other." That is how pagans identified Christians a century after John, the last apostle, had died in Ephesus.[2] Ellen White expands:

"After the descent of the Holy Spirit, the disciples were so filled with love for Him and for those for whom He died, that hearts were melted by the words they spoke and the prayers they offered. They spoke in the power of the Spirit; and under the influence of that power, thousands were converted."[3]

Are non-Christians today "melting" by words and actions that cannot but reflect the love of Christ in our hearts? Is *love* the first thing that comes to the mind when people think of Christians? The biblical record is clear about the early church:

"And the congregation of those who believed were of one heart and soul; and not one of them claimed that anything belonging to him was his own; but all things were common property to them. And with great power the apostles were giving witness to the resurrection of the Lord Jesus, and abundant grace was upon them all" (Acts 4:32, 33).

How far we have fallen.

The Early Rain

As we study the meaning of *early* and *latter* rain, we should keep in mind that we use these terms in two ways: in a historical-objective sense, focusing on time and the church—and in a personal-subjective sense, focusing on how this may affect us personally.

It was the early rain of the Spirit that made the early church become what it became. "The outpouring of the Spirit in the days of the apostles was the beginning of the early, or former, rain, and glorious was the result."[4] How glorious, exactly? The gospel was carried "to the uttermost parts of the inhabited world."

"Hearts yielded to the power of this message. The church beheld converts flocking to her from all directions. Backsliders were reconverted. Sinners united with believers in seeking the pearl of great price. Some who had been the bitterest opponents of the gospel became its champions. . . . Every Christian saw in his brother a revelation of divine love and benevolence."

Pretty amazing, isn't it? No wonder that "thousands were converted in a day."[5] Seventh-day Adventists have for decades now been waiting for the proverbial outpouring of the *latter* rain. But this cannot be until the early rain descends first.

What, exactly, is the early rain?

Most people would say it is the regenerating work of the Spirit in leading us to conversion. For a more complete picture, let's go to Joel 2:23. In my NASB Study Bible, it renders this as "Be glad in the Lord your God; for He has given you the early rain for your vindication. And He has poured down for you the rain, the early and latter rain as before." The problem is that the Hebrew word translated as "early rain" is *moreh*, which means "teacher," and not *yoreh*. *Yoreh* is correctly translated at the *end* of the verse as "early [rain]." So, *teacher*—not *rain*. The same word is found in Proverbs 5:13 and Isaiah 30:20, and it is translated "teacher" in both places. The Targums—interpretative renderings of Old Testament books when Jews began to forget the Hebrew language—and the Vulgate Bible, a third-century Latin translation of the Bible, also translate it as "teacher." The expression is really "teacher of righteousness."[6]

This makes sense, when you read Isaiah 45:8: "Rain down, O heavens, from above, and let the clouds pour down righteousness; let the earth open up and salvation bear fruit, and righteousness spring up with it." Or Hosea 10:12: "Break up your fallow ground, for it is time to seek the Lord until He comes to rain righteousness on you."

The prophets spoke of the early rain as the time of righteousness—the time when the goodness and justice of God would eventually be seen. Jesus, the Incarnate Son of God, came to show us just that. He, through the Holy Spirit, became the "teacher of righteousness" who at the time of Pentecost made all things clear to His disciples. He had promised: "The Holy Spirit . . . will teach you all things, and bring to your remembrance all that I said to you" (John 14:26).

So the historical-objective early rain was the revelation of Jesus as the second Adam who obeyed God perfectly (His righteousness), and who loved man supremely (His mercy at the cross). And this was the message of Pentecost to the world—the message which revolutionized it forever.

In a personal-subjective sense, the early rain "experience" would be our individual appropriation of such a message of love and obedience in Christ—something absolutely necessary if we are ever to experience the *latter* rain. This is the experience Ellen White had envisioned for Seventh-day Adventists in the wake of the 1888 message.

What, then, is the latter rain?

The Historical Latter Rain

Whereas the early rain kick-started the *Christian* era, God's opening work of reconciliation to *all* nations and not just simply through His chosen people, Israel—the historical-objective latter rain would close such work at the consummation, the end. What does all this mean, exactly? Ellen White says the outpouring of the latter rain will do several things: 1) It will prepare "the church for the coming of the Son of man,"[7] 2) it will give "power to the loud voice of the third angel," and 3) it will prepare "the saints to stand in the period when the seven last plagues shall be poured out."[8]

She also states that the latter rain cannot come "while the largest portion of the church are not laborers together with God," because "selfishness and self-indulgence" are still so obvious in the church.[9] And while she asserts she has "no specific time" when this outpouring would occur, in 1897, she wrote such a time was "now."[10]

That was over 110 years ago! If that is so, why have we not seen worldwide miraculous manifestations of the Almighty, in fulfillment of the promised blessing? Here, perhaps, is the best-known statement on the latter rain work of the Spirit at the end:

"The great work of the gospel is not to close with less manifestation of the power of God than marked its opening. The prophecies which were fulfilled in the outpouring of the former rain at the opening of the gospel are again to be fulfilled in the latter rain at its close. Here are 'the times of refreshing' to which the apostle Peter looked forward when he said: 'Repent ye therefore, and be converted, that your sins may be blotted out, when the times of refreshing shall come from the presence of the Lord; and He shall send Jesus.' Acts 3:19, 20.

"Servants of God, with their faces lighted up and shining with holy consecration, will hasten from place to place to proclaim the message from heaven. By thousands of voices, all over the earth, the warning will be given. Miracles will be wrought, the sick will be healed, and signs and wonders will follow the believers. Satan also works, with lying wonders, even bringing down fire from heaven in the sight of men. Revelation 13:13. Thus the inhabitants of the earth will be brought to take their stand.

"The message will be carried not so much by argument as by the deep conviction of the Spirit of God. The arguments have been presented. The seed has been sown, and now it will spring up and bear fruit."[11]

God's servant actually gave the reason the above lines remain largely unfulfilled:

"God cannot reveal Himself till those who profess to be Christians are doers of His word *in their private lives*, till there is oneness with Christ, a sanctification of body, soul, and spirit. Then, they will be fit temples for the indwelling of the Holy Spirit."[12]

Now we know that no cosmic alignment, no political liaisons, no ecumenical developments are delaying the outpouring of the latter rain. What is delaying the latter rain at the *time* of the latter rain—a time that has lasted over a century to date—is simply the church's unwillingness to surrender all. That is, the members' "private lives" must be watered by the early rain before the latter rain will do its work.

The Personal Latter Rain

Most of Ellen White's writing on the latter rain points to the personal work of the Spirit in our hearts. She viewed the latter rain as "the completion of the work of God's grace," bringing us "to perfection."[13] This is not the perfectionism brought about by legalistic tendencies or by a pentecostal infusion of overpowering miracle work, *in spite of* our lack of surrender. This "perfection" is total trust in and surrender to Jesus, our perfect Advocate. She also warns that we cannot share this "refreshing" unless we gain the victory over pride, selfishness, the love of the world, and "every besetment."[14]

This is, no doubt, strong medicine, and some may be tempted to give in to the disease called Sin, figuring they are simply terminally ill—too far gone to change *that* much. But we should never despair. We have a strong Helper in Jesus Christ. By His stripes (death) "we are healed" (Isaiah 53:5). He pardons all [our] iniquities," and "heals all [our] diseases," for "He redeems [our] life from the pit" (Psalm 103:3, 4). All we must do is go to Jesus and then choose to stay with Him! Every nerve within us, at times, may entertain unholy desires to leave Him and make of Self our substitute god. But nothing more is asked for, except to trust Him moment by moment. Jesus is our Savior, not *in* our sins but *from* our sins. Hallelujah! He will prove more than faithful to you and me. Through Him, "I can do all things" (Philippians 4:13). In order to receive the personal latter rain, we must "keep the vessel clean and right side up," ready to take in everything Jesus gives.[15]

But it is at this point that logic breaks down in the minds of some. Many Adventists simply assume that because the early rain was given at the time of Pentecost, and the latter rain at the end time, that there is a vast vacuum of the Spirit in the intervening centuries. They conclude that the Spirit is not with God's people today, although it would be more accurate to say that God's people are not with the Spirit today. They see God as "holding back His Spirit and that He must be worked on and persuaded to release the Spirit. The thought suggests that the spiritual shortcomings of God's people today are because they have not received the outpouring of the 'latter rain.' Insidiously, the blame is shifted to God, and we sit back waiting for Him to take the initiative in correcting things by pouring out the 'latter rain' of the Spirit. This kind of thinking is totally false."[16]

We must realize that the work of the Spirit is always ongoing. This is the great conceptual weakness of the neo-Charismatic Christian: waiting, longing, expecting a supernatural transformation which may be seen on the outside, instead of believing in—and paying the price for—the inward reformation of the heart. It is like wanting a magic pill from the Heavenly Physician to avoid pain now, rather than following His counsel calling for small steps that take time but which will eventually lead to a complete lifestyle make-over.

> "Many have in a great measure failed to receive the former rain. They have not obtained all the benefits that God has thus provided for them. They expect that the lack will be supplied by the latter rain. When the richest abundance of grace shall be bestowed, they intend to open their hearts to receive it. They are making a terrible mistake. The work that God has begun in the human heart in giving his light and knowledge, must be continually going forward . . . . It is God who began the work [justification], and he will finish his work [sanctification], making man complete in Jesus Christ. But there must be no neglect of the grace represented by the former rain. Only those who are living up to the light they have, will receive greater light. Unless we are daily advancing in the exemplification of the active Christian virtues, we shall not recognize the manifestations of the Holy Spirit in the latter rain. It may be falling on hearts all around us, but we shall not discern or receive it."[17]

What Now?

Admittedly, in vast areas of the western world, we are a church in decline. Our preoccupation for the things of the world, and our searing blindness to our true condition, have made of us—who have talent, resources, and much history in Jesus—a puny spiritual people. We really are terminally ill, but little do we know it. We've been medicating for so long that we don't know what health is like any more. Perhaps this sounds too harsh. Chances are that if you chose to read this book, you are open to the Spirit of God, if not already well on the way to His infilling.

But even if your particular situation is better than most, the angst this should cause is enough to send us to our knees and plead before the Father for immediate, yet lasting help. What we desperately need is a double dose of spiritual aid—a revelation of the character of Christ and a thorough baptism of the Spirit. Remember the lesson from Joel 2? The association between rain and the "teacher of righteousness"? We need a true revelation of the love and power of God, a true picture of His abundant grace and mercy, a view of His nature and grandeur.

"The message of Christ's righteousness is to sound from one end of the world to the other. This is the glory of God which closes the work of the third angel."[18]

You can make a difference right now. You, along with a few others, can see God transform you, your family, and your church.

"It was by the confession and forsaking of sin, by earnest prayer and consecration of themselves to God, that the early disciples prepared for the outpouring of the Holy Spirit on the day of Pentecost. The same work, only in greater degree, must be done now."[19]

God Himself will guide you to that "greater degree," for only He knows how that applies to individual disciples. The key is to start, to seek, to obey, to trust—to take the next step before the next is taken—to grow, as you fix your eyes on Jesus.

The prophet Hosea will have the last word:

"Come, let us return to the Lord. For He has torn us, but He will heal us; He has wounded us, but He will bandage us. He will revive us after two days; He will raise us up on the third day, that we may live before Him. So let us know, let us press on to know the Lord, His going forth is as certain as the dawn; and He will come to us like the rain, like the spring rain watering the earth" (Hosea 6:1–3).

NOTES:

1. Michael P. Knowles, *We Preach Not Ourselves* (Grand Rapids, MI: Brazos, 2008), 86.

2. As reported by Tertullian, an early Christian apologist, in his *Apologeticum*, ch. 39, p. 7 (in CSEL 69, trans. by Glover, Loeb edition). Accessed from http://www.tertullian.org/quotes.htm on January 30, 2011.

3. *The Acts of the Apostles*, 22.

4. *Ibid.*, 54, 55.

5. *Ibid.*, 48, 38.

6. See *The Seventh-day Adventist Bible Commentary*, vol. 4 (Washington, D.C.: Review and Herald, 1956, 1980), 945.

7. *The Acts of the Apostles*, 55.

8. *Early Writings*, 86.

9. *Review and Herald*, July 21, 1896, par. 2.

10. *Selected Messages*, bk. 1, 192, and *Review and Herald*, March 2, 1897. In paragraph 7 she wrote: "Pray most earnestly that now, in the time of the latter rain, the showers of grace may fall upon us," and in paragraph 14: "It is the time of the latter rain, when the Lord will give largely of his Spirit."

11. *The Great Controversy*, 611, 612.

12. Letter 139, 1898, p. 16, "To Elder A. T. Jones," December 16, 1898; also in *Manuscript Releases*, vol. 4, 365, emphasis supplied.

13. *Testimonies to Ministers*, 506.

14. *Early Writings*, 71.

15. Manuscript 35, Sept. 26, 1891, "Work and Baptism of Holy Spirit Needed," in *The Upward Look*, 283.

16. Paulsen, 135.

17. *Review and Herald*, March 2, 1897, par. 4.

18. Ellen G. White's letter to leaders in Battle Creek, in *General Conference Daily Bulletin*, January 28, 1893 par. 27.

19. *Review and Herald*, March 2, 1897, par. 4.

Questions for Reflection or Group Study

1. What do you see that is encouraging for spreading the three angels' messages into the whole world that was a far greater challenge to the church of the first century?

2. Based on Paul's declaration that the gospel "was proclaimed in all creation under heaven" (Colossians 1:23) within thirty years, do you think something similar is possible today? How?

3. What is the "early rain," exactly? How is it related to "righteousness?"

4. Identify the three things the latter rain will do in the church. Comment on them. Did you expect other things to happen?

5. What is holding back the coming of the latter rain? What does it mean to be "doers of the word" in our "private lives?"

6. Comment on this statement: "Unless we are daily advancing in the exemplification of the active Christian virtues, we shall not recognize the manifestations of the Holy Spirit in the latter rain." What does this mean for us today?

7. How only can we become overcomers in our life on this earth?

8. What is wrong with thinking that "God is holding back the Holy Spirit" today?

9. What is "the same work, only in greater degree" that Ellen White says must be done now?

10. What steps will you take to open the door of your life more widely to the Holy Spirit?

CHAPTER FIFTEEN

Babylon Rising

If you Google "I need a miracle," you will end up with five million hits. With Bing, it is over thirty million. Everything from prayer websites to New Age ideas to songs by The Grateful Dead—their title being an oxymoron, of course. Everyone needs a miracle. Everyone wants one. Everyone prays for one, when things don't go the way one wants them to go. Everybody likes to hear about miracles, even if they've never had one happen to them.

Ernie Knoll was a miracle man. Actually, he was a prophet—one followed faithfully by scores of Adventists, until very recently. He began receiving "visions" in 2005, and after over thirty of them, a consistent following developed, with a board, book sales, and a website inviting supporters to donate via any of the major credit cards. Reading his prophecies, you couldn't help but think his language was calculated to impress: a mixture of the book of Revelation and the Spirit of Prophecy combined but lacking much sense or specificity. The language and tone was there, but the content was not. A couple of my former students were attracted to him, but I warned them that my impression was that this was the result of an overactive imagination—of someone needing attention.

As it turned out, there was more to be learned. On July 22, 2009, a communiqué was sent by Knoll's ministry board, stating that what they had sincerely believed to be supernatural messages from God to Knoll for His people, they now believed to be from Satan. It went on to identify various deceptions, and it apologized to those who'd put their faith in these messages.

Everyone needs a miracle, and Satan is happy to supply it.

The Reason for Miracles

Miracles are not to make anyone believe—they can only confirm belief. But when it comes to religion, people often want miracles, as a spiritual shortcut. *If God could only write it across the sky, then I'd know for sure this is what He wants.* That is easier and faster than studying my Bible, praying, and thinking about what He is like so that I can discern His will for my life.

In His days on earth, Jesus performed many miracles. But He did this at a time when everyone believed miracles could only come from God, thus ratifying His divinity. He did them to show the merciful, kind character of His Father, in contrast to the popular understanding of the Almighty.[1] Christ never performed miracles as a shortcut to faith. For building faith, He gave a Bible study.

Remember the morning of His resurrection? Check out Luke 24. Those two disciples on the way to Emmaus were depressed—shocked that their Messiah would actually, suddenly, be put to death. They were confused and bewildered. If only they could see God's hand in all this. Christ knew their state of mind, which is why He went to them. But instead of appearing to them in the glory of the resurrection, they were "prevented from recognizing Him" (Luke 24:16). Instead of performing a miracle as they walked along the road, such as He'd done many times before, Jesus simply walked them through the Word. "Beginning with Moses and with all the prophets, He explained to them the things concerning Himself in all the Scriptures" (v. 27). It was only *after* their hearts "burned" within them with Bible-built faith (v. 32) that the miracle was performed: "and He vanished from their sight" (v. 31).

Time and again, the Jews asked Jesus, "Show us a sign!" (Matthew 12:38; 16:1; Mark 8:11; Luke 11:16). But the only sign would be His death and resurrection (Matthew 12:39, 40). When He told the parable of the rich man and Lazarus, Jesus clearly warned them that "if they do not listen to Moses and the Prophets, they will not be persuaded even if someone rises from the dead" (Luke 16:31). No greater miracle can be claimed than that of a resurrection. This will be Satan's last deception to the wicked raised after the thousand years are over (Revelation 20:7, 8, 5a): making them believe *he* resurrected them. Christ's crowning miracle while on earth was resurrecting His friend Lazarus, yet it failed to convince priests and Pharisees alike (John 11:45–47).

But our human tendency is to want a miracle rather than a change of heart. A miracle is exciting—it teases the senses. And Satan knows this very well. He is poised to exploit this to heights unknown, as the time of Christ's coming draws near. He already tested it successfully with post-disappointment Millerites.

Looking for Miracles and Excitement in Adventist History

Early in her ministry, while some Advent believers still practiced fanaticism and excess in the name of the Holy Spirit, Ellen White received a vision. Coming from a Methodist background, where some of these practices were not uncommon, she was not fully aware of the danger of such "exercises" as swooning, shouting, and dancing—perceived to be the result of the presence of the Spirit. But in vision, her angel showed her the beauty and order of heaven and said, "Follow it." She concluded that "the exercises were in great danger of being adulterated" and that "we should strive at all times to be free from unhealthy and unnecessary excitement. I saw that there was great danger of leaving the Word of God and resting down and trusting in exercises." She allowed for some excitement, but added a warning: "I saw that God had moved by His Spirit upon your company in some of their exercises and their promptings; but I saw danger ahead."[2]

Danger ahead was the problem. In the 1890s, along with powerful evidence of true revivals in the church in the wake of the righteousness by faith message, counterfeit revivals also surfaced. In 1884, Ellen White had already warned that "at every revival of God's work the prince of evil is aroused to more intense activity."[3] Three factors seemed to set the conditions for this deception. First, the religious liberty hearings on the Sunday law issue before the Senate, signaling to many members that the end of the world was near. Second, revivals among the remnant and a renewed sense that the latter rain had began to be poured out. And third, an increasing frenzy among Protestants in the Holiness Movement seeking "instant" sanctification.

By the summer of 1897, revivalist A. F. Ballenger began to call for the baptism of the Holy Spirit at every camp meeting where he preached. He saw this as the necessary follow-up to the message of righteousness by faith.[4] However, his emphasis was a call for instant holiness—a miraculous, instantaneous cleansing of self from sin—countering Ellen White's teaching that sanctification "is the work of a lifetime."[5] The excitement spread like a prairie fire on a hot summer day, and it became known as the "Receive Ye the Holy Ghost" movement.

Ballenger's message turned more radical. He required people to stop sinning immediately before they could receive the Holy Spirit. He became convinced that the baptism of the Spirit was a second work of grace in order to obtain power for witnessing. Then, he taught that the third phase of the Spirit's work was to grant people spiritual gifts—particularly the gift of healing.[6] And his tone became radical:

"I have told our people to either clean up or get out of the church of God. Brother, I dare do that; . . . and thank the Lord, some are getting clean, and some are getting out. . . . I must have a clean church to invite the people into, before I can stand before the people to give the loud cry in all its glory. . . . The Lord says we can not have the baptism of the Holy Ghost until we get the victory over every besetting sin."[7]

To be fair, much of what Ballenger shared in those years was correct biblical teaching—even if a bit extreme—and it led many people to surrender to God. However, his penchant for the supernatural, for instant sanctification, and for salvation from disease[8] gave a wrong slant to his message—a slant that proved disastrous in Indiana.

S. S. Davis, an evangelist in Indiana, and R. S. Donnell, the conference president, were duly impressed with Ballenger's message and emphasis. They became convinced that the Pentecostals had the Spirit and the Adventists the truth—and that a marriage of the two was necessary. Donnell also came to believe that when people are born again, they are born with holy flesh; that is, perfect from sin, just as Jesus was. Thus arose the teaching of "translation faith."

In churches all over Indiana, members began to gather in cleared basements to dance and shout and lift their hands "in the Spirit." As soon as someone would faint from the exercise, others would gather round him or her, shouting, singing, and praying all the more. When the faint revived, it was evidence they now had "translation faith"—they were made perfect in a wink.

The Holy Flesh Movement found its climax in the Indiana camp meeting of 1900, where much of what I described was taking place, accompanied by "a bedlam of noise" and confusion. Still in Australia, Ellen White became convicted by the Spirit of God to return right away and meet this delusion: "The teaching given in regard to what is termed 'holy flesh' is an error," she shared with church leadership. "All may now obtain holy hearts, but it is not correct to claim in this life to have holy flesh. . . . No human being on the earth has holy flesh. It is an impossibility." Then she penned some of the most relevant warnings regarding spiritual delusion pertaining to the time of the end:

> "The things you have described as taking place in Indiana, the Lord has shown me would take place just before the close of probation. Every uncouth thing will be demonstrated. There will be shouting, with drums, music, and dancing. The senses of rational beings will become so confused that they cannot be trusted to make right decisions. And this is called the moving of the Holy Spirit.
>
> "The Holy Spirit never reveals itself in such methods, in such a bedlam of noise. This is an invention of Satan. . . . I was instructed

to say that at these demonstrations demons in the form of men are present, working with all the ingenuity that Satan can employ to make the truth disgusting to sensible people."[9]

The question is, have we learned? Are we as a people really ready for the coming deception? Don't get me wrong. I'm not against experience or excitement, as we relate to God. In fact, I got into the study of the Holy Spirit's baptism for that very reason: I wanted the power of God's Spirit in my life. I wanted Him to overwhelm my life. And the Bible makes clear that if the Spirit is in your life, it should be evident to others (Acts 6:3; 19:2; 1 Thessalonians 1:5). Fortunately, the Lord gave me excellent opportunities to study and pray about it, seeking God's wisdom on the matter. I remember, after spending a weekend in the mountains on a personal retreat, driving back home disappointed that the Spirit had not fallen on me all that time, in spite of my praying and pleading. Moments later, as I continued to pray and drive, the thought came to me clearly that *what Jesus wanted me to do about Him is to trust Him, not to feel Him.*

The New Ecumenism

We know that shortly before Christ comes, Satan will galvanize his resources for one last major and sustained assault on the souls of men. He will lead the whole world to worship the beast (Revelation 13:4), and through the image of the beast, he will perform "great signs," in order to deceive the entire earth (vv. 13, 14). So two things will happen to "the whole world": the world will worship the beast, and the world will be deceived by miracles.

How, exactly?

Many religious leaders hope that one day humanity can come together in ecumenical (from the Greek *oikoumene*—the inhabited world) solidarity, forgetting doctrinal differences and focusing on essentials such as worshiping God. Some Adventists fear this ecumenical movement, to the point where they highly criticize their church for sending observers, for example, to major assemblies of the World Council of Churches. But their zeal may be misguided. For it is very unlikely that denominations ignore their theological distinctives to such an extent as to blend together in one. What brings people together is not a *lack* of something, but something new—something that catches everyone's attention.

For that, we need to turn to the book of Revelation.

We find in Revelation 16 that everything at the end will culminate in the battle called Armageddon. But what precedes the battle is just as important to understand as the battle itself.

"And the sixth angel poured out his bowl upon the great river, the Euphrates; and its water was dried up, that the way might be prepared for the kings of the east" (v. 12).

Jesus, the King of kings, is coming, and the political support given to His opposing beast power is coming to a low ebb, symbolized by the drying of the Euphrates. In 539 B.C., when the head of the Medo-Persian army, Cyrus, dried the Euphrates, the life source to the city of Babylon, he was able to take over the city (Isaiah 44:27 – 45:1; 11:15b; Jeremiah 51:36, 37).

Satan knows history, and he knows it is now or never. Revelation 12 shows his failed attempts to overcome the enemy. He failed to persuade most angels in heaven to turn against their Maker (vv. 7–9). Next, he failed to destroy the Messiah, in spite of the fact that the kingdom ruling the world at the time was Rome, firmly under his control (v. 4). Then, he failed to drown the woman—God's faithful people—during the 1,260 years of apostasy, with the "river" of coercion he poured out of his mouth (vv. 13–16). Last, he turns his wrath against the remnant of God; that is, you and me today (v. 17). Note one thing: *every aggressive attempt is through the use of his mouth.*

How is he going to try to overwhelm God's remnant? First, he rebuilds the sea beast once again—the power of Rome (Revelation 13:1–8). Next, he forges a lamb-like beast, the legislative power of the United States of America, with which he can promote his substitute Sabbath to the world (Revelation 13:11–18). However—and follow this carefully—the entire demonic religio-political structure needed to stamp out "the very elect" is not in place until we come to chapter 16. The time is finally come for the dragon, that old serpent called the devil and Satan (Revelation 12:9), along with his reliable side-kick, the beast, to do something big. And nothing is bigger than playing God!

"And I saw coming out of the mouth of the dragon and out of the mouth of the beast, and out of the mouth of the false prophet, three unclean spirits like frogs; for they are the spirits of demons, performing signs, which go out to the kings of the whole world, to gather them together for the war of the great day of God, the Almighty. . . . Armageddon" (Revelation 16:13, 16).

The prince of this world now sees he finally has everything in place to be king *of this world.* Not just a prince anymore, but total domination. The waiting is over. *The demonic trinity has finally become one—just as God is One.*

Am I going too fast? OK, who is this unholy trinity? The *dragon* is Satan, particularly through his miraculous powers, or spiritualism; the *beast,* of course, is the papal institution; and the *false prophet* is apostate

Protestantism. In one of her most oft-quoted statements, Ellen White prophesied:

> "The Protestants of the United States will be foremost in stretching their hands across the gulf to grasp the hand of spiritualism; they will reach over the abyss to clasp hands with the Roman power; and under the influence of this threefold union, this country will follow in the steps of Rome in trampling on the rights of conscience."[10]

When this triad showed up before as the dragon, the sea beast, and the lamb-like beast, they were not as much in sync as we see them now to be in Revelation 16. In Revelation 12, the dragon's mouth was ready to devour the child, while in Revelation 13 the beast's mouth utters blasphemies, and the lamb-like beast used its mouth to speak like a dragon. But in Revelation 16, what came out of each of their mouths was identical: "spirits of demons like frogs."

What About the Frogs?

Like frogs? Like frogs!

The frogs remind us of the second plague on ancient Egypt as God sought to deliver His people from bondage and teach the Egyptians the inadequacy of their own gods. A Jewish legend tells of how Egyptian magicians were able to bring forth frogs with the help of demons.[11] The Egyptian goddess, Higit, was symbolized by a frog. She was supposed to be a goddess of fertility. Exodus 8 tells us that, as the result of the plague, frogs were even in their houses throughout "the land of Egypt" (vv. 11, 6). No doubt there was religious irony in the fact that the goddess of fertility was seen preventing fertility, by occupying beds and bedrooms throughout Egypt! Thoughtful Egyptians couldn't have missed the point. Satan had been able to copy the miracles done by Moses, such as turning sticks into snakes and water into blood. But frogs were the last of Satan's miracles—the maximum extent of his miraculous abilities. And Exodus says that the Lord destroyed all those frogs.

Why would Satan want frogs again, since he failed memorably with that stratagem once before? My guess it's because he can't let go of that earlier defeat in Egypt. The frogs of Revelation 16 are symbolic. He wants a second chance, and he believes he can make it this time. And since, in ancient Egyptian spiritualism, frogs represented fertility, he will use his unholy offspring to go head to head with God's remnant, the children of the woman (Revelation 12:17). His children against God's children.

But here is an interesting common denominator: the frogs come out of the dragon's mouth, the beast's mouth, and the false prophet's mouth. The most identifiable characteristic coming out of anyone's mouth is speech.

In ancient times, frogs were symbols of deceptive spirits, because of their loud but meaningless croaking.[12] And "the Jews of the first century came to associate frogs with charlatans and demonic water spirits."[13] What do we have here? We have an unholy alliance between spiritualists, Romanists, and apostate Protestants, the objective of which is to deceive the leaders of the whole world by means of "signs," or miracles—even miracles of bringing fire down from heaven, such as Elijah did. But how could three such disparate religious groups ever come together? Their common denominator is not doctrine but miraculous speech! False speech: *glossolalia* and *false prophesyings.* And the fire from heaven is the supposed Holy Ghost fire.

Here the old contention comes full circle. In Genesis 11, Satan is behind the attempt by men to build a tower—Babel—that reaches to heaven in order to avoid the judgments of God in the form of another Flood. They declare themselves to be the enemies of God. They have *one* speech and speak as *one.* God "visits" them—a biblical expression for judgment—and confuses their speech to thwart their plans. Satan has waited thousands of years to undo God's interposition. He now leads mankind to join in *one* spiritual speech—false, miraculous speech. That's one reason why John the Revelator no longer sees simply a lamb-like beast who speaks like a dragon (Revelation 13:11). The beast has morphed into a false *prophet*, speaking for a false god.

The Impact of the Charismatic Movement

The impact of the Charismatic Movement cannot be underestimated in these last days. Though not all Charismatics speak in tongues, miracle-seeking Charismatics are the fastest-growing religious group on the planet, numbering some 600 million adherents worldwide. It took the Catholic Church over 1,000 years to reach those numbers, but barely 100 years for Pentecostals and Charismatics to do so. An estimated 85 percent to 90 percent of all Christians in the third world are Pentecostal or Charismatic.[14] Who is vulnerable to becoming a Charismatic? According to sociology-of-religion experts, it is those experiencing socio-economic deprivation but who also experience personal stress and have a religious disposition.[15] That would mean incredibly large population masses experiencing poverty and stress, and comprised of those convicted of the central place of religion in their lives.

And if you think that people in the West may be exempt because they are more likely to be post-Christian and are not really poor, think again. Westerners today, unlike the Third World or the Arab World, seek a spirituality that is eclectic and personal—they are just as religious, even if self-centered. It would be shocking for many readers to realize how many mainstream evangelical thinkers, even *theologians* and respected authors with PhDs, speak in tongues as part of their personal spirituality. You won't catch them doing so in public, but as the adage goes, "You are who you are when no one's looking."

In addition, the Pentecostal Movement, with the gift of tongues—the so-called baptism of the Spirit, cutting through every denominational barrier once thought impossible to overcome—has managed to be the most important factor for ecumenical bonding. Cecil Robeck, Jr., a top authority on the movement, has pointed out that the twentieth century would be evaluated by church historians as a century in which the Holy Spirit birthed two great movements: the Ecumenical Movement and the Pentecostal/Charismatic Movement. Walter Hollenweger, arguably the greatest authority on this movement, asserts the following:

> "The uniqueness of the charismatic renewal [is] in the fact that for the first time since the Reformation, an Ecumenical grass roots has emerged which has crossed the frontiers between Evangelicals and Catholics. This indeed is of great significance. The basis of this ecumenical approach is the fact that Christians have discovered a common experience, which is at the heart of their spirituality—and this, in spite of their differing theologies and interpretations of this experience."[16]

The basis for union is their common experience. Professor Hollenweger has studied Pentecostals and Charismatics all over the world for over forty years. He has demonstrated that the roots of Pentecostalism have much in common with African animism and Korean shamanism, as well as with other pagan religions, making Pentecostalism ideal for a "theologically responsible syncretism."[17]

Babylon is rising to the height of its power. Behind her is the mastermind, the prince of this world. So very many have found in Pentecostalism the answer to a dead church experience, as well as to a Christianity steeped in tradition and becoming increasingly irrelevant to people's personal issues. Pentecostalism offers healing from disease; a real spiritual high when gathered for worship; and a powerful experience such as speaking in tongues or warm "presence," which makes experience the gauge against which religion can be measured. In addition, this is a happy religion and one that does not worry much about doctrinal differences. It means getting close to God, and that is all anyone ever needs. Isn't it? Everyone likes miracles.

Most converts to the Charismatic Movement are real converts. They have felt that, finally, they have come from death to life. And anything to the contrary tends to elicit a strong reaction, like a hungry dog when challenged by another nearby, after he finally found some food to eat.

"You resort to Greek translations and fancy words to explain away what the Holy Spirit is doing in the church today," barked a woman who'd become a Charismatic at a radio talk-show pastor who challenged her beliefs. "Let me give you a piece of advice that might just save you from the wrath of Almighty God: Put away your Bible and your books and stop studying. Ask the Holy Ghost to come upon you and give you the gift of tongues. You have no right to question something you have never experienced."[18]

How can you question experience? Just put away your Bible to make room for the Holy Ghost. Wow! If it were up to Satan, he'd give to that idea a hearty Amen!

NOTES:

1. For example, healing the paralytic lowered through the roof by granting him forgiveness (Mark 2:1–9, or raising Lazarus for the sake of the few yet to decide on His divinity (John 11:27, 45). See also *The Desire of Ages*, 406, 367.

2. Manuscript 11, 1850, in *Manuscript Releases*, vol. 13, 299, 300.

3. *The Spirit of Prophecy*, vol. 4, 411.

4. Calvin W. Edwards and Gary Land, *Seeker After Light: A. F. Ballenger, Adventism, and American Christianity* (Berrien Springs, MI: Andrews University Press, 2000), 35, 36.

5. *Review and Herald*, June 17, 1890, par. 14.

6. Edwards and Land, 46–51.

7. Quoted in Arthur Patrick, "Later Adventist Worship, Ellen White, and the Holy Spirit: Further Historical Perspectives," in *Missionärem*, September 2005, 2.

8. See Herbert E. Douglass, *Messenger of the Lord: The Prophetic Ministry of Ellen G. White* (Boise, ID: Pacific Press, 1998), 205.

9. *Selected Messages*, vol. 2, 32, 36, 37.

10. *The Great Controversy*, 588.

11. G. K. Beale, *The Book of Revelation*, NIVGTC (Grand Rapids, MI: Eerdmans, 1999), 833, 834.

12. *Ibid.*, 832.

13. Jacques B. Doukhan, *Secrets of Revelation: The Apocalypse Through Hebrew Eyes* (Hagerstown, MD: Review and Herald, 2002), 152.

14. Walter J. Hollenweger, *Pentecostalism: Origins and Developments Worldwide* (Peabody, MA: Hendrickson), 300.

15. *Ibid.*, 358.

16. *Ibid.*, 3, 4, 163.

17. *Ibid.*, 132ff.

18. In John F. MacArthur, Jr., *Charismatic Chaos* (Grand Rapids, MI: Zondervan, 1992), 23.

Questions for Reflection or Group Study

1. Why did Jesus use God's Word to engender faith, instead of performing miracles?

2. What were the problems with Ballenger's revivals and the revival in Indiana? What is the bottom-line issue here?

3. Why do you think "it is an impossibility" to be perfect in this world?

4. The chapter proposes that the final worldwide Ecumenical Movement will not be based on theological agreement but on spiritual experience. Do you agree? If so, why?

5. In what ways do Satan and his allies evolve from Revelation 12 to Revelation 16? Why should we be concerned about it?

6. Why is the symbolic false trinity, depicted as spirits like frogs in Revelation 16?

7. Do you agree with the assessment that false religious/spiritual speech will be the means to deceive the world at the end? Why?

8. Why do you think the Charismatic Movement is the fastest-growing religious movement ever?

9. Do you think the elevation of experience over what the Bible teaches is affecting Seventh-day Adventists?

10. How can you have confidence so that you will not be caught up and deceived by an experience?

CHAPTER SIXTEEN

The Voice of the Spirit

The greatest natural disaster in a third of a century took place the day after Christmas, 2004. Likely, you remember watching CNN reports or YouTube clips of massive tsunami waves discharging all their fury on villages, all the way from Indonesia to the coast of Eastern Africa, following an intense earthquake in the Indian Ocean. It seemed as if the entire area was plunged into madness.

Again, in March 2011, these scenes would be repeated, after a similarly catastrophic earthquake and tsunami struck Japan.

Three years after the Indian Ocean quake, our daughter Stefani and I flew to Chennai, southeastern India, for some meetings with pastors. As they drove us south of the city along the Bay of Bengal, I kept noticing empty patches of cement for miles on end. When I inquired about them, one of the pastors said: "Oh, that was the tsunami. There were homes in all those patches before the waves came. There is nothing now."

The Asian Tsunami took the lives of nearly 230,000 souls. Months after the disaster, British seismologists published a report on the phenomenon. The quake that started it all, the Sumatran-Andaman earthquake, registered between 9.1 and 9.3 on the Richter scale, literally shaking the entire globe by at least half an inch back and forth. This quake was the longest ever recorded in history—over ten minutes long. It left an 800-mile long crack on the ocean floor. And the force of the quake was equivalent to a 100-*gigaton* bomb.[1] A gigaton is one billion tons. Don't ask me what *that* is like—but it's just the biggest "boom" humans have ever experienced.

Out of that catastrophe came a story hard to believe yet validated by journalists the likes of Christianne Amanpour and Anderson Cooper. Daylan Sanders, the director of The Samaritan Children's Home, by the beach in Sri Lanka, had come back from the U.S. to help abandoned children have a chance at life. At 8:45 that morning, while reading His Bible and praying, he heard a frantic voice calling out: "The sea is coming!" Without thinking, he shouted orders for all twenty-eight children and the staff to head to the boat at the beach! They all did just that, finding that the outboard engine had been left on the boat overnight—normally an oversight. A thirty-foot wall of water was coming at them. You would think instinct would scream at you to run as fast as you can in the opposite direction. Sanders, however, accelerated the motor, having decided to face the wave! As he did, a verse from his beloved KJV Bible came clearly to his mind: "When the enemy comes in like a flood, the Spirit of the Lord shall raise up a standard against it" (Isaiah 59:19).

He tells the rest of the story:

"That massive wall of water, it stood! I am not one given to exaggeration, I saw as if something hold [sic] it back, some invisible force or hand . . . it just stood."

Witnesses perched on tree-tops confirmed later how, amazingly, that little boat simply went up the massive wall of water and over it, as if that were the most natural thing in the world.[2]

This is the kind of story that makes you pause to pray, to think, or to cry. Don't tell me that having that kind of relationship with God and His Word is not experientially powerful. Here is the voice of God at work, because the Word of God is that real to that man. Because Sanders assimilated the written Word, God was free to apply it at the right time, in the right place. Here is a miracle, but on God's terms and based on His Word.

"Many Will Say to Me on That Day..."

In the previous chapter, we looked at the unholy trinity's last-day plan. We saw that Protestantism, which once held high the voice of Scripture, turns into the false prophet; that Romanism, which holds high the voice of authority, is the beast; and that spiritualism is simply the fire-breathing dragon leading the world through its miracle voice. We explored the great danger of getting entangled with emotional religion, which will constitute the satanic glue to hold the world together.

But the question remains: If sensory experience can be so powerful, how can you really know whether a revival comes from God or from the enemy?

Matthew 7 gives us the key, I believe. Jesus said:

"Many will say to Me on that day, 'Lord, Lord, did we not prophesy in Your name, and in Your name cast out demons, and in Your name perform many miracles?' And then I will declare to them, 'I never knew you; depart from Me, you who practice lawlessness.'" (vv. 22, 23).

When the Bible uses the phrase *on that day,* it refers to judgment day, or the coming of the Lord. "On that day" people will come to the Lord with powerful credentials: prophesying, casting out demons, and performing miracles. However, Jesus will tell them they don't belong to Him. Why? Because, He says, they "practice lawlessness." The King James Version says that they "work iniquity," but the original word there is *anomia,* which literally means "lawlessness." Jesus is not implying that we focus on the law in order to stay away from the deceptions of the end. "Lawlessness" is here related to whether or not people actually *know* Him. "I never *knew* you." You . . . who? "You who practice lawlessness."

What does *knowing* Jesus have to do with lawfulness? Everything! The night Christ introduced the coming Spirit to His disciples, He also told them: "You are my friends if you do what I command you" (John 15:14). In English that sounds harsher than it needs to be, but the idea behind it is that *knowing* Jesus means *following* Jesus. He is perfectly loving, wise, and powerful, He is deeply interested in me and my life and has done everything for me. Does knowing this leave me indifferent? Of course not. I surrender in obedience to such Love!

An intimate relationship exists between Christ's law and Christ Himself, easily demonstrated by a little-known story in His life. Jesus was once accused of casting out demons by the power of Beelzebul. Beelzebul was a Syrian god, a demon, and for the Pharisees, that was another way of saying Satan. Christ's answer to them was, basically, that it wouldn't make sense to have Satan fight against himself, so what was happening was the work of a totally different Power. The story is found in two of the gospels, but the specific wording Jesus gave in each of them is instructive. "If I cast demons by the Spirit of God, then the kingdom of God has come to you" (Matthew 12:28). Note the slight difference in the next gospel. "If I cast demons by the *finger* of God, then the kingdom of God has come to you (Luke 11:20, emphasis added).

What do we learn from this? God's Spirit is likened to God's finger. Now, we shouldn't be too literalistic here but should simply note the Bible's point. Can you think of anything the Bible says about God's finger? Of course, He wrote the Ten Commandments with His finger. "And He [God] gave Moses the two tables of the testimony, tables of stone, written by the finger of God" (Exodus 31:18). So the writing of the Ten Commandments was done by no one else but the Spirit of God!

The Spirit: Author of God's Words

This has tremendous implications in our study of the Spirit, as it relates to the time of the end. Why? Because most Charismatic people easily dismiss the law in the Christian's life, arguing that once we're anointed

202 • ADVENTISM'S GREATEST NEED

with the Spirit, the law becomes irrelevant to a Spirit-filled Christian. I remember giving Bible studies to a man with a Charismatic background, and after studying the Bible Sabbath for some weeks, he happily accepted it as truth. But I noted that it didn't make a tangible difference in his life. He still wouldn't keep the Sabbath holy. So one day I gently confronted him on it. He looked back with a surprised expression and said, "Oh, I know this is what the Bible says. But I'm waiting for the Spirit to tell me this is what I should do."

I think I was so shocked that I couldn't think of a come-back, which, of course, should have been: "My brother, the Spirit is the one telling you in the Bible what to do!"

Peter makes that clear, doesn't he?

"For no prophecy [what the Bible records is what the prophets said] was ever made by an act of human will, but men moved by the Holy Spirit spoke from God" (2 Peter 1:21).

The Bible was authored by the Holy Spirit. So whenever we're following what the Bible teaches, we're being men and women of the Spirit. And whenever we refuse to do so, we're no longer so—we're simply men of flesh.

In this context, we find Paul quoting Jeremiah:

"For this is the covenant that I will make with the house of Israel after those days, says the Lord: I will put My laws into their minds, and I will write them on their hearts. And I will be their God, and they shall be My people" (Hebrews 8:10).

When will God be our God? When His law—His character—is written by His Spirit in our hearts.

You see the point, don't you? At the time of the end, many will be claiming to belong to Jesus because they are in some association with miraculous powers. However, those Jesus will recognize are people whose hearts reflect His character, His law. For *that* is the true work of the Spirit, not spiritual rhetoric or remarkable miracles.

This was Lucifer's problem. He wanted to be God without being *like* God.

"Had Lucifer really desired to be like the Most High, he would never have deserted his appointed place in heaven; for the spirit of the Most High is manifested in unselfish ministry. Lucifer desired God's power, but not His character."[3]

God's power, but not His character. Ellen White wrote:

"Satan is willing that every transgressor of God's law shall claim to be holy. This is what he himself is doing. He is satisfied when men rest their faith on spurious doctrines and religious enthusiasm; for he can use such persons to good purpose in deceiving souls. There are many professedly sanctified ones who are aiding Satan in his work. They talk much of feeling; they speak of their love for God. But God does not recognize their love; for it is a delusion of the enemy."[4]

This is an end-time scenario. Babylon is leading a counterfeit movement of the Spirit, by pretending to exercise heavenly power without yielding to the heavenly law—the law of self-sacrificing love. And many Adventists, I fear, are vulnerable, and the reason is lack of Word power.

The Power of God's Word

I was privileged to teach at an undergraduate Adventist university for fourteen years. Every year, except for one, I taught a freshmen-level course, on the life of Christ, that had between 70 and 110 students. It gave me an opportunity to monitor the pulse of Adventist young people. I was inspired to see how many of these 18- and 19-year-olds came from good Adventist homes: good values, understanding of right and wrong, wholesome attitudes, and intelligent about many things. However, during a decade and half, I saw a declining trend. Each year, the Bible literacy of the students seemed to diminish. Because of that, it took longer for some to reach logical conclusions about right and wrong, because, in the absence of a solid foundation, everything became relative.

Oh, that we would understand the power and joy of Bible study! Its pages are a treasure chest of wisdom. When I conduct public evangelistic meetings, it doesn't take but two or three nights for the guests to be convicted that what they came to hear is something special. And that is not because of the speaker, for I tend to be both slow and long of speech. Rather, it is because of the Word. God's speech leaps off the pages to them, like "apples of gold in settings of silver" (Proverbs 25:11). As I greet them afterward at the door, I see in their faces a certain fullness, a contentment that satisfies, as if they're saying, "This will last me through the night, and I should have some left over for the morning." And then they come back for more, surrender to the Author of the Word, and take their place with the people of God.

Every time I do evangelism, our very own people come to me, with surprise, telling me that they thought they knew our distinctive truths but didn't expect there was so much more to it. And we're talking about members who've been Adventists for decades! This tells me little is going on by way of personal study, so that when real Bible study is made, light comes through with brilliance they had never imagined.

The Word of God can become to you something more powerful than the sensory realities so many crave, when it comes to religion. Listen to Peter's assessment:

> "So we have the prophetic word made more sure, to which you do well to pay attention as to a lamp shining in a dark place, until the day dawns and the morning star arises in your hearts" (2 Peter 1:19).

Let's analyze this a bit. The words of the prophets—the Bible—are compared to increasing light, as long as you pay attention to them. Imagine total darkness, to the extent you can't see your hand before your eyes. Then a faint glimmer of light appears in a crack under the door, so that minutes later, you detect contrasts. Then this increases so you can discern shapes. You get the picture. And finally, the place gets as bright as the sun shining squarely in your face!

Was this hyperbole, exaggeration, on the part of the apostle? Not if you take in the full context.

> "For we did not follow cleverly devised tales when we made known to you the power and coming of our Lord Jesus Christ, but we were eyewitnesses of His majesty. For when He received honor and glory from God the Father, such an utterance as this was made to Him by the Majestic Glory 'This is My beloved Son with whom I am well-pleased'—and we ourselves heard this utterance made from heaven when we were with Him on the holy mountain" (vv. 16–18).

Peter, of course, was referring to the experience at the Mount of Transfiguration (Matthew 17:1–6). And of that amazing incident, he said they were "eyewitnesses of His majesty," and they themselves "heard this utterance from heaven." Can you imagine? Hearing the voice of God—seeing Christ as bright as the sun at noontime. Would you ever forget that?

Back to verse 19: "We have the prophetic word made more sure." That's a statement of comparison: more sure than something else. More sure than what, Peter? Are you ready? *More sure than what his eyes witnessed that day and his ears heard from heaven.* Peter is saying that God's Word can be a greater reality to our lives—something more sure—than what we may see with our eyes and hear with our ears. Now, tell me if that is not power!

The Word of God exists to make you what you were meant to be. It is:

> "Profitable for teaching [what is right], for reproof [of what is wrong], for correction [making the wrong right], and for training in righteousness [staying on the right]; that the man of God may be adequate, equipped for every good work" (2 Timothy 3:16, 17).

You get the distinct impression that it is like building a structure, piece by piece, until you have a solid edifice. That's what the Word does. That word translated "equipped" or "thoroughly furnished" in the KJV, is the Greek *katartizo*. This is the word used for setting right a dislocated bone or for mending broken nets. That is, the Word is meant to put you and me back together as we were once meant to be!

Faith Is the Byproduct

One more thing now, I'd like to share about the power of God's Word: the Bible will produce faith in God. "So faith comes from hearing, and hearing by the world of Christ" (Romans 10:17). "The words which you gave Me" Jesus prayed, "I have given to them . . . and they believed that You sent Me" (John 17:8). "And this is the victory that has overcome the world—our faith" (1 John 5:4). Remember that "faith" is far more than believing that Jesus died on the cross! Far more, too, than knowing which day is the Sabbath or where we go when we die! *Faith* is a simple New Testament word to describe what happens when a person recognizes that Jesus is indeed our Savior and that He is worth trusting. We are saved by grace through faith (Ephesians 2:8); that is, by what Jesus has done—grace—giving us the chance to respond—faith. To have faith means that we will do whatever He asks us to do, because He has done whatever it took to save us. Faith is saying Yes to God. And *that* is brought about by exposure to the Word.

Do you see how critical it is to internalize the Word of God? "Every failure on the part of the children of God is due to their lack of faith," wrote Ellen White.[5] And Paul taught that "whatever is not from faith is sin" (Romans 14:23).

Exercising faith, then, is a matter of life and death. And obtaining faith is a matter of Bible assimilation.

A few years ago, before CDs and MP3 players or iPods became a standard part of our lives, I used to listen to the Word of God on cassette tapes. I did that every day as I drove to and from work and as I ran in the mornings. Listening for about thirty or forty minutes each day would allow me to cover the entire Bible in three months. And then I would start over again. I did not leave aside the more intentional, careful study of Scripture, but this practice allowed me the bird's-eye view of things. What a blessing that was for my life! It was as if my mind was bathed with God speaking to me each day. And I was surprised and delighted by the results: My confidence in God became all the stronger; my assurance grew that His promises stood as solid as a rock that can take the constant beating of angry waves. I remember one day listening to Jeremiah 33:3, "Call to Me and I will answer you, and I will tell you great and mighty things, which you do not know," and thinking, *Wow! The King of the universe is willing to be so available to me, lowly me! And He really wants to share major things with me, even me!* Another day, after listening to 2 Kings 17:7–41, on the reason Israel was taken captive, it made me deeply sad. It helped me see how I was no different than wandering Israel and that God had done all in His power to love me and care for me and provide for me, yet I still strayed away from His gracious dealing with me! This caused me to ask forgiveness and to surrender anew to the same loving God active in the lives of people millennia ago.

Such regular exposure to God's holy Word led me *to know* that God loved me, that He was in absolute control of my life, and that He had plans for even me. God desires this for each of us, to engender faith in Him, absolute trust in Him. And this amazing development can only happen when taking in the Word.

"The words that I have spoken to you are spirit and are life," said the Master (John 6:63). When we eat to live (versus living to eat, a common disease in our midst today), we obtain the necessary physical energy to accomplish our work. Likewise, when we feed on God's Word, we receive faith, the necessary spiritual "energy" needed to face a world of sin. This is why the Bible teaches Christians to live by faith and not by sight. The operating word there is *live*. Christians don't vegetate by faith, they actually *live*—are alive—by faith.

Herry Mhando is a remarkable evangelist from Zimbabwe. He lives by faith and not by sight. He believes bringing people to Jesus depends on "kneeology." "Asking" has to do with initiative, "seeking" with determination, and "knocking" with action (Matthew 7:7). He has often contracted soccer stadiums in Africa to hold his meetings, and this, without money. He has gone to wealthy business people in town to fund the evangelistic campaign, and some of them are *former* Adventists! But they are so impressed with his conviction that he is on an errand for the Almighty, that his faith is contagious! A former student of mine, after visiting with him for a couple of hours, summarized his impressions for me: "he is a humble man of faith."

"After setting a goal," he once said, "I believe that I should work hard to reach it. As long as at the end I will not take the glory, God will bless my efforts and I will reach my goal."[6] And reaching his goals is what he does. His meetings often begin with a few thousand, leaving large parts of the stadium empty. But each night, word-of-mouth brings more people, so an opening night attendance of "merely" 2,000 ends up with a closing night attendance of 20,000. His biographer gives the reason: "Much of the treasure that Mhando has mined from the Bible [and preached in his meetings] is evidenced by the choice of rarely cited passages."[7] His evangelistic success is rare these days. For example, even though he was a full-time doctoral student at the seminary at Andrews University, he committed to doing seventeen evangelistic series during the five years it took to complete the degree. The result? Over 25,000 baptisms for Jesus!

But there is a secret screaming out of Mhando's life that underlies the reason for his success. It's what he does with his time every morning, between three and seven. He studies God's Word.

You may not need to begin with four hours in the morning, but you may need to begin. Time with God will be the power breakfast needed for the rest of that day. Seek Him early in the morning, before engaging with work, exercise, or other necessities, and He will be waiting for you. What we will need for the last push through to the end is Word food. Only His words can do something inside of us which nothing outside can touch. This is the work of the Spirit.

To Be Men and Women of the Spirit

God's original plan was to spend time with us each day face to face. This was His practice with Adam and Eve "in the cool of the day" (Genesis 3:8). But when the first pair chose to trust the words of Satan over the words of God, their natural proclivity to come to God was exchanged for a natural tendency to walk away from Him. They found themselves naked, which is exactly how we all are without the covering of God. They had shed their robes of righteousness and exchanged them for filthy rags (Isaiah 64:6).

Mankind could no longer be in the presence of God and live through it (Exodus 33:20). Sin robbed us of our most precious privilege as creatures—to be with our Creator. The few exceptions to this rule took place with people such as the prophets, completely given over to God. But even before them, God had to veil His glory so they would not evaporate instantly. Their normal reaction was, "Woe is me!" (Isaiah 6:1–5). How could a sinner stand before sheer Holiness!

Deprived of face-to-face privileges with human beings, God's nearness to us is through His Spirit, who invisibly whispers in our ears, "This is the way, walk in it" (Isaiah 30:21). But even that can be counterfeited by the devil, intent also to whisper in our ears. So what God did is very simple: He spoke to those who had made it a life-long practice to listen to His voice—His prophets—and shared messages of love, instruction, and warning through them for us. The record of those messages is what we call the Bible.

So if you want to be a man or a woman of the Spirit, you must become a man or woman of the Word. This is exactly how you listen to a holy God. If you want to know what it is like to be in the presence of God, don't close your eyes, cross your legs, and hum. Open your eyes to read, ponder, and engage with His Word. He speaks to *you* through its pages. And the more of the Word of God you choose to internalize, the greater are God's options to speak to you when you are *away* from the Word: when you drive, when you work, when you live your life. A direct correlation exists between internalizing the *written* Word, with the ability to hear the Spirit *apply* the Word in your life.

George Müller was legendary for his life of prayer. He committed every need before God in prayer, trusting that the Almighty Provider would give everything His children needed. When he started taking care of orphan children in Bristol, England, he sustained them with prayer. When that ministry grew to caring for over 2,000 children—including a staff of several hundred, and several large buildings still standing today—that was sustained by prayer. You see, Müller had no charitable foundation, he didn't ask for money, and there was no church or mission board underwriting those large daily expenses. But he believed in a mighty and loving God who would supply every need "according to the riches of His glory" (Ephesians 3:16).

Müller's walk with God was very real. But he learned something early in his ministry that put all this in perspective. Listen to his own words:

"Before this time my practice had been, at least for ten years previously, as an habitual thing, to give myself to prayer, after having dressed in the morning. Now I saw, that the most important thing I had to do was to give myself to the reading of the Word of God and to meditation on it, that thus my heart might be comforted, encouraged, warned, reproved, instructed; and that thus, whilst meditating, my heart might be brought into experimental communion with the Lord, . . . It often astonished me that I did not see the importance of meditation upon Scripture earlier in my Christian life. As the outward man is not fit for work for any length of time unless he eats, so it is with the inner man. What is the food of the inner man? Not prayer, but the Word of God—not the simple reading of the Word of God. . . . No, we must consider what we read, ponder over it and apply it to our hearts. . . . Through His Word our Father speaks to us. . . . The weaker we are, the more meditation we need to strengthen our inner man."[8]

The man known the world over for his life of prayer and faith was actually a man of the Word. And this was the reason for his success. He became a man of the Spirit by becoming a man of the Word.

And so can you. And so can I.

NOTES:

1. Excerpted from http://lucernarium.wordpress.com/2008/08/11/ on February 2, 2011.

2. Story details accessed from http://goodnewschristianministry.org on February 18, 2006.

3. *The Desire of Ages*, 435.

4. *Review and Herald*, June 26, 1900, par. 5.

5. *Patriarchs and Prophets*, 657.

6. Nkosiyabo Zvandasara, *Herry Mhando: The Man and His Methods of Evangelism and Church Growth* (Berrien Springs, MI: Leslie Books, 2001), 33.

7. *Ibid.*, 21.

8. *The Autobiography of George Müller* (Springdale, PA: Whitaker House, 1984), 139, 140.

Questions for Reflection or Group Study

1. Thinking of the story of Daylan Sanders and the Asian Tsunami, is your relationship with God such that you could recognize His voice?

2. What does knowing Jesus have to do with lawfulness, or the keeping of the law?

3. What do you think about the idea that God's law was written by the Holy Spirit? Are there any implications for the way we live our lives today?

4. Lucifer's problem in heaven was his desire to have God's power without having His character. Is that ever our problem? In what way?

5. Share or articulate some time when the reading of God's Word became more real to you than sensory experience.

6. If the reading and internalizing of God's Word is meant to produce faith in God, why do we spend so little time with the Bible?

7. Reread 2 Timothy 3:16, 17. Reflect on what "equipped" or "thoroughly furnished" may mean for your life.

8. What do you think would happen in our lives if we were to spend as much time with God each morning as Herry Mhando spends daily?

9. Do you think it's possible to live lives of faith today such as George Müller did?

10. What are you planning to do that would allow you more time with God's Word every day?

CHAPTER SEVENTEEN

A Church Empowered By the Spirit

In the days right before the collapse of communism, life was tough for Romanian Adventists. Lack of available goods, rampant political corruption, and poverty dominated people's lives. But my friend Pavel was a rich man. He'd been faithful to God in everything he knew, risking education, advancement, and opportunities, to honor the Sabbath and other Bible teachings.

God rewarded such faithfulness by placing him as the owner of a sewing business which made serious money. He was taking in more than half a million dollars a year and was poised, in association with a German company, to quadruple that income. As they were asking God whether or not to take that step in business, the conference called him to be a full-time pastor. They had no clue what he was making. A pastor's salary was $250 a month, a tenth of 1 percent of his potential income.

He and Dana, his wife, decided to surrender all to Jesus. They sold their nice home and cars and gave away practically everything they owned. They bought an old Russian jalopy, a little box on wheels, so as not to make their members envious. But they found their four-church district to be a complete mess. Jealousy and gossip ran high, and struggles for leadership power were the business of the day. Acrid argumentation was common over small items such as the worship service. The churches appeared to be everything except a community that followed Jesus. The new pastor wondered how he could bring new people to *those* churches?

He decided to practice the fundamentals. He encouraged families to gather together for seasons of prayer. As they knelt together, they begin to realize the true condition of their own hearts, and this led them to confession and surrender. "As a body of believers, they entreated the healing power of the Holy Spirit to rule supreme in their personal lives as a blessing to the church."[1]

Within two years the membership doubled. As they reached out to friend and neighbor, they added a new congregation and two new companies to the district. This kind of progress doesn't go unnoticed by the enemy of souls, and he prepared a counterattack to strike just two weeks before the start of Pavel's next evangelistic series of meetings.

As he drove outside of Otelu Rosu one day, a teen decided to cross the highway without looking in his direction. The car struck the boy's hip and leg and sent him flying straight up into the air, only for him to land right in front of Pavel, too late to avoid his hitting the boy again, this time on his head and shoulders. The teenager's body was a crumpled mess, with blood running out of his ears, nose, mouth, and eyes. He was rushed to the hospital. His brain hemorrhaged profusely; his spine was broken in two places; one of his lungs was punctured; and he had a broken hip, arm, and leg. A team of physicians did their best to save him but without success. After he died, they covered him with a sheet, and each one filed out of the emergency room, leaving the boy, Mene Mene, to be taken to the morgue later.

Poor Mene Mene had been a 19-year old, well known in town. Suffering from motor coordination deficiencies, he couldn't control his arms or legs well and had come close to being killed crossing the street on more than one occasion. People had given him his nickname to ridicule his stuttering problem. Now, the Adventist pastor had killed one of the best-recognized characters in town. And Pavel was devastated by the loss of that innocent young life and the damage to God's cause, at a time when the Spirit was blessing them so much.

Pavel remained next to Mene Mene's bed, praying for him.

"God, what are the people of Otelu Rosu going to say when they hear that I killed a young man just beginning his life? They know I'm a pastor. What will they think? If need be, I am willing to exchange my life for his. I know You are able to bring him back to life if You choose. I'm asking You—please bring him back. Please, God—please!"[2]

One of the doctors caught him praying and told him to go home. He assured Pavel that the boy was very dead and that it was too late to pray for him now.

"Just face it—it's over," he said.

But Pavel believed in a bigger God than those communist doctors had ever dreamed of. Back home, he and his wife spent the entire night pleading before God, that if there was any way to restore the young man's life for God's honor and glory, to please do it. And they accepted God's will, whichever way it went.

In the morning, Pavel returned to the hospital to meet with the family but instead found a commotion around Mene Mene, who was now sitting up in bed, eating! He was alive! A host of medical professionals crowded into the room, bewildered, comparing x-rays from that morning with the ones taken the day before. To the inexplicable amazement of everyone, the new x-rays showed absolutely no damage whatsoever to the brain, spine, hip, or lungs. The young man had only a broken arm and leg. In addition, his speech was perfect for the first time in his life. The stutter was gone. And when the teen was discharged, they saw that he had full control of his arms and legs. Another miracle.

You can imagine the news in town. And when the evangelistic meetings began, the whole area turned out for them, packing the church, with many staying for questions after each presentation. The result? The church doubled its membership again.

This is not simply a great story, it is a great life lived by someone who's chosen to live the Spirit-filled life to the fullest. Pavel was my student and is currently my colleague in ministry. His 250-member church (he now pastors in Kentucky) is giving over 150 Bible studies to people in the community, at the time of this writing. The same Spirit at work in communist Romania is the One at work in the southern United States.

Blessings in Proportion to Self-Sacrifice

When Jesus sought to fill the heart of the rich young ruler with His Spirit, he called him to "sell all that you have and give it to the poor" (Luke 18:22). This is what Pavel did, and God blessed him beyond his wildest dreams. The history of the New Testament church gives evidence of the same thing: They surrendered all, and heaven became their supplier (Acts 4:32–35). From the Corinthian believers, the apostle Paul raised funds to help the churches experiencing famine in Judea. He told them that "he who sows sparingly shall also reap sparingly; and he who sows bountifully shall also reap bountifully" (2 Corinthians 9:6). And then he added: "Now He who supplies seed to the sower and bread for food, will supply and multiply your seed for sowing and increase the harvest of your righteousness; you will be enriched in everything" he promised, "for all liberality, which through us is producing thanksgiving to God" (vv. 10, 11). Did you catch the subtle point? True thanksgiving does not come from what we have, so much as from what we can give!

How much of what you have in your attic or your garage or the spare room in your home will you be taking to heaven? How much of what we spend for our various collections could be used to bless others beyond all computation? Those who are poor in Spirit are those who will inherit the kingdom (Matthew 5:3). That is, those who recognize the need for more of the Spirit in their lives, not those who feel they need more *things* in their lives.

To her son Edson and his wife, Ellen White wrote about full surrender, saying, "Before giving us the baptism of the Holy Spirit, our heavenly Father will try us, to see if we can live without dishonoring Him."[3] How much more of the Spirit we would see in the church if the things holding us to the world were to be released!

> "The church is asleep as to the work it might do if it would give up all for Christ. A true spirit of self-sacrifice would be an argument for the reality and power of the gospel which the world could not misunderstand or gainsay, and abundant blessings would be poured upon the church."[4]

Many churches in North America barely exist. They are reminiscent of the valley of dry, dead bones described in Ezekiel 37. They have good, decent people in them, but they are devoid of the Spirit. They subsist with few resources, a limited pool of talent and youth, and they have not won a soul to Jesus in years. Their days are filled with complaints or corporate pity. They make absolutely no lasting impact on the surrounding community. But if they really wanted, this situation could change radically.

The servant of the Lord gives us the diagnosis, as well as the prescription, for our condition in these churches:

> "The promise of the Spirit is not appreciated as it should be. Its fulfillment is not realized as it might be. It is the absence of the Spirit that makes the gospel ministry so powerless. Learning, talents, eloquence, every natural or acquired endowment, may be possessed; but without the presence of the Spirit of God, no heart will be touched, no sinner be won to Christ. On the other hand, if they are connected with Christ, if the gifts of the Spirit are theirs, *the poorest and most ignorant of His disciples will have a power that will tell upon hearts.* God makes them the channel for the outworking of the highest influence in the universe."[5]

And again:

> "The disciples did not ask for a blessing for themselves. They were weighted with the burden of souls. . . . They claimed the endowment

of power that Christ had promised. Then it was that the Holy Spirit was poured out, and thousands were converted in a day. So it may be now. Let Christians put away all dissension and give themselves to God for the saving of the lost. Let them ask in faith for the promised blessing, and it will come."[6]

The diagnosis is dissension and lack of interest in the Spirit, allowing other *things* to crowd out God. The prescription is connection with Christ and a desire to ask for the Holy Spirit so as to be a blessing to others. Jesus promised:

"Truly, truly, I say to you, he who believes in Me, the works that I do, he will do also; and greater works than these [His miracles] he will do; because I go to the Father" (John 14:12).

Greater works? I shall never forget when, years ago, discouraged, I casually opened my Bible to 2 Kings, to pass the time. I was soon taken in by the life of Elisha, who gave such clear evidence of the double-portion blessing he'd asked of the Lord. He did not merely ask for that to which he was entitled, he asked for a double portion of the Spirit (2 Kings 2:9). In ancient times, all sons obtained a single portion of the inheritance, and only first-born sons received a double portion. Elisha believed his Father to be rich and generous, and he asked accordingly. And he lived his life accordingly. Even after death, he kept blessing others. How so? you ask. After Elisha died, they buried him in a cave, as was the custom of the day. Years later, they were burying another man nearby, and the place was not quite ready, when Moabite raiding bands came suddenly upon the mourners. With no time to think, they tossed the man's body into the cave where the bones of Elisha were, and the Bible says, "When the man touched the bones of Elisha he revived and stood up on his feet" (2 Kings 13:20, 21). The infilling of the Spirit is a blessing that keeps on giving.

These Scenes Shall Be Repeated

In reference to the very powerful work of the New Testament church in the world—the fact that thousands were converted in a day, that backslidden members returned to the church, and that the heathen flocked to God's people searching for the Pearl of Great Price—Ellen White simply says:

"These scenes are to be repeated, and with greater power. The outpouring of the Holy Spirit on the day of Pentecost was the former rain, but the latter rain will be more abundant. The Spirit awaits our demand and reception. Christ is again to be revealed in His fulness by the Holy Spirit's power."[7]

But haven't many faithful followers of Jesus been praying now for centuries for a mighty outpouring of God's Spirit, such as seen at Pentecost, on His church? Thousands, no doubt. One of them was a pastor and Bible worker who consistently led souls to Jesus. Her name was Mrs. S. M. I. Henry, and she corresponded with Mrs. White frequently. In one of those letters she expressed her great burden that they had been praying and pleading for the Spirit of God to fall on them, but it didn't seem to happen. How long before the latter rain would fall? Sister White answered her with wisdom and encouragement:

"Of the prayers that have been ascending for the fulfillment of the promise—the descent of the Holy Spirit—not one has been lost. Each prayer has been accumulating, ready to overflow and pour forth a healing flood of heavenly influence and accumulated light all over the world."[8]

God Will Finish the Work

Have you ever wondered about the millions and billions through the centuries who've never been reached by a piece of literature or the hopeful words of a missionary? Well, 2,000 years ago, the Spirit made clear to Paul that "God has not left Himself without a witness" (Acts 14:17).

Take, for instance, the well-known story of the Davis Indians. In 1910, reports kept coming to the British Guiana Mission office that there was a tribe perched in the Roraima Mountains, bordering with Venezuela, which kept the Sabbath. The following year, O. E. Davis, the mission president, made the hazardous weeks-long journey by canoe and on foot to find the tribe. Before he arrived, he was weak and feverish with malaria and decided to stop at a mining camp to regain his strength.

One day, while sitting outside and reading his Bible, a group of Indians saw him and started running toward him.

"We have been waiting many years for you to come!" they said excitedly. "An angel told chief Auka [or Owkwa] that a white man with a black book would come and teach us more, so sit down and teach us now!"

Davis tried to put them off until later, but they would have none of it. As he opened his Bible, he learned that they already knew about the Sabbath, healthful living, and even the sanctuary ministry! He returned to Georgetown to recover from malaria but promised them he would return, which he did, months later. This time, he taught them everything else they didn't already know, and then he died.

Elder Davis was expected, because Auka, the major chief of all those Roraima mountain tribes, when he became chief, prayed to the Great Spirit for days to help him be a good chief for his people. Shortly after his request, while speaking to the people, he received his first vision. He stopped breathing, his eyes turned to glass, and when they tried to make him lie down, he was immovable as a boulder. When he came out of vision, he told them that "a person like a bright light came and talked to me, telling me things we should do."

Auka received many visions, and he went around the various tribes teaching each what the heavenly messenger had told him. They learned about the Sabbath, about clean and unclean meats, about how to pray, about Satan, the coming of Christ, and many other Bible teachings. Angels taught Auka hymns in multi-part harmony so he could teach them to his people—songs such as "Shall We Gather at the River," "There's Not a Friend Like the Lowly Jesus," and others. He was told not to rule by force and not to kill, introducing Auka to a whole new way of life. So much transmission was taking place between heaven and earth that they made a special bed for Auka, and whenever he didn't know what to do, he lay on the bed, asking the Great Spirit to show him what to do.

Before Davis died, he told the tribes, "God will send another God-man to you." In 1927, Alfred and Betty Cott became full-time missionaries to the *Davis* Indians, as they preferred to be called. They found all the tribes in the area keeping all of the Adventist Bible teachings. Today there are over 3,000 Adventist Davis Indians who worship in twelve churches and twenty groups—the result of one heathen chief asking help from the Great Spirit.[9]

But what about the Middle Ages? What about the Americas before the Europeans discovered there was an entire world waiting there for them? What about tiny islands in the Pacific, which for centuries had no contact with the outside world?

Perhaps one of the most worthwhile books for Christians to read is the now-classic *Eternity in Their Hearts.* Don Richardson, a Christian missionary among the Sawi people in Southeast Asia, and a scholar, relates story after story of how various groups in the world came to know God, sometimes centuries before they saw their first Bible or met a missionary.

In 1763, some 800,000 Karen people of today's Myanmar were very ready to encounter the first white man with the Bible and to accept all the Christian teachings. The reason? They had a system of belief that, apparently, predated both Judaism and Christianity. Their belief in a supreme deity called Y'wa (very close to the Old Testament *Yahweh,* "Lord"), however, was incomplete by their own reckoning. But the Karen people expected their religion to be complete when "white foreigners" came to share it with them. "The sons of Y'wa, the white foreigners, obtained the words of Y'wa . . . the words of Y'wa anciently," intoned one of their ancient religious songs.[10] For hundreds of years, the Karen people had a group of teachers called Bukhos, who did not speak for the commonly accepted evil spirits but for Y'wa, the true God. These were the ones who taught biblical concepts to the Karen people via a number of songs, pointing to a Creator, a Satan, a first pair tested in a garden, the forbidden fruit, the Sabbath, and the fact that due to Tha-nai's (Adam) and Ee-u's (Eve) failure to trust Y'wa concerning the forbidden fruit, now the race is weakened, unable to naturally obey Y'wa!

But the Karen people would still have to wait. The 1763 encounter with a British military man was a disappointment—he had no Bible. Finally, in 1817, missionary Adoniram Judson disembarked in Rangoon. When he shared some of the Scriptures with a rough Karen character called Ko Thah-byu (he'd killed thirty people already), the man recognized it as "the lost book." After he accepted the Gospel and was baptized, he began sharing what he found with every Karen village he could. And they, in turn, shared with many others all over the mountains bordering Thailand, India, and China. It's a fascinating story. Hundreds of thousands of Karen, Lahu, Wa, Lisu, Kachin, Shan, Mizo, and other peoples have readily accepted the Gospel and the teachings of Christianity through just a few decades, because the Karen, as well as those other groups, had a basic understanding of the God of heaven, of sin and righteousness, and of a Deliverer, and were simply waiting for more.[11]

The truth is that God gives us the Great Commission for our own sake, as much as for the sake of the lost. He is perfectly capable of finishing the work all by Himself, but making us partners in this endeavor helps us become more like Him.

Today, many Adventists consider the Muslim world the toughest challenge to the spreading of the Gospel. In many countries of the Middle East and central Asia, *sharia* law—Islamic life practice—is the law of the land, superseding even their national constitutions. To be a Muslim is a matter of national as well as religious identity. And if you leave Islam for the sake of another religion, it is a great affront, if not a death sentence. But what few recognize is that well over half of all world Muslims now live in the Western world. The freedom of religion in those countries makes the work of God much more accessible.

To Show Himself Strong

But even if the situation were absolutely forbidding, nothing is impossible with God. All He needs, all He longs for, is someone "through whom He may show Himself strong" (2 Chronicles 16:9). Golden Lapani is such a man. Some may remember him being introduced at the 2005 General Conference session, in St. Louis. His story is worth sharing.

Lapani grew up a Muslim in Malawi, a Muslim country. But after he became so sick that he was sent home to die, he had three dreams, in which Jesus appeared to him and told him to become a Christian and that he would be healed. He began reading a Bible, accepted Jesus as his Savior and Lord, and was completely healed. Immediately, he quit his work as a biology teacher, bought some land to farm, and dedicated almost all his time to work for Jesus. As a result of his decision, he has been stoned, burned, and poisoned. Enemies and former friends have tried to put him to death at least twenty-five times since 1982. But his work has continued undeterred, to the point where everyone in his family is now an Adventist. In every town where they tried to kill him there is an Adventist church today.

One time, the chief of the village where he wanted to hold Bible meetings was murdered, and his body disappeared. Some in town accused Lapani of the murder. He, along with other believers, fasted and prayed for twenty-one days that God would reveal the truth and that His name be exalted. On day twenty-one, the chief's body floated up from the bottom of the river, even though it was attached to the large rocks the assassin had used to sink him to the bottom! "Your God is a miracle God," people said. Now there is a church with eighty members in that village.

Lapani's method is similar everywhere he goes: He asks permission from the village chief or elders to visit the community; he brings them food, medicine, and clothes for the children; and he prays for them (and sees many answers to prayer). Then he starts giving Bible studies, and after some time, asks permission to hold evangelistic meetings. After creating so much good will in town, he is hardly refused, and after a group has been baptized, making up the new church, he leaves five Bible workers continuing to instruct and equip them for six months, before they move on to another town.

The absolutely remarkable thing is that Lapani, in twenty-five years of data available to me, has led over 18,000 souls to baptism, half of whom are Muslim.[12]

With God all things are possible. "You are our letter," Paul wrote the Corinthians, "known and read by all men; . . you are a letter of Christ, cared for by us, written not with ink but with the Spirit of the living God, not on tablets of stone but on tablets of human hearts" (2 Corinthians 3:2, 3). We are God's men and women of the Spirit, and through us, God intends to change the world.

The Church Triumphant

Everything I've read in Scripture and in the Spirit of Prophecy, plus the many stories I've come to know or even experienced, have led me to a composite picture of what God can and will do for His remnant people. Please indulge me in a bit of reverie, as I dream of what can be.

The economy in the West gets weaker and less able to rebound to pre-viously known levels. For the first time, people who never knew suffering begin to wonder where they can put their trust. At the same time, enter-tainment and technology have so advanced that living in a fantasy world has become the only reality for millions. The spirit of evil, selfishness, and survival of the fittest has intensified, but so has the Spirit of God, convicting people all over the world to seek the true God for answers to their real-life questions.

Many Seventh-day Adventists have mingled with the world for so long that even though they wish to make changes, they feel trapped by habit and are unable to discern much from the Word of God. They want relief—but not total transformation. They seek peace of mind—but not a change of heart. On the other hand, more and more people in the world, some with a religious background and some without one, are genuinely open to the God of the Bible, to the point where they are ready to pay whatever price is necessary in order to know Him. The activity of angels in dreams is increased. Life-turning moments for people in search of God multiply. And many previously Laodicean believers turn over their whole lives to God. Consecrated Adventists begin to downsize, while giving more and more to the cause of Christ. They spend more time on their knees and in the Word, giving help and being a blessing to others. They sacrifice what only shortly before they could never part with. They find that the joy of Jesus is the only longing in their hearts—to be like Him and to work for others as He's worked for them.

Conditions in the political and financial world worsen so much—along with increasing natural disasters worldwide—that religious groups are finally taken seriously when they propose to set aside Sunday as a mandatory day of rest, in order to appease an offended God. Other na-tions follow through, due to the apparent immediate success this is caus-ing in the USA. Adventists then know that only a little time is left. But their concerns are no longer to huddle in isolation to wait for the Lord to come but to take an urgent, last-day message of love and truth to neigh-bor, friend, and co-worker. By the thousands, Adventist young people, young professionals, families, couples, the middle-aged, and the elderly share—with faces lighted up with the glory of God and in the power of the Spirit—the beautiful truths Jesus has made so clear.

Thousands more seem to grasp in a short time what before would have taken years to understand. Miracles will be reported of God's in-tervention, as we share the good news of Jesus with the world, in the power of the fourth angel of Revelation 18. The corporate latter rain is finally here. The beauty of Jesus' character is seen, oh, so clearly! The love of God shines through every sincere heart. The power of the Spirit is so obvious that any thoughtful person perceives we "have been with Jesus" (Acts 4:13).

At the same time, Satan mobilizes his forces for the last great deception. He shows up as Jesus in Jerusalem, in Rome, in Shanghai, in Cairo, in New York, in Sao Paulo. He appears to raise the dead and to heal by the thousands. He looks just like the pictures of Jesus seen in so many churches. He speaks with clarity, assurance, and kind tones. He intervenes in the global economy. He teaches that his new day is Sunday, a day of allegiance to him. His power of persuasion and conviction is so great that even many life-long Adventists can't help believing him. There is a great religious revival, with miracles, and tongues, and great happiness in everyone. But there is no reformation. So the revival somehow rings hollow.

Probation closes. And those who've learned to walk with Jesus trust Him, in spite of how they feel. Satanic agencies work overtime to take away our assurance in Christ, but they do not succeed. The Word of God stored in the heart becomes a source of great comfort at that time. Others will realize with foreboding that the end is at hand, yet it will be too late to see real transformation of character. Terrible plagues fall, one after the other, but all over the world, the people of God remain calm, hopeful, and surrendered. As major natural disasters unleash global catastrophes, we discern the coming of the Lord Jesus with His holy angels. "Behold," we cry, "this is our God for whom we have waited the He might save us . . . . Let's rejoice and be glad in His salvation!" (Isaiah 26:9).

We see Jesus and His unmistakable kind and noble bearing. He seems to be smiling, as if we were the only ones in the universe. We witness, with excitement and joy beyond description, as angels dart from place to place, calling to the dead to rise in the name of the Lifegiver. We rise to Jesus, our eyes fixed on Him, certain we'll never lay eyes elsewhere again. We see people rise with immortality, then note that we too have changed, in the twinkling of an eye. The joy of the millions involved in the happy journey is simply indescribable. All sacrifice, all pain and sorrow, appears so far away and so foreign to our experience. "And we shall ever be with the Lord" (1 Thessalonians 4:17).

My dear reader, there are days when I clearly see that I have not yet given all to Jesus. At times, I'd still rather do my will than His. Sometimes, I prefer His gifts over Himself. But Jesus knows the weakness of my heart. He hears my prayer, when I cry that He create in me a greater desire for Him and His glory than for me and my comfort. Jesus hears!

"I love the Lord," the psalmist sang, "because He hears my voice and my supplications" (Psalm 116:1). I want to come to the point in my life that Jesus is my all in all—that nothing else in this world matters to me but His happiness. I'd like to please my Savior, for He's loved me to the end.

And all this is the work of the Spirit, silently, steadily, humbly, and powerfully changing and purifying us. Let the Holy Spirit have His way in more and more of your life. For some, you need to stop delaying—you so well know already what the Spirit wants to change in your life. Let Him in. Remember that character-building takes time. Let Him in now, and tomorrow you'll notice a new you. Let Him in now, for you will never be as happy as when fully surrendered.

Let's let Him in today. He has been waiting a long, long time.

He is ready to bless us. He is ready to bless His church.

We will never regret it.

NOTES:

1. Greg Budd, *One Miracle After Another: The Pavel Goia Story* (Hagerstown, MD: Review and Herald, 2009), 134.

2. *Ibid.*, 137.

3. Letter 22, 1902, pp. 9, 10. "To Elder and Mrs. J. E. White," February 1, 1902; also in *Manuscript Releases*, vol. 2, 43.

4. *Testimonies*, vol. 4, 483, 484.

5. *Christ's Object Lessons*, 328, emphasis supplied.

6. *Testimonies*, vol. 8, 21.

7. *Christ's Object Lessons*, 121.

8. Manuscript 1532, July 19, 1899, "To Mrs. S. M. I. Henry;" also in *Manuscript Releases*, vol. 21, 155.

9. Excerpted from Adriel Chilson, "The 'Davis' Indians" in *Adventist Review*, January 10, 1991, 10; Sahara de Almérida, "A Dream and a Harvest," and Bob Norton, "Angels Prepare the Way for Gospel to Reach Indians in South America" in http://4hispeople.org/chief_auka.htm, accessed February 5, 2011.

10. Francis Mason, *The Karen Apostle* (Boston: Gould & Lincoln, 1861), 21, in Don Richardson, *Eternity in Their Hearts*, rev. (Ventura, CA: Regal, 1984), 84.

11. Richardson, 73–108.

12. I've heard Lapani's story from various oral sources in formal Adventist meetings, as well as in informal conversations with those who know

him personally. One written source I found sometime in 2007 was on the Internet—a story evidently published in one of the union or division papers in South America. I don't have the date of publication or the accession date, but the story was written by Charlotte Ishkanian, entitled "Um homem e seu Deus" (A Man and His God).

Questions for Reflection or Group Study

1. What stands out to you about the story of Pavel and his wife?

2. Comment on the statement: "True thanksgiving does not come from what we have so much as from what we can give." Why would that be?

3. How is it possible for the church to do "greater works," according to the promise of Jesus?

4. If the Spirit awaits our demand and reception, what are we waiting for?

5. Why should we not be discouraged if we do not see our prayers answered right away concerning the outpouring of the Holy Spirit?

6. What common thread do you see in the stories of the Davis Indians, the Karen, Lahu, Wa, Lisu, Kachin, Shan, Mizo and other peoples?

7. What can we learn from Golden Lapani about how to work with others to win them for Christ, even under the most forbidding circumstances?

8. Reread 2 Corinthians 3:2, 3. Comment on the thought that it is through us [that] God intends to change the world.

9. As you look at the world today, what evidence do you have that Jesus may be coming very soon?

10. What is the most important decision you are making as a result of reading this book?